Praise for

CRAFTING STORY MOVEMENT

"Kathryn Craft's background in dance and choreography adds a delightful and fresh insight into developing characters, emotions, and story structure. Filled with illustrative examples and usable prompts, *Crafting Story Movement* is a valuable resource for new and experienced novelists alike."
—Shelley Noble, *New York Times* bestselling author of *The Tiffany Girls* and *The Colony Club*

"Drawing from the world of dance and movement, Craft takes us on a deep dive into the energy that drives a story forward and draws a reader closer. Full of examples from successful books, and practical suggestions for utilizing the material, *Crafting Story Movement* is a welcome, hands-on guide for fiction writers in any genre."
—James Scott Bell, International Thriller Writers Award winner and author of *Write Your Novel from the Middle*

"Brilliant! *Crafting Story Movement* should be on every writer's desk. Kathryn Craft, former dancer turned author, begins each chapter with inspirational words from noted choreographers and dancers, setting up stellar examples on how to propel a story forward with energy, passion, action, restraint, and nuance. A remarkable book with a stunningly unique perspective."
—Julie Maloney, author of *A Matter of Chance* and founder/director of Women Reading Aloud

"The movement of a dancer across a stage and a reader whose eyes race across the page seem an unlikely duo, yet the connection is laid bare in *Crafting Story Movement: Techniques to Engage Readers and Drive Your Story Forward* by the inimitable Kathryn Craft. The author's talent of drilling into the heart of notable books to explain what works and why is a gift every author, no matter their aptitude, will treasure."
—Barbara Conrey, *USA Today* bestselling author of *Nowhere Near Goodbye*

"With *Crafting Story Movement,* Kathryn brings insight, common sense, experience, and a sense of joy to the process of writing a novel. This should be on every writer's bookshelf!"
—Jonathan Maberry, NY Times bestselling author of *NecroTek: COLD WAR* and *RED EMPIRE*

"*Crafting Story Movement* will set your story in motion. Informed by the world of dance, Kathryn Craft invites you—chapter by chapter—into the deeper choreography of transformation. You'll never experience your own narrative quite the same way again."
—Therese Walsh, author of *The Moon Sisters* and editorial director of Writer Unboxed

"Brilliant, perceptive, and just what every writer needs. I never connected dancing with storytelling until now. Craft (so aptly named) offers plenty of useful examples of how to get your story moving, and I already know I will keep this guide by my side as I write my next novel!"
—Nancy Johnson, bestselling author of *People of Means* and *The Kindest Lie*

"Kathryn Craft has turned her long experience with dance to great advantage. By focusing on movement, and with numerous excellent examples from a wide range of novels, she manages to reveal the parallel progression of the author through her material and the reader through the story. In so doing, she provides both fundamental guidance for beginning writers and a fresh, illuminating perspective for old hands. Few are the writing guides that can teach old dogs new tricks. *Crafting Story Movement* is one of them—and one of the best."
—David Corbett, author of *The Art of Character*

"Brimming with insight and wisdom, Kathryn Craft's *Crafting Story Movement* entertains and informs while illustrating how the fine art of movement applies to story. A compelling how-to guide for novelists at all levels to devour, absorb, reread and savor."
—Terez Mertes Rose, author of the Ballet Theatre Chronicles series and blogger at The Classical Girl

"Through the metaphor of dance, *Crafting Story Movement* does the near impossible—it brings fresh perspective to the craft of writing. Full of deep and rich insights as well as practical exercises, Craft delivers her advice in a motivating voice that made me itch to get back to writing!"
—Lainey Cameron, award winning author of *The Exit Strategy* and host of The Best of Book Marketing Podcast

CRAFTING STORY MOVEMENT

TECHNIQUES TO ENGAGE READERS AND DRIVE YOUR NOVEL FORWARD

KATHRYN CRAFT

Copyright © 2025 by Kathryn Craft. All rights reserved.
Published in the United States by Craft on Craft, LLC
www.kathryncraft.com

ISBN Paperback: 979-8-9991425-1-1
ISBN Hardcover: 979-8-9991425-0-4
ISBN Ebook: 979-8-9991425-2-8

All rights reserved. No part of this book may be reproduced in any form or by any electronic or mechanical means, including information storage or retrieval systems, without permission in writing from the publisher or author, except by a reviewer who may quote brief passages in a review.

Library of Congress Cataloguing-in-Publication Data has been submitted.

Cover Design and Interior by Donna Cunningham of BeauxArts.Design
Author photograph by Alexandra Reckless

*To my dance mentor and constant inspiration,
Lana Kay Rosenberg,
who first encouraged me to tell stories through movement*

Contents

Foreword   vii

Introduction: Travel on the Diagonal   1

Part I: Set Your Story in Motion

   Chapter 1: Spark Your Curiosity   7
   Chapter 2: Choose a Compelling Perspective   15
   Chapter 3: Pressure Your Protagonist to Act   30
   Chapter 4: Incite a Specific Story Goal   43
   Chapter 5: Aim Toward the Inciting Incident   58
   Chapter 6: Engage the Reader with Your Opening Lines   66
   Chapter 7: Plunge into Genre   83
   Chapter 8: Motivate Your Protagonist   93
   Chapter 9: Head Forward by Looking Back   100
   Chapter 10: Stage the Story Against an Interactive Setting   117

Part II: Propel Your Protagonist Through a Gauntlet

   Chapter 11: Determine Relevant Conflict   131
   Chapter 12: Harness the Forces of Action   140
   Chapter 13: Refresh Tension   149
   Chapter 14: Push Your Reader Off Balance   165
   Chapter 15: Say Less, Do More   175
   Chapter 16: Interweave External and Inner Arcs   189
   Chapter 17: Sharpen Your Stakes   206

Part III: Drive Your Protagonist Toward the End

Chapter 18: Push Your Characters to the Limit	219
Chapter 19: Demonstrate Emotion	229
Chapter 20: Combine Strategies to Adjust Pacing	240
Chapter 21: Summon the Darkness	253
Chapter 22: Grant Your Protagonist the Ultimate Fight	260
Chapter 23: Point Beyond "The End"	268
Chapter 24: Keep Your Story Moving Within You	284

Conclusion	292
Epigraph References	295
Endnotes	298
Bibliography of Excerpts	302
Index	308
Acknowledgments	314
About the Author	316

Foreword

BEGINNING NOVELISTS OFTEN GET ONE THING WRONG. They believe that when a protagonist is presented with a problem, or has a goal, that will propel the reader through the hundreds of pages that follow. They imagine that everything that "happens"—what we can visualize in our mind's eye—*is* the story, and so long as we readers can "see" what is happening, we are automatically immersed and excited.

Nothing can be further from the truth. A novel is events, true enough, but the *experience* of a story happens in the heart and mind of the reader. The reader imagines, feels, thinks, judges and reacts. The reader first engages and then, we hope, keeps going. What keeps the reader going is a sense that things aren't yet finished. Anticipation is stirred and there is an urgency to the words on the page.

There is also a feeling that the story is constantly moving. Motion is hypnotic. It is the reason we can't take our eyes off the rushing water of a river, a neon green ball on a tennis court, or dancers on a stage. In a novel, however, there is no water, tennis ball, or body in motion. The sense of motion must be generated in other ways, and if plot events alone are not enough to do that, what else is needed?

That brings us to Kathryn Craft's excellent guide *Crafting Story Movement*. This is a book of fiction method like no other. Kathryn comes by her expertise honestly, not only as a longtime dancer, choreographer, movement teacher, and critic, but as a novelist, teacher, and writing coach. Her in-depth program *Your Novel Year*, and her blog posts at the online writing community *Writer Unboxed,* convey a depth of experience and present a perspective on fiction that is utterly unique.

Get ready. What you will discover in the pages ahead are scores of insights and practical suggestions for, first of all, engaging readers, and then mesmerizing them with constant motion: motion generated not just by action, but by the curiosity, pressure, desire, genre expectations, origins, worldview, hidden objects, unexpected elements, unwanted change, new courage, understatement, emotional turning points, character limitations, and (wonderfully) the act of "summoning the darkness." Most of all, you'll realize that motion flows most from the energy, commitment and purpose of the writer.

When Kathryn writes, "Movement is a transfer of energy," or explains why movement on stage is most gripping on a diagonal, she is not just spinning fancy metaphors for writing. She is opening practical approaches to creating story momentum. I love this book. You might think, at this point, that there is nothing new to say about the craft of fiction, but there is, and Kathryn is saying it here.

That is not all. Kathryn's insights come from in-depth reading, which she shares herein in a parade of examples that incontrovertibly illustrate her points. If you don't get what Kathryn is saying—and begin using it right away in your fiction—well, then that's on you. But I don't need to caution you. Read on and discover a realm of fiction craft that will enrich your writing, our reading, and our literature.

Donald Maass

Surrey, British Columbia
June, 2025

Introduction

Travel on the Diagonal

This is the key factor: the communication between artist and audience. This is what creates that indefinable electricity, which is essential to theatre.
—Donald McKayle, dancer and choreographer

THIS BOOK IS A MOVEMENT STUDY for novelists. That a dance critic turned developmental editor—especially one with my last name—would write a book on the craft of story movement might seem an inevitability, but I was slow to come to the idea. It wasn't until preparing a presentation for an online conference run by author Therese Walsh, co-founder of the acclaimed *Writer Unboxed* blog, that my backgrounds in dance and story converged to illuminate the contribution I might make to the already robust canon of how-to-write-fiction titles: the way every single aspect of craft I'd studied held the promise of story movement.

Sometimes it takes a few decades to realize that the journeys you've compartmentalized could converge as a perspective worth sharing.

From my dance training, I learned that movement is a transfer of energy—from one muscle to another, dancer to partner, the earth to the body, the mind to the body to the surrounding space, performer to audience member. The choreography that coordinates that movement is not a series of steps any more than a story is a series of black marks on a page. What captivates is the intention the mover brings to the connection between steps, just as story movement relies on the energy between words. It is in a novel's spaces that author and reader interact, through questions raised, expectations managed, and ideas allowed to resonate.

By focusing on how to harness the energy that drives a story forward, I hope to encourage you to discover the "why" that will connect storytelling "steps" you may have learned elsewhere. As this book's twenty-four chapters suggest, aspects of story movement manifest in many ways. We'll start with how you-as-author move toward your story. We'll look at how you invite the reader to share in its experience and how to keep them invested. We'll look at how energy is exchanged within scenes and how this drives a protagonist's inner change.

My movement background may have primed me to think of story in terms of impetus and destination, but this doesn't mean nonstop action. A reader's pulse can be elevated with only a single question riveting them to the page. As choreographer Lucinda Childs has said, "The diagonal gives a three-dimensional feeling to dancers that cannot be achieved when they are only front and back. On the diagonal, more movement is automatically visible."[1] Imagine tension on a page like a diagonal pass across the stage—a longer path to get from back to front, yes, but whose shadows and partial truths invite interest.

My goal is to energize the discussion of basic story craft with a movement specialist's perspective; wisdom from exceptional dance artists and stellar excerpts from published novels in a range of commercial and upmarket genres will be our guides.

The techniques you find on these pages will help you create and sustain movement among many layers of story craft. I offer no rules for their use, because rules are fixed and immutable. Nor will I offer you a writing method, which like a stiff shoe may not be a good fit for your way of walking. Fixed, immutable, stiff—such adjectives will be of no use when applied to a creative endeavor that must conjure movement from the flat surface of a page. I intend to impel, provoke, and electrify as we look at the many ways your story interacts with your reader.

The only rule is to do what it takes to achieve story movement.

But let's not dawdle right here at the opening, as that is a death knell for any writing that hopes to engage its reader. The sooner we plunge in, the sooner you can start applying fresh awareness to the movement in your manuscript.

PART I

Set Your Story in Motion

1

Spark Your Curiosity

The artist must be ecstatic about something; he burns at a brighter flame; he vibrates at a higher level of intensity. And he must feel that what he's got is something he must share with you.
—Ted Shawn, modern dancer

PICTURE YOURSELF AT THE END of your manuscript's journey. It is now a published novel, and you stand holding it in a bookstore while looking out at a gathering of family, friends, fellow writers, and avid readers. The room is abuzz with love, pride, and anticipation. In the best-case scenario, much of that positivity is emanating from you.

Why? Because love sells books.

Yet by the time your once-beloved novel is ready for publication, you may be sick to death of it. This attitude can curb your promotional efforts. But the fatigue is real. After generating multiple drafts, then rewriting and revising, you will have pored over every word dozens of times, making this the novel you've reread more than any other—and well before the story's power has been brought to fruition. Until then, you must hold in your heart and mind an unshakable belief in its potential.

Prepare in advance to be the first reader hooked by the story you plan to write.

What about your main character's predicament arrests you, puzzles you, or enthralls you so much that you are willing to put in the year(s) it will take to write and shape it? What about this story touches you in a place so deep that you'll keep writing, even when the going gets tough? Writing is hard and its monetary reward too uncertain to write a novel unless it will give you something you need. Something you can then offer your reader.

Each of the following novels drew me in as a reader. This had me wondering what had sparked the author's abiding devotion to the project. Let's see.

Solve a character's problem

What if you could live forever, but no one would remember you? This question occurred to V. E. Schwab while walking the hills in England's Lake District, as her grandmother was succumbing to dementia. "I remember walking through Ambleside, feeling very intensely aware of my aloneness and thinking about what it would be like to move through a world where you couldn't leave a mark,"[2] Schwab said in an *Entertainment Weekly* interview. Her character's conundrum kept churning within her over the next ten years—and once the resulting novel, *The Invisible Life of Addie LaRue* was released into the world, it hit all the bestseller lists.

Respond to the call

After the success of her *New York Times* bestselling novel *The Unlikely Pilgrimage of Harold Fry,* British author Rachel Joyce had publicly and repeatedly claimed that her next book would *not* be a sequel to sixty-year-old Harold's pilgrimage to see Queenie Hennessy, a long-estranged friend dying of cancer, who Harold came to believe he was keeping alive by walking the 500 miles to visit her. But then, while she was working on a different project, the thought struck Joyce that she wasn't finished with Queenie's story after all.

"The realisation came fully dressed, as if it had been around a long time," Joyce told *The Guardian*—and *The Love Song of Miss Queenie Hennessy* was born. "No sooner had I had it, than I also got the book's title, its form, and sentences, hundreds of them, cramming my head. There was nothing for it but to abandon the piece I was working on and start on Queenie's story, right from her very beginning."[3]

Honor a voice

Being present when you hear your character's first, distinctive words can result in a powerful invitation to tell their story. Roland Merullo first heard the voice of the protagonist in his novel *The Talk-Funny Girl* during an incident he witnessed between a woman and her little boy at a Vermont convenience store. "The mother grabbed him and shook him and said, in a loud voice, something so racist, so illogical, so hurtful, that I can't repeat it here,"[4] he says on his website. If he'd had children of his own then, he added, or had been a little braver, he might have stepped in and told her to take it easy. Instead, he wrote a novel about a teenage girl raised in an abusive, backwoods community, where speech could serve to both isolate her and ultimately become a barometer of change.

Her voice isn't revealed until after these opening lines from the prologue:

> I am a grown woman now, married and raising children, and happy enough most of the time. Underneath that happiness, though, showing its face every now and again, is a part of me still connected to a time when I was a girl living with her parents in the New Hampshire hills. That girl was not treated well, and when anyone is hurt like that—especially a child—the hurt burrows down inside and makes a kind of museum there, with images of the bad times displayed on every wall.

Astute readers will note the disconnect this narrator creates between her current self and her teen self, referred to above as "that girl." We soon find out why. On the third page of chapter 1, we encounter this same narrator's first lines of dialogue as a seventeen-year-old girl seeking a job. The first one reads, "I come for a try for paying work." A few paragraphs later, she clarifies the kind of work she's looking for: "Any of a thing for pay."

Why is this teenager using such garbled syntax, when the prologue clearly shows she'll end up capable of eloquently describing her pain as inhabiting a museum within her? The voice that attracted Merullo to his character also attracted this reader.

Unpack a disturbing situation

In the thriller genre, author Kaira Rouda has a penchant for channeling chilling first-person voices. Rouda told me that it only took her two months to draft her voice-y thriller, *Best Day Ever*. "Paul popped into my head fully formed and demanded to tell his story. You'll know from reading—he's persuasive."

The novel's opening is innocent enough—almost:

> I glance at my wife as she climbs into the passenger seat, sunlight bouncing off her shiny blond hair like sparklers lit for the Fourth of July, and I am bursting with confidence. Everything is as it should be.

The clues were subtle at first, but the word "confidence" piqued my interest and "should" inspired foreboding. As the couple gets underway on their weekend getaway to their second home, in an area that will be sparsely populated this early in the spring, Paul's voice continued to repulse and intrigue me—as if he was someone I didn't dare look away from until I knew what he was up to.

Look through a prism at a timely theme

In *My Sister's Keeper,* Jodi Picoult explores the family dynamics that arise when an adolescent, who had been genetically predetermined to be a bone marrow donor for her ill older sister, sues her parents for the rights to her own body. In an interview with *Bookreporter,*[5] Picoult, who admits she is no ethicist, said she approached this complex issue by picking apart the emotional threads of this family's relationships.

Once she realized how many characters were personally impacted by the story events—among them the sick daughter, her lawyer, the sister-donor, the older brother who wasn't a match, and the mother who just wants her first-born daughter to live—she knew that multiple points of view would strengthen the emotional storm drawing her into the story.

Follow a seductive path

Colum McCann was inspired to write his National Book Award-winning novel *Let the Great World Spin* by his fascination with Philippe Petit's 1974 high-wire walk between the World Trade Center towers. After the 9/11 terror attack brought down the towers, the intimate novel he'd envisioned was no longer possible.

"If you're a writer, you know there are ways in which we don't know what we're doing at all,"[6] McCann said in an interview on Oprah.com. "We're working out mysteries in a sort of poetic realm, and hoping that if a story is honest, if you're dragging the deep truth out of yourself, then something good and profound might come out of it. Often, and in this case, it's after I finish the novel that all the pieces join together with what I want to say. Then again, it might be a whole pile of shite. You can't be too holy with this stuff."

What McCann called "an organic outgrowth of the creative experience" became a sweeping novel of disparate stories that pivot around a single node of connection—those who'd witnessed Petit's stunt—just as the stories of the strangers killed in the terror attack tragically converge.

Promise a friend

At the outbreak of the world war in July 1914, many hoped the conflict would be resolved by Christmas. This notion led Hazel Gaynor and co-author Heather Webb to conjure a group of friends making plans for that Christmas—plans horribly interrupted, since four Christmases would come and go before the soldiers returned home. Their epistolary novel, *Last Christmas in Paris,* resulted—and their collaboration drew them deeper and deeper into the story.

Gaynor's website describes the process this way: "The book was written through a literal exchange of letters. Hazel would wake up in Ireland, pen a letter from one of her characters, and wait for a reply. Several hours later, Heather would wake in the U.S. to find mail in her inbox. She would respond in kind, sending her characters' words over the e-waves."[7]

The surprises the authors discovered in their inboxes, bolstered by their social accountability, created a powerful hook that saw them through to the end.

Search for the "why"

In an interview with BookBrowse, Diane Setterfield admitted she doesn't know where she got the inspiration for her novel *The Thirteenth Tale.* "This book took three years to write and its real genesis was longer still: there was no single moment when I thought: *Aha! What a great idea!* Rather there was a slow and gradual accumulation of numerous small ideas."[8]

While Setterfield delivers the kind of big reveal readers love, that was not what beckoned her toward the novel's collaboration between enigmatic author Vida Winter, who as the novel opens has completed the twelve-book arc she'd promised her readers, and Margaret Lea, the reclusive young biographer to whom Vida entrusts the truth about her violent past—the story that will become her thirteenth tale.

"I had been considering what it must be like to know oneself to be one kind of person, whilst consistently giving in public the impression of being an entirely different kind of person," Setterfield said. "I was moved by the loneliness such a person might feel, and in one of those exhilarating rushes of inspiration (I wish there were more of them) dashed down a piece that later became Miss Winter's letter to Margaret. At that stage I didn't even know if it was the voice of a man or a woman." The mystery drew her in.

Delve into a situation you can't look away from

If a situation grabs on tight and won't release you, chances are you'll go the distance—and find readers who'll do the same. During an in-person event, author Bryan Reardon spoke about the setup for his debut domestic thriller, *Finding Jake*. When stay-at-home dad Simon Connolly is notified that there's been a shooting at the high school, he rushes to a rendezvous point in the church across from the school. One by one, anxious parents are reunited with their children—until Simon is all alone. His son, Jake, is missing—and accused of being the shooter.

Are you kidding me? From this early twist to its unexpected ending, it took Reardon only four months to draft his propulsive, *New York Times* bestselling debut.

The story that will beg the reader's interest from beginning to end must first beg your own—*from beginning to end*. The craft of story movement begins inside the author—in many cases, before any actual writing has been done. Take time to identify what sparked your interest in your novel and then fan its flames. The power of your writing (and your self-promotion, for that matter) cannot hope to exceed your love for your protagonist and their predicament.

→❊ Try This ❊←

Before powering up your story—or later, when your writing mojo flags, and you need to be reminded—answer these questions:

- What about your protagonist's predicament hooks your mind, heart, and spirit?

- What spark ignited the flame of conflict within your story?
- What about your character has earned your enduring loyalty?
- What is this story's dramatic imperative—meaning, why must their story start right here and now? What will it offer you, as well as today's reader?
- When journaling in your protagonist's first-person voice, can you reach a level of immersion into character that feels so true you feel you owe it to them to tell their story?

2

Choose a Compelling Perspective

I had daydreamed through many performances of Swan Lake, thinking the dancing tutus only ever conveyed one aspect of swans: their beauty gliding on water. I wondered what it would be like to use male dancers and bring out swans' aggressive, muscular side.
—Matthew Bourne, choreographer

NOVELS OFFER THE READER the opportunity to experience countless paths not taken, places unexplored, situations never encountered, beliefs and prejudices never felt, and possibilities they never would have conceived. The protagonist you choose to be your reader's guide won't be "everyman"—they will have a unique genetic makeup, physicality, spirit, and personality, as well as specific societal influences and past experiences.

Blend these specifics together, pour them into an observant character, and you arrive at perspective. Many people read books simply *because* it will grant them access to a perspective they hadn't previously considered.

Perspective is a blade that cuts into a story on a certain angle. Jack and Jill may have gone up the hill to fetch a pail of water and then fallen down the hill quite innocently, sure. But why did Jack fall and break his crown, anyway? Chances are, Jack and Jill would have different notions of what happened. And did anyone interview the next-door neighbor? She may believe she had witnessed a murder.

To expand the reader's perspective is one of literature's highest callings. Memoir would be pointless without it. It pervades a journalist's best quotes, energizes speeches, makes history worth reading about. If you didn't believe a dancer-author had a perspective worth considering, you wouldn't be reading this book.

In a novel, the path that will lead you to a dramatic core capable of changing minds and hearts runs straight through perspective.

Your protagonist's perspective will determine how your story's premise will play out, so make this important determination early on. As you'll see from my following browsing experiences, the promise of a compelling perspective can also drive sales.

I picked up *The Girls* by Lori Lansens because each intriguing line of its opening rowed me further from the shore of familiarity, raising questions about whose perspective was guiding this work.

> I have never looked into my sister's eyes. I have never bathed alone. I have never stood in the grass at night and raised my arms to a beguiling moon. I've never used an airplane bathroom. Or worn a hat. Or been kissed like that. I've never driven a car. Or slept through the night. Never a private talk. Or solo walk. I've never climbed a tree. Or faded into a crowd. So many things I've never done, but oh, how I've been loved. And, if such things were to be, I'd live a thousand lives as me, to be loved so exponentially.

If you guessed that our narrator is a conjoined twin, you're correct.

Since conjoined twins are extremely rare, most of us don't have a clue what it would be like to live in this way. We might assume it would be a nightmare from which you could never wake. And yet right up front, protagonist Rose Darlen delivers a startling assurance: she has been loved so deeply that if given the chance, she'd chose the same life all over again. Her sister Ruby may agree to this point, but the chapters in Ruby's voice reveal a strikingly different life experience. This story's promise left me eager to learn what it had to say about the human condition.

Lansens is not a twin of any sort, so what drew her to the topic? In an interview on BookBrowse, Lansens shares the following conversation with her three-and-a-half-year-old son that hooked her on an emotional level. After reading him a story, he had pressed his cheek to hers:

> I quietly enjoyed the warmth of his little face and soon felt the quickening of his cookie-breath. "I wish we could be glued like this, Mommy."
>
> I got goose shivers.
>
> "I wish we could be glued with our heads like this."
>
> "Why, baby?" I asked. "Why do you want to be glued to Mommy?"
>
> "Because then we would always be together."
>
> We were quiet for a moment.
>
> "But," Max realized suddenly, "we couldn't see each other." He strained with his eyes to prove it.
>
> Then he sighed. I understood his longing. And felt it, too.

For Lansens, the understanding this moment engendered became a jumping-off place for her novel. She called it "a truth I felt I could take to the edge."[9]

After that, Rose and Ruby Darlen revealed themselves—and they didn't slip through the curtain quietly to take center stage. "They charged through it in all their brilliant conjoined glory," Lansens wrote. "But only after shouting at me from the window of their ramshackle farmhouse. And waving madly from their spot on the bridge over the creek. And screaming from Frankie's basement, where that unimaginable thing happens."

Extreme point of view is also the undeniable draw of Garth Stein's book club darling, *The Art of Racing in the Rain*. Here is its opening:

> Gestures are all that I have; sometimes they must be grand in nature. And while I occasionally cross the line into the world of the melodramatic, it is what I must do to communicate clearly and effectively. In order to make my point understood. I have no words I can rely on because, much to my dismay, my tongue was designed long and flat and loose. It is a horribly ineffective tool for pushing food around my mouth while chewing. And an even less effective tool for making clever and complicated sounds that can be linked together to form sentences. And that's why I'm here now waiting for Denny to come home. He should be here soon. I'm lying on the cool tiles of the kitchen floor in a puddle of my own urine.

By the end of this paragraph, this protagonist had already won my empathy, and I had fully accepted the story's mode of delivery. I believed this dog's perspective would help me experience aspects of my world anew.

What drew Stein to this perspective? At his website, he credits learning of the Mongolian belief that dogs are reincarnated as humans, as well as hearing Billy Collins read a poem from the perspective of a dog. "When Billy Collins finished reading, I knew I had to write a story from the point of view of a dog," he wrote. "And my dog would know the truth: that in his next incarnation, he would return to earth as a man."[10] Then, the framework of Denny's need took shape:

> A close friend of mine, who is a semi-professional racecar driver but who supplements his racing by working behind the counter at an upscale automotive repair shop, was going through some personal difficulties. His plight wasn't Denny's, but it gave me some ideas about what happens to families when

one member suddenly passes away. I developed a story that would really put my main character, Denny, through his paces, and then it was all there for me.

Lansens spoke of taking her story of conjoined twins *to the edge*. Stein spoke of putting his racecar driver *through his paces*. Even in these early stages, perspective was actively driving these stories.

So many novels have been set during World War II, one might reasonably wonder what's left to write about. Yet the war's breadth offered a rich background of conflict against which to set diverse cultural tales. Three of the less obvious settings grabbed me with the promise of distinct perspectives.

Sarah's Key by Tatiana de Rosnay is set in France at the time when the local police, under orders from the Nazis, were rounding up Jews and holding them in the Paris Velodrome before shipping them to concentration camps. In *Sarah's Key,* while the police are giving a young girl, Sarah, and her mother ten minutes to pack before taking them from their apartment, Sarah's younger brother crawls unseen into a hidden compartment where the children often played. This snip is from Sarah's point of view.

"Are you afraid in there?" she said softly, as the men called out for them.

"No," he said. "I'm not afraid. You lock me in. They won't get me."

She closed the door on the little white face, turned the key in the lock. Then she slipped the key into her pocket. The lock was hidden by a pivoting device shaped like a light switch. it was impossible to see the outline of the cupboard in the paneling of the wall. Yes, he'd be safe there. She was sure of it.

The girl murmured his name and laid her palm flat on the wooden panel.

"I'll come back for you later. I promise."

Swept up in the purge, Sarah was never able to return to retrieve her brother. This heart-wrenching perspective, of a heroic child who must deal with the ramifications of her actions while ensconced in her own fight to survive, is powerful due to its extreme inner conflict. The mother in her called her to write it, de Rosnay told the Mother Daughter Book Club. "I was appalled by what I discovered concerning the roundup, especially about what happened to those 4,000 Jewish children, and I knew I had to write about it. I needed to write about it."[11]

In a story set halfway around the world from Paris, Tess Uriza Holthe looked at the Second World War through a child's perspective. In *When the Elephants Dance,* Alejandro is the sole provider for an ill and starving family hiding beneath the floorboards of their house in the Philippines. But note the difference in the voice, and its promised perspective.

> Papa explains the war like this: "When the elephants dance, the chickens must be careful." The great beasts, as they circle one another, shaking the trees and trumpeting loudly, are the Amerikanos and the Japanese as they fight. And our Philippine Islands? We are the small chickens. I think of baby chicks I can hold in the palm of my hand, flapping wings that are not yet grown, and I am frightened.

This novel speaks directly to the power of story. Throughout their ordeal, the family shares mythical tales, feeding "their bellies with words and images because they cannot fill them with food,"[12] Holthe said in a BookBrowse interview. By embodying the ideals of honor, family, religion, and patriotism, Holthe's original folk stories help the family persevere against the brutal horrors of war.

At the heart of another World War II tale, *The Last Rose of Shanghai* by Weina Dai Randel—this one set in China—is the moving story of forbidden love between Aiyi, a young Chinese heiress and businesswoman, and Ernest, a penniless displaced German Jew riding the incoming wave of refuge-seekers in Shanghai's International Settlement. That Aiyi has been long betrothed to a wealthy Chinese man is the first of many obstacles between them as the Japanese move in, violence escalates, and fortunes are reversed. Randel keeps the blade of her story's perspective sharp by whetting it with the differing perspectives of Aiyi and Ernest.

"Shanghai holds a special place in my heart as I used to work and study there,"[13] Randel said in an interview at *China Daily*. "I used to walk past a red brick building on the way to school, and it was inscribed with 'church' in Chinese characters, which I found out later was a synagogue." She knew from the start it would be a love story between people whose perspectives were informed by different cultures. "Because of the restraints of tradition, the shackles of history, and the strife of war, their story would be an uphill battle sprinkled with resilience, hopes, and self-discovery."

Randel seduced me with the promise of a high-stakes tale of forbidden love. Her authentic experience as one who had lived in Shanghai, which allowed her to immerse the reader in its sights, sounds, and smells, was a bonus.

Choose how you'll illuminate your story

Related to perspective is its conduit, point of view (POV). Both are necessary to move your story forward. To grasp my point, let's look at the ways POV illuminates a story—just like a theater light.

For the audience to see what's going on, you first need a source of bright, white light. To focus it on the plot unfolding on the stage below, that light must be constrained by a metal housing that will send it in only one direction. To add interest, a colored gel is slotted in front of the white light.

In my analogy, the brilliant white light will represent the limitless potential with which your protagonist (or other POV character) was born. Its brilliance is notoriously hot—as hot as an urgent desire—but that can also cause dramatic complications. The metal housing represents the backstory that has formed this character's way of looking at the world. By limiting its direction of travel, this housing runs the white light of this character's thoughts, beliefs, and feelings through the limitations of her past experiences. The gel represents the perspective that will color how this character perceives the action on the stage below.

As an example, let's look at Roland Merullo's *The Talk-Funny Girl*, introduced in the last chapter. By the time teen protagonist Marjorie begins relating her story, the bright light of her potential has already been narrowed by parents who lived in a cult so removed from society that they had developed their own way of speaking. Marjorie goes to school in town and knows how to get by in both worlds but chooses to withstand teasing at school and sound ignorant when looking for work over the possibility that word might get back to her parents, since any hint of assimilation results in severe abuse. This informs Marjorie's burning desire to live a life built from her own choices and results in the perspective—the gel that will color every aspect of plot after that—that no one can be trusted to have her best interests at heart.

This backstory is fixed; she can't change its metal housing. The purpose of the story is to add experiences (plot that takes place on the stage) that heat up her desire to accomplish a story goal that will require that she access more of that light—so that, in the end, you can show how and why the gel changes color. Once her perspective shifts, her POV—her way of looking at the world—can also shift.

Once you have a bright white light, buzzing with potential and set in motion by desire, funneled through the housing of past experience and then colored by the perspective the character will shine on the action, you can rely on point of view alone to provide a template for story movement—and you'll invite the reader to move into your character's experience of it.

To find your POV's impact on movement potential, you need to understand the backstory that narrows their perspective. The encampment where Marjorie grew up provided such an extremely limited "housing" that Merullo included only six pages of forward-moving plot before devoting three pages of backstory that showed how her family ended up in this community, but this will not be the need in every story. In the first energized line of Edgar Allan Poe's "The Tell-Tale Heart," written in 1843, we gain full access to his POV character's perspective: "True!—nervous—very, very dreadfully nervous I had been and am; but why will you say that I am mad?" The whole point of Poe's short story is to pull us so close to the bright light of a tormented mind that it feels dangerous to be there.

Let's look at various ways compelling perspectives can drive conflict in long-form fiction.

Pass the baton

An effective way to ensure conflict between different-yet-relatable perspectives is to tell the story from more than one character's point of view.

In *House of Sand and Fog,* author Andre Dubus III uses alternating first-person accounts to set up the core conflict. Behrani is a deposed Iranian colonel starting over in the United States, and Kathy is an American struggling to get by. Their lives intersect when Kathy's house goes up for sheriff's sale and Behrani purchases it for a song. The colonel is thrilled to provide a home for his family with his meager resources, but Kathy is devastated to lose her only connection to her deceased father. Kathy seeks the help of her new lover, married policeman Lester Burdon, to correct the administrative error that cost her the loss of her home.

For more than two hundred pages we follow these first-person accounts. Then, in a new chapter, we read:

> It was dark now, and Lester had been sitting on the fish camp's porch for over two hours. The fog was thick in the trees, and it made the black woods around the cabin appear to be under a milky water. He could still smell the maple he'd cut, split, and stacked, and twice he heard a car go by...

Huh? The author abandons his own mode of story delivery to allow Lester's third-person intrusion. This was jarring, to be sure, but let's look at why this shift didn't stop story movement cold.

Up to this point, the first-person perspectives have allowed the reader to empathize with both Behrani and Kathy. But their conflict, born of presumption and cultural misunderstanding, has come to somewhat of a standstill. Here, Dubus wants to dig deeper into the character of Lester Burdon, the married deputy sheriff who's fallen for Kathy, to set him up as an agent of change. Lester's backstory arrives at this conclusion:

> Lester began to feel as inauthentic a man as possible, living in a marriage he no longer felt, working as a law officer when he'd never been able to face any man down on his own, to serve or protect anyone without the San Mateo County Sheriff's Department behind him.

Let's look at how Dubus gets away with this jarring shift without losing his reader, as it will offer a useful lesson in why to introduce an additional POV character.

He has a genuine, story-relevant reason to shift the perspective. By this point Dubus has earned our empathy for both his primary characters, but they are so ensconced in their perspectives that resolution seems unlikely. This twenty-five-page chapter in Lester's POV allows access to his backstory and inner conflict, suggesting that he might be the agent of change. This added characterization proves critical to our understanding of the tragic storm to come.

He raises questions the reader wants answers to. Since Lester has already pulled off some shady stunts on Kathy's behalf, the reader is eager to learn why a law enforcer might act that way. Managing reader expectation like this can build curiosity and anticipation.

He tweaks his story's structure to accommodate a rule change. Dubus didn't throw his POV rule out the window—he modified it and indicated this by creating "Part II." New section, new rules. The addition of Lester's perspective gives this second part a more prismatic build toward the climax.

He uses the intrusion to subtly underscore meaning. Lester got involved where he didn't belong. He wasn't part of the original conflict; his third-person status demonstrates this. By further destabilizing the situation, Dubus uses Lester to raise the stakes in a story that explores how we defend the right to pursue the American Dream.

From a writer's standpoint, not all POV decisions can be executed perfectly. Dubus's alternating first-person POVs worked fine until his story demanded the reader know something that only a non-POV character was experiencing. Picoult anticipated that her multiple points of view for *My Sister's Keeper* would be so hard to track, that she put each character's chapters in different fonts.

I could tell you never to do that because it's cheesy, and goes against all principles of good book design, and a sign that your novel is too confusing and requires simplifying, but here's how much readers care about such opinions: *My Sister's Keeper*, which came out in 2004, still carries a rating of 4.6 out of 5 and an impressively high ranking on Amazon. And Dubus's novel, with that glaring POV switch, was an Oprah pick, a National Book Award finalist, and a #1 *New York Times* bestseller.

File these examples under "anything can work if you can make it work." The most important takeaway here is that the perspectives these novelists chose served their stories by continually cranking up the kind of tension that keeps readers turning pages.

But how far, realistically, can you push a reader? Would they hang in there for *sixteen* perspectives? Consider Bryn Greenwood's novel, *All the Ugly and Wonderful Things.* If passing off POV is like a relay race, Greenwood made off with all the POV batons, sending her novel straight to the *New York Times Best Sellers* list.

Why would she even attempt that—and how did she get away with it?

Capitalize on perspective in multiple POVs

In her story, Greenwood touches on a volatile cultural taboo: the age of sexual consent. Most people would come down hard on the side of punishing adult predators who assault minor youth. Case closed.

But what if a much greater danger comes from the child's own parents?

To raise this question in her readers' minds—all while respecting the emotions of readers whose opinions are entrenched—Greenwood chose a loose POV structure that allowed her to dip into the best perspective for illuminating that part of her story.

Her opening gets right to the heart of the story's theme of judgment by introducing the protagonist, Wavy, through another character's perspective. From Wavy's cousin Amy, we learn that Amy's mother took in five-year-old Wavy when her own parents were in jail. From the outset we see Wavy the way others do: voiceless (Wavy rarely speaks) and odd (she won't eat in front of other people). The second chapter moves to the perspective of Wavy's next caretaker, her grandmother. We're two dozen pages in before we finally hear from Wavy, and by this time, the novel's very structure is suggesting how hard Wavy will have to fight to make her own opinions matter in the world.

At the tender age of eight, as her parents resume "guardianship," Wavy becomes her baby brother's main caretaker while her father cooks meth in a nearby barn and her mother sleeps the days away in a drugged-up haze. This situation is discovered by one of her father's drug runners, twenty-four-year-old Kellen, who is obliged to Wavy for helping him after a motorcycle accident. He starts to check in on her. Takes her to school. Pays her school fees. Cleans up the house. They stare up at the stars together; learn the constellations. They grow to love one another—nothing lurid to make us look away.

Who else should we hear from? Kellen, of course, so we know his motivations aren't of the creepy pedophile variety. Wavy's teacher gives us an important outside perspective, as she believes Kellen is Wavy's father. Two of Wavy's real father's girlfriends, determined to win her father's favor through sex, give us a look at the dysfunctional world in which Wavy learns to be female. Later, when teenaged Wavy wants to prove her love for Kellen, the perspectives of the police officer who arrests Kellen for statutory rape and the judge who jails him provide legal context.

In the end, Greenwood shows considerable restraint by sticking with sixteen perspectives—to fully explore her story, she originally wrote it from the POVs of dozens more of her characters. This excerpt from an interview at the back of the book gives us material pertinent to our discussion of whose POV can support story movement, and why.

> Wavy's parents didn't make the cut, because they were so focused on themselves that their narratives derailed the story I wanted to tell. Although Aunt Brenda is the natural antagonist to Wavy, her narrative turned out to be redundant. Aunt Brenda doesn't need to speak, because the average reader knows exactly what she's thinking. It's what we would be thinking if we were in her shoes.

By sticking to unexpected perspectives chosen for the way each could drive the story forward in the most eye-opening way, Greenwood keeps her story humming. To help orient the reader to this potentially confusing compilation of perspective, her chapters do not flip back and forth through time, nor is any one event explored through multiple perspectives; you can rely upon this story to drive relentlessly forward, and trust Greenwood's POV choices to effectively deliver it.

What a POV character needs to drive story movement

To create impulsion in your story, a secondary POV character needs a scene purpose other than allowing the reader access to information the protagonist doesn't have. They deserve development like your protagonist's, complete with backstory motivation that brought them to this scene and a story goal they're moving toward.

If any two of your characters are motivated by the same factors to achieve the same thing for the same reasons, you don't need them both. Their parallel paths will never intersect. And don't be fooled by your character's insistence that her supportive best friend would never cause conflict. Conflict does not have to slam into a protagonist at a 90-degree angle; it might take the form, for example, of gentle redirection when the protagonist is about to do something ill-advised.

While we all want our characters to come across as real people, thinking of your character as a perspective instead can help you develop your story's core conflict. Referring back to the theater light analogy, a secondary character can play a key role due to the way their own backstory has limited their "white light" of self and arrived at perspective of a different color. This character needs to be invested enough that we understand his perspective—as in the case of Dubus's Lester Burdon—which means he needs a story goal. Lester's desire to help his lover is a good start, but adding his shame at never having faced down a criminal adds more gas to the psychological through line driving his actions at the end of the book.

You'll enhance the dramatic tension of your novel if each of your characters has a reason for acting the way they do, no matter how many POVs you inhabit. When characters enter a scene for different reasons, conflict is bound to occur. This animates the scene regardless of its emotional tenor.

We often connect conflict with anger and when drafting a novel, it's not a bad place to start. Anger is a potent fuel, and it certainly spurs conflict. But it's also obvious. I urge you, at some point, to dig deeper. Marianne Williamson, in her 1992 book *A Return to Love,* posits that all human emotions are based in either fear or love.[14] Consider these emotions—not anger—as emotional bedrock. Anger may originate in the fear that justice will not prevail, or in a fear of abandonment. Jealousy can surge when someone else benefitted from luck that bypassed your character. Satisfaction comes from loving one's current circumstances. Awe overtakes us when beauty or grandeur inspires an intense response of love.

If every character in your novel is angry, your cast will feel redundant. Delve deeper and you might find perspectives born of poverty, entitlement, or abuse, allowing you to expand that one-note anger your characters share into an array of perspectives that will expand the breadth and depth of your story.

Manipulating POV is also a means by which you can allow your characters to keep their motives or plans secret, to be revealed later.

By whisking the reader from the limitations of their own perspective, POV delivers what readers seek: fresh experience of our world. As you read the excerpts in this book—even those meant to exemplify other techniques for getting your story moving—watch for the many ways that a compelling perspective is also at play.

Perspectives are powerful because you are writing from deep within your characters' essential selves. A strong POV can deliver the bitter taste of a bigoted character's words to your reader's own tongue. If your character is nervous, your reader will hear a vocal tremor without being prompted to do so. Make these choices carefully, and the bright white light of your character's potential, funneled through the backstory experiences that have limited it and the opinions and prejudices and feelings that color it, will coordinate to give the reader a distinct impression of story movement.

⇥ Try This ⇤

Having trouble trying to figure out who gets a POV, and how their perspective will help drive story action? Follow the energy.

- Define the unique makeup of your protagonist's "white light"—their spiritual, emotional, moral, ethical, and genetic core. What backstory has focused that light? What desire will inspire their actions? What is the resulting perspective that will color their perception of all plot points? And this one is key: Does this character interest and engage you? If not, keep working until they do.
- Journal about the story from the perspective of each of your major characters. If any two of them are on a parallel path, combine them. They aren't both needed. Work on this until each character brings a unique perspective to your premise.
- Can you deepen the remaining perspectives?
- If this is a big story, with plot powering up all over the world, consider using multiple third-person POVs, since multiple first-person POVs can be hard for a reader to track. If it's an intimate study, consider a first-person account.
- Practice telescoping your POV—your theater light—until you can fluidly move from illuminating the entire stage of story to zooming in on small details that will expose inner conflict.

3

Pressure Your Protagonist to Act

[The dancer] spikes his day with nerves, tensions, restlessness, anticipation, doubt, and a host of other irritations to keep his body-warmth up. Heat, or lack of it, is of primary concern to the dancer.
—Murray Louis, modern dancer and choreographer

WHEN TRANSLATING THE STORY in your mind to the page, it's easy to leave out proof of your protagonist's agency. This is so key to your reader's ability to bond with your protagonist that it would behoove you to keep this question in mind when first setting fingertips to keyboard: How can your character convince your reader (and sometimes your own self!) that they have what it takes to deliver on your novel's promise?

Most modern readers want to read about the kind of character evoked in this quote, which is widely attributed to artist Frida Kahlo: "I'm the type of woman that if I want the Moon, I'll get it down myself." A protagonist who takes decisive action will prove they have what it takes.

Let's examine a perspective that strengthens both character agency and story movement.

Evoke an outsider's pain

Belonging is an essential human need. By necessity—not desire—the outsider seeks the code that will lead to acceptance and let him rest easy in his skin. There are so many ways a character can feel hopelessly shut out from human companionship. Perhaps your protagonist is smarter than their peers, and acceptance would require them to pretend otherwise. Maybe your protagonist is sickly, neurodiverse, or suffering from family dysfunction. Has a different skin color or body type or speaks a different language.

However they are shut out, this character wants in. The answer will not be found by wallowing in their bedroom; they must become a keen observer of locked doors and curtained windows. They won't spend a whole lot of time devising a strategy; they'll start picking locks and breaking glass.

This active pursuit of acceptance, no matter how reckless, shows an agency to which your reader will relate—and, perhaps, even aspire. The added benefit is that through action, your character has revealed himself to the reader. As choreographer Doris Humphrey once said, "Nothing so clearly and inevitably reveals the inner man than movement and gesture."[15]

The following two novel openings overcome page-one inertia by showing an outsider thrust straight into action.

Case study 1: Show the protagonist in action on page 1

In *Fugitive Colors,* Lisa Barr introduces her protagonist with the first two words of her prologue, set in Chicago:

> Yakov Klein slowly ran his finger over the cover of the art book he was about to steal from the library, as a burglar would a precious jewel just snatched from a glass case. Pressing the book to his face, he inhaled the familiar dusty scent of his latest prize: *Gustav Klimt.* It was a delicious moment, but one he

would have to savor later, in the secrecy of his bedroom once the lights were out and his parents were sleeping. Right now, he had to get out of the library without getting caught.

Right away, through touch and smell, we can feel Yakov's forbidden desire. The very first sentence establishes his scene goal; the last sentence attaches stakes. Even without yet knowing why we should care, we are wondering: Can he get away with this?

In the next paragraph, we see him tuck the book beneath his overcoat and make a beeline to the exit. Then:

> From the corner of his eye, Yakov saw a little girl, no more than five, holding her mother's hand and watching him. He knew what she saw—what everyone saw when they looked at him—the long black wool coat, the tall black silk hat that was still too big, and the *payis*—long sidelocks—that Jewish custom had required him to grow his whole life. It was a uniform borne of a different century. Yakov, son of Benjamin, raised as an Orthodox Jew, wore some version of the same clothing every day—black and white, a wardrobe devoid of color or change—and he hated it.
>
> That's why he stole the art book. If truth were told, that was why he had been stealing art books since the week after his bar mitzvah, nine months earlier. He desperately needed color.

Ah, motivation revealed. And the stakes spread as "Yakov, son of Benjamin" extends the shame of getting caught to his family as well. When his mother discovers sketches that Yakov has been making, she begs him to stop, knowing his father and the rabbi would forbid it.

As this prologue continues, every sentence moves this outsider along a specific trajectory while setting up hidden motivations that will propel this budding young artist to Paris where, six years later and now calling himself Julian Klein, he will make it his mission to expose Nazis confiscating "dangerous" modern art—including Klimt's—during World War II.

Case study 2: Build up the outsider's entrance

Must your protagonist appear on page one? Not necessarily. Your protagonist may be the gateway to your story, but as with all things creative, there's no one way to construct the gate. But don't be coy—ensure that all signs point toward your protagonist's imminent entrance. Manipulating where you shine the light of story will build anticipation, and anticipation is a form of story movement.

In *A Prayer for Owen Meany,* John Irving chose not to bring Owen on scene right away, but to bring him to life through his narrator, John Wheelwright, who builds him up as a bit of a folk hero:

> I am doomed to remember a boy with a wrecked voice—not because of his voice, or because he was the smallest person I ever knew, or even because he was the instrument of my mother's death, but because he is the reason I believe in God; I am a Christian because of Owen Meany.

Wheelwright follows this testimony with vignettes showing how he and his other friends bullied Owen for being so small; while seated in Sunday school, they couldn't resist picking him up and passing him back and forth overhead. In one scene, the boys are swimming at a quarry, following Mr. Meany's rule to always swim one at a time with a rope tied around their waists. When Owen plays a prank by slipping the rope and hiding to see what will happen, he is deeply disappointed—no one panics enough to dive for him. Owen complains to his tormentors, his dialogue rendered in ALL CAPS to remind us of the trials of his wrecked voice, but he never rats on them or retaliates.

As this forty-two-page first chapter heads toward its dramatic reveal, in which we learn how Owen becomes the instrument of his friend's mother's death, Irving ratchets up anticipation by dropping this question from Wheelwright into its own paragraph at the end of a section, allowing it to resonate:

"How could I have known that Owen was a hero?"

Overcome your own inertia

How you'll establish your protagonist's agency is something you must think about each time you begin a project. This is especially true if you spend a good deal of your initial word count probing the protagonist's memories and thoughts in search of the inner conflict propelling their story.

That's called "starting to write"—not "opening a novel"—but writers often conflate the two.

Only you need early access to your protagonist's interiority—their innermost thoughts. Your reader will simply assume your protagonist has a good reason for doing what they're doing. Searching for hints along the way is part of reading fun. Besides, any reader who has met with an unreliable narrator knows a character's actions will speak louder than anything she is willing to tell us anyway. To earn your reader's faith and investment, your protagonist must be willing to act.

As early as 1687, storytelling guru Sir Isaac Newton hinted at the necessity of getting your protagonist off their duff with his principle of inertia, which (sort of) states, *A protagonist at rest will stay at rest, and a protagonist in motion will stay in motion until the story's problem is resolved, unless acted on by an external force.* Newton's second law describes the effect force will have on a body—it will accelerate in the direction of the force. And once your character has revealed the nature of the journey ahead, Newton's Third Law of Storytelling (oh, why not?) promises *for every action there is an equal and opposite reaction.*

To overcome the inertia that a blank first page can represent, try making your protagonist an "actor"—one who acts. But are all characters capable of "doing" something? Let's look at three increasingly challenged protagonists.

Anne Shirley

At the outset of Lucy Maud Montgomery's 1908 novel *Anne of Green Gables*, Anne, a preteen, is waiting at a train stop for her new foster father to pick her up. When he approaches, she starts talking so fast and at such length he can't possibly pose the objection that he had specifically asked for, and had expected to meet, a boy.

Due to countless cruelties suffered in an orphanage and previous foster placements, Anne could easily come off as a victim. But when seized by nightmarish flashbacks, she bolsters her optimism by imagining heroic characters in "fantastical" scenarios. She loves to learn and relentlessly defends herself when mocked at school for her lack of formal education.

In her new, kinder placement, she does not let obstacles like lack of money, isolation due to the rural setting, or an inability to ride a horse or drive a buggy keep her from reaching the ferries and trains that will allow her to achieve her goals in other towns.

As a "doer," Anne exhibits more agency than many adults I know. Through her, Montgomery teaches us that when it seems like a protagonist lacks the power to act, the writer must imagine a way for her to do so.

Susy Hendrix

When we first meet Audrey Hepburn's recently blinded character, Susy, in the 1967 film *Wait Until Dark,* drug dealers looking for a heroin-filled doll are hiding in her apartment as she calls to tell her husband at work to say she was "the best in blind school today." After she decides to "tap her way over" and meet him at a coffee shop in his building, she blithely tells him she'll be the one reading *Peter Rabbit* in braille. With her first words she's already showing us she has handled an extreme obstacle like a champ. But how about when the story comes to a head and Susy, trapped alone, must defend herself against the violent thug who returns for the doll?

During the long climactic fight, she:

- continually finds ways to put her antagonist at a disadvantage by plunging the apartment into darkness by breaking lightbulbs, disabling the emergency light, and unplugging the refrigerator;

- asks if he's looking at her—and when he says yes, throws a chemical at his face;
- douses him with gasoline and threatens him with lit matches while making him tap the floor with a cane so she knows where he is;
- tries to scream for help, and
- arms herself with a kitchen knife, saving herself from rape by stabbing him.

Certainly, courage can't replace eyesight—or can it? In the end, Susy rewards our early faith in her.

Joe Bonham

The anti-war novel *Johnny Got His Gun* by Dalton Trumbo, which won the 1939 National Book Award for Most Original Book, pushes the envelope of establishing agency all the way to an unforgiving wall. Trumbo's protagonist, a World War I draftee, is as severely compromised as a living human can be—an explosion took his arms, legs, and face along with all its associated senses—yet his heart didn't know to stop beating. How can a person with no sight or hearing or speech—and with no way of knowing if he is awake and remembering, or asleep and dreaming—"do" anything? This novel creates an interesting case study in story movement because by necessity, most of the novel plays out in Joe's mind. His agency manifests as relentless striving against impossible odds. Though it takes him more than a year, he learns to distinguish day from night by the distinct vibrations made when different people walk into the room.

In this state, even suicide is impossible. Condemned to live, Joe deeply desires to take the necessary steps to connect with another human being. He tries to communicate with a nurse by banging his head against the bed but is repeatedly drugged for this "agitation"—until a Christmas relief nurse realizes he's tapping in Morse code and fetches a former army doctor to interpret it. What happens next, after living for years around people without connection to them, is one of the most powerful statements on what it means to be human I've ever read in a novel.

If a character with no appendages or senses can convince us of his ability to act, so can your character.

Now, did you note those publication dates? These three stories, whose characters found a way to act in the most trying of conditions, have stayed in my heart for decades. Wouldn't you love to have your protagonist linger in your reader's heart for that long?

Use your secondary characters to create movement

Let's say your protagonist, Mike, is depressed. Will it woo your reader to show him wallowing in the scent of his unwashed body and thinking desperate thoughts over the course of several chapters? I think not. That would be like spending money for a ticket to get on board, only to learn this story train will remain in the station.

To get this story moving, it might be helpful to invite a more active secondary character to carry the scene. Enter George.

Although Mike won't be capable of exhibiting much agency at first, starting in his POV will help establish him as the protagonist who will serve as our gateway to story:

> First ringing in his ears, now pounding in his head. Life was getting more intrusive by the day.
> More pounding.
> "Ignoring me won't work forever, Mike. Open the door or I'm calling the police to do a wellness check."

When Mike peels himself from his shroud of sheets and opens the door, George's reaction can tell us a bit about Motionless Mike.

> "Dude, what the hell? Your hair looks like pickup sticks. That's it, you're coming with me to the rec center." He picks up dirty clothes from the floor and drops them in a pile on the bed.
> "Volunteering with kids is for people who have something to give," Mike says. "I've got nothing."

George goes in the bathroom and turns on the shower. Strips the bed. "We leave in one hour. Shave while you're at it. Laundry in the basement?"

George's entrance allows the reader to perceive Mike in contrast to George, who barges in and solves problems at a clip.

Maybe Mike can't manage the shave, but he smells better, and George finds a paisley shirt and some pants in the closet. On the subway ride to the city's south side, Mike listens to George's yammering with half an ear as he watches the other passengers, wondering what's going on in their lives. He wonders if the laughing girl talking to the pimple-faced boy is hiding her real feelings. If her father is ashamed of her torn pants.

Let's pause and assess what relying on George's actions tells us about Mike without Mike having to describe himself to the reader or reveal backstory in the opening:

Even though Mike is in stasis, his "more" in the second line, bolstered by "forever" in George's first dialogue passage, assure readers they've joined a story already in motion.

- We experience Mike's stasis through George's reaction.
- Mike feels comfortable enough around George to let him see what's really going on.
- Mike either cares what George thinks of him or believes life will simply be easier if he lets George take the lead.
- Mike fears he has nothing left to give.
- Mike is observant on the bus.
- Mike's thoughts suggest his father will be ashamed of him.

The action in this scene raises a series of questions:
- Why does Mike consider life "intrusive"?
- Might Mike have something left to give after all?
- What would happen if he lost George's support?
- Why did Mike wonder about whether the girl on the bus's father would be *ashamed* of her torn pants?
- What might it take for Mike to turn his life around?

Compare what we've learned in this opening versus an opening delivered through Mike's despairing thoughts as he lies in bed. All we'd really have is the question of whether he was a reliable narrator of his woes. Chances are, Mike doesn't know why he's feeling so low anyway and will have to undertake this story's journey to understand its genesis. Through George, readers get what they need to know for now on the fly, and without long passages of description or interiority from Mike or George. Your reader will tolerate such passages much better once they're oriented to your character's story.

Look to your secondary characters to move the story any time your protagonist is incapable of acting on their own, whether because they're tied up and stuffed in a closet, paralyzed in body or soul, or caught in the grip of fear. The movement will direct you toward relevant plot complications and help your reader get on board with your story.

The most compelling reason for launching action and story together is to convince your reader that your character *has* character—and is worthy of the story. Your protagonist has no skin in the game while huddled within the cocoon of his own mind. It's only once he risks acting from a place of deep desire, and is met with a confounding obstacle, that your reader will start thinking, *Oh no, what will he do now?*

With that question, your reader becomes a co-creator in story movement.

Show action—and reaction

Active scenes create story logic. Their cause-and-effect, action-reaction chains create momentum. Try to move beyond the obvious; *he spit in her face —> she was appalled* is much less interesting than *he spit in her face —> she laughed*. Because unexpected reactions shake things up, learn to surprise yourself.

In his book *You Can Be Happy No Matter What*,[16] Dr. Richard Carlson poses a situation in which a group of people are held at gunpoint during a bank robbery. All resolves peacefully, but hostage reactions run the gamut. One of them might leave and bank online for the rest of her life. One might need to talk about the situation nonstop for several weeks until she processes that in the end, she was fine. Another might get up from where he was told to lie, brush off his pants, and say, "As long as I'm here, can I cash this check?" Your characters' differing perspectives can be delivered through such action-reaction chains.

No reader will invest in an inert protagonist. A reaction shows that a character's action has changed something in the story. If a plot point has no impact on the forward movement of the story, you must ask yourself why it was there in the first place.

Evoke potential energy

Even when a dancer strikes a pose, their entire body is alive with energy. Beneath the appearance of stillness, their muscles are engaged and on standby as energy builds toward their next kinetic movement. You can suggest this same movement potential with a character in stasis. This next excerpt is the opening of K. L. Going's young adult novel, *Fat Kid Rules the World*, a Michael Printz Honor Book:

> I'm a sweating fat kid standing on the edge of the subway platform staring at the tracks. I'm seventeen years old, weigh 296 pounds, and I'm six-foot-one. I have a crew cut, *yes a crew cut,* sallow skin, and the kind of mouth that puckers when I breathe. I'm wearing a shirt that reads MIAMI BEACH—SPRING BREAK 1997, and huge, bland, tan pants—the only kind of pants I own. Eight pairs, all tan.
> It's Sunday afternoon and I'm standing just over the yellow line trying to decide if people would laugh if I jumped.

Let's look at what we have here. A character in his head. Waiting. But rather than lying on a beach somewhere conducting a lazy life review, we find him in a tense situation—literally teetering at the edge of life and death—in active decision mode. Is this character exhibiting agency? Look how his deprecating self-assessment controls the reader's eye from crew cut to bland pants to foot placement. This kid's awareness of his outsider status is so acute that he even wonders if people would laugh if he jumped. Putting such high stakes into immediate play trumps the lack of physical story movement as this character's inner turmoil infects the reader, who will now move straight into this story to see what happens next.

Once you've brought your protagonist on scene, your goals as author need to fade into the background so your character's well-motivated actions can take the lead as they head toward the incident that will blindside them and change the nature of their goal.

→✵ Try This ✵←

Your protagonist's goal will transform an amble through time and space into a pointed trajectory, infusing your plot with an energy born of desire and purpose. Here are some ways to identify that energy.

- What scene goal could your protagonist be pursuing at the opening of your novel? Show us that this goal matters to them and why it is unfolding here and now. Then, show us how they react when achieving that goal proves to be complicated. Your protagonist's choices and reactions will orient your reader to the story while effectively gaining their interest.
- Think about the ways you have felt like an outsider and endow your character with the painful emotions that experience engendered.
- Are you resting easy in your skin these days? Stop that! Stay in touch with the outsider perspective by trying something you don't know how to do—alongside people who do. Then take notes on how you felt. Your disadvantage will be useful research for the outsider perspective. Your stories will be better for it.
- How might you foreshadow your protagonist's "potential energy"? How might some hidden quality be used to drive your story forward?
- Does a secondary character have an outsider status you could feature? In her novel based on family trauma and secrets, *No*

Place I'd Rather Be, Cathy Lamb hands off one of the novel's key emotional moments to a secondary character described as having Asperger's, Kyle Razolli, who's been jotting notes on human behavior his entire life in hope of understanding it. While he is surrounded by family members who supposedly have an emotional advantage, he is the keen observer who figures out what everyone truly needs to heal. The scene where he does so is profoundly moving.

- If things get slow, try asking yourself, WWJBD? (What Would James Bond Do?) Once James Bond enters the scene he will not sit down somewhere and get lost in his head. He will set a goal. Do not fear stating this goal overtly—it will ramp up suspense and remind you to push your story forward.

4

Incite a Specific Story Goal

Does not the power, the magnificence of all creative art lie in knowing how to force chaos into form?
—Mary Wigman, dancer, choreographer

I KNOW SOMETHING ABOUT YOU: you love lying on a couch with a book in hand as the walls of the room fall away and you step into a completely different world. Your toes are digging through hot sand; you're sipping a piña colada—and your stomach is in knots because standing at the edge of the water, chatting up a younger, thinner, barely clad version of you, is your spouse.

Wait…I mean, your protagonist's spouse.

In her book *Wired for Story: The Writer's Guide to Using Brain Science to Hook Readers from the Very First Sentence*, Lisa Cron lets us in on the science beneath the special bond between the protagonist and a reader. A study she cites, based on functional magnetic resonance imagery conducted while subjects were reading a short story, revealed, "the areas of the brain that lit up when they *read* about an activity were identical to those that light up when they actually experience it." [17] If the writer has removed all obstacles standing between the reader and their ability to experience the story, the reader can become one with the protagonist. Smell what they smell, hear what they hear, and feel the things they touch. Without having to be told, the reader can also sense the protagonist's emotions.

There's nothing automatic about this special bond. If you want your reader to come closer to your "slowly rising character," pretty language won't do the trick. The bond is created by your protagonist's movement toward a deeply desired goal.

Let's develop that beach scene I opened the chapter with for how it might serve as an inciting incident. A spouse, Jordan, is flirting with someone who looks like our protagonist, Lee—or so Lee says. But is this reliable narration of what is happening? Lack of confidence, or fear of losing Jordan, could be skewing Lee's perception of an innocent conversation. Except for one thing: Jordan's goal-oriented behavior is a giveaway. Jordan leans a little too close; with touch that lingers too long. And Lee recognizes that hungry look, having been the object of it when they were first dating. That look had made Lee's toes tingle—at least until Jordan's drinking caused the accident that stole all sensation from Lee's legs. Lee would put an end to Jordan's flirtation right now if it weren't for the wheelchair left behind near the boardwalk. Jordan had carried Lee onto the hot sand and promised to return with a cool drink. That was an hour ago.

Lee tries once again to tap into gratitude for Jordan's care: this day by the sea, the umbrella tilted to protect Lee's fair skin, the sandwiches Jordan had packed. But this time, it doesn't work. Why must Lee watch while Jordan scratches that interminable itch to seduce? It's over—this time Lee is going to walk away (this incident has "incited" the protagonist's story goal). The reader wonders: how can Lee walk away without being able to walk (the reader's story question)? Through goal and question, story unites protagonist and reader.

Inciting incident isn't just some jargon you need to learn to hang out with the literati. This plot point launches your story. Let's explore what an inciting incident is, what it isn't, and how it can serve as a springboard to set your story in motion.

Inciting incident, defined

This is something that happens to your protagonist that so alters the expected course of their life that it *incites* them to enact a plan to get back on track. Because there's too much to lose to sit idly by, this incident provides a dramatic imperative—this character *must act* in pursuit of a goal to set things right, despite any obstacles.

A plot develops when the effects of the inciting incident spread to others (which is usually other people, but could also be animal or plant characters, or even aspects of setting). For Lee, Jordan's flagrant infidelity has created a dramatic imperative by pressuring Lee into ending the relationship. Jordan may not want this; flirting might not be fun anymore without Lee watching. And what is that third character feeling? They might enjoy the flirtation while thinking Jordan is married but feel differently when Jordan shows up at their door with suitcases in hand

Beyond inspiring your protagonist to pursue a story goal, let's look at all the other contributions this all-important plot point will make to story movement. It will:

- suggest the nature of the protagonist's need for inner change;
- inspire the protagonist to act;
- raise a question in the reader's mind that invites their participation in the protagonist's story;
- establish genre, which will in turn raise reader expectation for a particular type of story;
- suggest initial stakes so the reader will know why this story matters;
- introduce the threat from an antagonist, whether external or internal, that will try to obstruct the protagonist's efforts; and
- point all action toward the dark moment, which will feel like the opposite of success.

Whew. That's a lot! But it's what's needed, because story is about change, and change is hard. Ask anyone who's tried to stop any ingrained habit.

The inciting incident contains the rocket fuel that will give your story the thrust it needs to inspire your protagonist to act toward a desired goal, no matter the obstacles faced. When well designed, it will also convince your reader to set aside their disbelief and buckle in for the experience your story will provide. Since this inciting incident must accomplish a lot, its moving parts are not always easy to craft.

Let's look at how that happens, so you can burn this fuel in your own stories.

Craft an inciting incident

Let's say you're at a cocktail party, wandering among a couple of conversational groupings in search of a good story. Martha and Dot are trying to interest people in hearing about strikingly similar experiences. Which grouping would you want to join?

You hear Martha say, "Did I ever tell you about the time I climbed Mount Kilimanjaro?"

A few feet away, you overhear that Dot had climbed that same mountain. "Did I ever tell you that when my husband died, just three weeks before our fortieth anniversary climb of Mount Kilimanjaro, I went ahead and made the climb anyway?"

Both women accomplished an impressive feat. Which grouping would you want to join?

Here's my take.

When Martha announced her climb, I'd either think, "Listen to you, bragging about your world travels and your fitness level"—or, if I knew her, maybe, "Yeah, yeah, you say this at every party."

With the added context Dot provides, I'd already have questions forming in my mind—or, if I knew her, I'd think, "She's so inspiring I'll listen again, since a great story never grows old." Rather than give Martha another thought, I'd lean toward Dot, waiting for her to go on.

Let's pause here to examine why Martha's story didn't hold as much promise as Dot's.

For all we know, Martha simply had an *idea* to climb the mountain and acted on it, whereas Dot had a well-motivated desire to climb the mountain, and when met with an unexpected complication, she made a new goal along with a plan to enact it.

In other words, Martha delivered information. Dot set a story in motion.

In large part, that works because we sense that the death of Dot's husband was not foreseen. When something happens to us out of the blue, as most inciting incidents do, we feel discombobulated. It's as if we're trying to work in our own kitchen but someone has rearranged all the drawers and cupboards. Our patterns are disrupted. We madly reshuffle priorities and expectations. We can't carry on this way—we need to put our house in order. So we set a goal to do so and enact the necessary steps to achieve it. The same will be true of your protagonist.

Is this important? Look at the crowd reaction when Dot spoke—don't you want readers flocking around you?

These people will hang with Dot's story because they want to know, *Will grieving Dot be able to complete the climb?* And that won't be their only question. They'll also want to know, *Why on earth did she do it? How did she summon the fortitude? What was it like? How did the climb change her?*

Compare that with the question raised by Martha's story. Oops, wait, there wasn't one. She already told us she succeeded in making the climb. Her information delivery hasn't piqued our curiosity about her adventure.

Dot promises a story because *something happened to her* that stood in the way of her initial goal. This incident incited her to seek a *story goal* she hopes will restore some semblance of meaning in her life, which then raises a related *story-worthy question* in the reader's mind: *Can Dot achieve her goal?* And a natural extrapolation of that question is, *If Dot could do it, could I?*

By arousing both the protagonist's desire and the reader's curiosity, the inciting incident creates an emotional bond between them that, if successful, will last until the goal is met and the question resolved at book's end. You'll have drawn your reader into your story's movement.

Identify your inciting incident

The inciting incident is not simply one of many things that happen in a story. It is *the* thing that "happens to" your protagonist that sets your story in motion and will establish a standard of relevancy for every other aspect of your novel. Every other event in a cogent story will either be brought about by your protagonist's decisions and resulting actions, or by some person or force trying to obstruct or influence their progress toward their goal.

Your first draft may have evolved from your imaginative meanderings, but your success at organizing events into a structural spine that raises, dashes, and rewards expectations will depend on a well-crafted inciting incident. These efforts determine how closely the reader will connect with your story. On a marketing level, the inciting incident will help you boil your mass of words down to a short pitch you can use to interest agents, editors, and others interested in your work. For this reason, pitches often begin with the inciting incident: "When her husband died just three weeks before their fortieth anniversary climb, Dot…"

Since this mega plot point launches all story movement—both the external action and the protagonist's inner arc of change—let's take a closer look.

Check for these characteristics in your inciting incident

Inciting incidents across genres have qualities in common that contribute to story movement. You can check your own work against this list:

The inciting incident happens in scene. It's extremely rare that an inciting incident is implied rather than shown. Why? Because scene structure offers up powerful tools that can dramatize the destabilizing effect this plot event has on your protagonist: scene goal, dialogue, inner monologue, action-reaction, setting, stakes, and exposition. Each of these tools will attract interest in a story that's clearly on the move. If you simply delivered your inciting incident in summary, your reader could easily skim past its importance.

The inciting incident happens within your story's current timeline. A key to getting your story moving is its dramatic imperative. Your story must begin—now—or some undesired consequence will come into play. This example will show how this works.

Let's say you begin with a prologue showing the ancient burial of a talisman that had fallen into the wrong hands and caused mayhem. In chapter 1, set in our era, the talisman is accidentally unearthed during new construction. A crew supervisor brushes it off and tosses it into their truck to give to their child, thinking they'd clean it up and play with it. Which event is the inciting incident? Only one of the two creates a dramatic imperative: the modern unearthing. Written well, the backstory burial is a key setup, but it will only create a general sense of foreboding for what will happen thousands of years later. The modern unearthing has imminent stakes. Once the child unleashes this ancient destructive force, the supervisor is going to have to set a goal to once again put it to rest.

The inciting incident <u>incites</u> the protagonist to create—and act upon—a goal. Let's say your protagonist, Mina, is lying on the road bleeding out after a devastating car accident. There is dramatic imperative, because something must *happen now*—but that will come in the form of lifesaving measures and the long, tense wait for news of Mina's condition. While Mina is fighting for her life, no reader would reasonably expect her to be setting a goal. But once she is well enough to digest the extent of her life's disruption, have her act toward a goal as soon as possible. That will most likely require some pre-inciting incident setup. Perhaps Mina had just landed her dream job as head women's basketball coach at her alma mater, and the accident that has left her paralyzed from the waist down happened during the long drive necessary for her to relocate. Will she resign and shift her life's focus, or will she adapt to her new reality and try to stay the course so she can achieve her dream?

The inciting incident inspires a story question. As soon as your reader recognizes "the big disruption" in your protagonist's life, this plot point will raise a question in the reader's mind. If the question is simply whether Mina will walk again, the answer will be a simple yes-no, which is about as involving as Martha's braggadocio. To go the distance, your story question needs more complexity.

This is where introducing antagonists (a person, an institution, nature, the character's own self, or even a friend) can shore up story potential. Let's pick up Mina's story again. Where is her agency here, as protagonist? Mina can't pop out of bed and start rearranging her life. Her earliest "actions" may come in the form of decision-making. "Would you like a bed bath?" a nurse might ask. "No," she might say, simply because when confronted with helplessness, it feels good to exert her will. Feeling helpless, Mina says no just to exert her will. But doing this feels so good that she calls a friend and asks if she wants to go on a road trip—to the university. On the drive, her friend discourages Mina from taking on the stress of this job. Mina herself is unsure what she'll do when she arrives, but she's determined to say it in person.

When the athletic director greets Mina and learns she still wants the job, he may have second thoughts. Not because he's a horrible person, but because he's caught between his hopes for a winning team (which will protect his own job) and his adherence to the institution's diversity and inclusion practices. Then they are joined by the woman who subbed in for Mina while she was in the hospital—a Black woman who was the best player on the championship team Mina had captained. While fending off internal antagonists, such as the missing confidence her body once inspired, Mina sees that while she won't let go of her dream without a fight, she doesn't want to be the reason her friend and colleague fails to achieve her dream.

Once a major obstacle or two are identified, you can raise a much more specific question in the reader's mind. "Will Mina realize her dream goal of coaching a winning basketball team at her alma mater, given her self-doubts, adversaries, and the possibility she may never walk again?" By refining the question raised, each obstacle pulls the reader deeper into the story, allowing the psychological bond between protagonist and reader to strengthen.

At this point, the story question creates an effective barometer by which the reader (and you!) can measure relevant story progress. Let's say Mina digs in and her goal remains the same. She will—she *must*—take this coaching job, and no uninsured, distracted driver is going to stop her. The reader will now be looking around every turn to see how Mina is progressing toward her goal. After two weeks in the hospital, when she still feels nothing in a pin-prick test, the reader will think, "Oh no, it's not looking good for Mina right now!" When her upper body strength allows her to transfer from bed to wheelchair to car, restoring a semblance of hope, the reader will think, "Thank goodness! Mina really needed a break."

Your reader has become invested in your character's goal, and your story is off and running.

Finding an elusive inciting incident

If it took you a while to warm up your writing muscles at the start of your project, you might not find your inciting incident near the beginning, where it belongs. Its exact location will depend on the specific needs of your story, but you certainly don't want to launch your story halfway through. Your inciting incident might happen when your character is middle-aged, but it will be tied to a specific period of significant change beyond which nothing will ever be quite the same—not her life's chronology. That's why we use backstory: to weave in detail from the character's past that will be made pertinent by the inciting incident.

So where is your story's true opening? Let's look at Dot's story once again.

Is it the day Dot boards the plane for Africa?

Is it at her husband's funeral?

Is it the day Dot's husband died?

Is it the day he started feeling unwell?

Or is it even earlier, say, the day Dot and her husband booked the anniversary trip?

Wait! It could also open with a prologue, in which they scramble to the top of the mountain as a couple of twenty-year-old kids, and he drops to one knee as if out of breath—and then proposes.

Come to think of it, your story is chock full of turning points beyond which nothing will ever be the same for your character. How do you know which one is the inciting incident? Search for these clues.

1. *Fill in the blank.* "It all began when..." Okay, maybe not "all." When did *this specific story* begin? What forced your character to take an action driven by desire and motivated by backstory?
2. *Work backward.* After drafting the book, if you have a sense of what overarching story question it is you've answered by telling your tale, go back and look for the specific incident that would have raised that question in the reader's mind.
3. *Ask your characters.* Try journaling in the first-person voice of your protagonist or someone close to them—one of them might tell you something you need to know. *What is it, dear character, you really wanted, and how did you come to know this? How must you change? What will apply the necessary pressure on you to incite that change?*
4. *Apply an outline.* As you peruse each outline-worthy event, ask: Does this feel more like a story event (an obstacle your protagonist encounters on their quest for the story goal) or more like an inciting incident (the event that inspired the goal)?
5. *Identify the dramatic imperative.* Why must this story be told *now*? The answer might point you to the inciting incident.
6. *What is the worst possible thing that could happen to my protagonist?* If your character fails to achieve their story goal, what's the absolute worst that could happen? Examining this loss could lead you to understanding what your character truly desires. Which informed their story goal. Which can lead you back to the incident that incited it.

Interweave premise and inciting incident

Let's go back and zero in on the all-important question you may have glossed over in the first item above, despite my use of italics: When did *this specific story* begin? What is its nature, exactly? The nature of the story you want to tell can be communicated concisely through its *premise* (its point, or *raison d'être*). However you choose to define it,

Dot's story will be told through the lens of an aging woman who takes on a challenging climb. That's the plot (reflecting her external goal—what she *wants*). But the story premise will also incorporate a major emotional turning point in Dot's arc of inner change, which shows what she *needs*). If you can create an inciting incident that inspires a goal that your protagonist desires, while also showing that they are eminently unqualified to achieve it, we'll have a sense of both the inner and outer arcs. See if you can find the suggestion of both inner and outer arcs in the following premises, based on very different stories that could be incited by the death of Dot's husband.

Enduring love

Premise: While climbing a mountain to spread her husband's ashes, a grieving sixty-year-old woman learns that death need not end their love story.

Let's say you want to tell a story about active grieving. The sudden death of Dot's husband, just three weeks before their fortieth anniversary climb of Mount Kilimanjaro, is marked by a strange phenomenon: even as his lifeless body lies before her, she feels him take her hand and say, "We can do this. Bring my ashes." Fearing her tether on reality loosening, Dot decides to do the climb to get her mind off things. But her grief journey will require that she face things, not escape them—because when she gets to Tanzania, the ghost of her dead husband is one of her fellow climbers.

The goal: Her husband's death raises a story goal for Dot. She will climb the mountain and scatter his ashes.

The story question: This goal raises a question: *Will Dot be able to make the climb at age sixty, so she can spread her husband's ashes?* The reader will keep this story question in mind while constantly assessing Dot's progress.

The stakes: Dot wants to fulfill his request to scatter his ashes on the peak where they shared their best memory, but the closer she gets to meeting her goal, the more his ghost fades beside her.

Note how specific the inciting incident must be. If the climb hadn't already been scheduled at the time of the husband's death, the reader wouldn't have linked the two; this linkage will be crucial to sustaining reader interest in the climb. If you included his death in the backstory, and we didn't have access to either Dot's reaction to it or her husband's paranormal resurrection, the incident would hold less power. The reader has never even met the man! As you can see, the story question needs to be strong enough to see the reader through to the end of the book. I think this one is.

Freedom from abuse

Premise: After hastening her husband's death, an abused woman climbs a mountain so she can taste true freedom—and learns of its cost.

In this story, Dot's glad her husband is dead. All suffering in their marriage has been hers until he is felled by what she deems a well-deserved heart attack. But he's too stubborn to die—so she helps death along a little.

This inciting incident would need a different flavor, don't you think? I picture her standing over his inert body, holding a vial. Later, at the funeral, her face carefully composed, she greets people politely, tugging repeatedly at her sleeves to keep her bruises covered. Occasionally she fingers the plane ticket hidden in her pocket for the trip that will prove her strength—but this time, to herself.

Story goal: After being on the receiving end of the abuse that inspired Dot to hasten the end of her husband's life, she decides to make his scheduled climb on her own so she can spread her arms at the summit and feel truly free.

Story question: After cowering within a long, abusive marriage, is Dot strong enough to climb Kilimanjaro so she can feel truly free?

Stakes: The police are on to Dot and have evidence implicating her in her husband's death. This increases her desperation to get to the top so she can experience at least one moment in which she truly feels free.

Triumph of the human spirit

Premise: A grieving, husband-dependent wife honors his faith in her by undertaking a mountain climb they'd meant to do together—and learns of her own inner strength.

How might the inciting incident launch a triumph of the human spirit story? The story might start with a scene in which she pulls up her shirt and turns her head as her husband gives her the insulin shots she can't bear to self-administer. His actions allow her to reframe the injection as a gift born of love instead of a daily reminder that she's a hair's breadth away from death. Maybe she only said she'd do the climb to humor him; someone with type 2 diabetes couldn't be expected to make such a climb. After he succumbs to a fatal cardiac arrest, she's off the hook. But she keeps hearing his final intelligible words after the EMTs revived him: "You're stronger than you know." Weary as she is, she picks up the phone and orders extra insulin. She's going to be away for a while.

Story goal: To bolster her courage to live beyond the loss of her husband, sixty-year-old Dot heads to the mountaintop to affirm her independence.

Story question: Can Dot make it up the mountain with diabetes, considering in sixty years she's never even given herself her own injections?

Stakes: Looming medical peril as she balances rigorous activity with her dwindling insulin supply.

The inciting incident for each of these stories is the death of Dot's husband, but I've barely scratched the surface of the many different stories his death could spawn. The premise is a capsulized look at what point you hope to make in your novel, through use of external plot and inner character growth. You don't need to worry about getting it wrong. While a character will often state a scene or story goal overtly, the premise is a guiding light for you alone.

Where to place an inciting incident

Regardless of genre, it is rare for the inciting incident to unfold on a novel's first page. It is possible, though—especially if the story situation calls forth an expected human reaction, such as terror when the sounds of war grow close, the desperation of begging for a loved one's life, or falling in love at gunpoint at a gas station minimart.

Wait, what?

That last one is the opening of Joshilyn Jackson's novel, *Someone Else's Love Story:*

> I fell in love with William Ashe at gunpoint, in a Circle K. It was on a Friday afternoon at the tail end of a Georgia summer so ungodly hot the air felt like it had all been boiled red. We were both staring down the barrel of an ancient, creaky .32 that could kill us just as dead as a really nice gun could.
>
> I thought then I had landed in my own worst dream, not a love story. Love stories start with a kiss or a meet-cute, not with someone getting shot in a gas station minimart. Well, no, two people, because that lady cop took a bullet first.
>
> But there we were, William gone as still as a pond rock, me holding a green glass bottle of Coca-Cola and shaking so hard it was like a seizure. Both of us were caught under the black eye of that pistol. And yet, seventeen seconds later, before I so much as knew his name, I'd fallen dizzy-down in love with him.

This opening draws the reader in by tapping into a universal fear of finding oneself at the business end of a loaded gun. Two paragraphs later, our protagonist-narrator backpedals to tell us what had happened at her mother's house that led to the stop at the minimart; she then backs up further to offer context for the events of that morning. But the reader will wait, because we soon learn that her young, super-smart son is at the minimart with her, raising the stakes to the point that the reader will climb on board for this story's entire journey.

In teasing out part of her inciting incident in her opening, Jackson wasn't "breaking rules" so much as raising a strong question that will keep the reader glued to the page until the full inciting incident reappears with an answer.

To knock a protagonist off her rails, we need to know the nature of those rails—how the desire they bring to the first scene and the worldview to which they cling defines the expected course of their life. That's what we'll explore next.

→ Try This ←

Don't fret if you don't have all the answers to the following questions right away. Envisioning a novel is hard work—you may come up with ten ideas and reject nine. But the questions will still be here to help guide your decision-making as you strive to align a story structure that will promise movement.

- In your work-in-progress, what is the destabilizing event that will launch the story?
- What desire did your character bring to this inciting incident that will help your reader understand just how destabilizing it is?
- What is your story's dramatic imperative—why must it start *now*?
- What external story goal will your protagonist strive to achieve in this novel?
- Have you suggested inner and external challenges that will raise a story question powerful enough to beg your reader's involvement until "the end"?
- If these answers remain elusive, try thinking of a completely different story that could be inspired by your inciting incident, as I did with Dot. Maybe the same incident that motivated your protagonist to enter the sex trade might inspire another woman to become a nun. How would the inciting incident need to differ? What details would need to be included in the inciting incident to promise this other story type? If you found that exercise easier, use it as a template for the decisions you must make for the sex worker story you truly wanted to tell.
- How could you encapsulate the above answers into a one-line premise that suggests both inner and outer arcs? This one-liner can help you assess the relevancy of choices in both arcs as you write.

5

Aim Toward the Inciting Incident

But remember that intent is everything. One does not just jump, one lifts into the air, one rises.

—Agnes de Mille, choreographer, dancer

What do you call it when a character is knocking around, thinking of this and that, with no real goal in mind? One might call it puttering. Another might call it procrastinating.

Readers call it boring. If your readers wanted to be bored, they wouldn't read.

To entice readers to hop on board, you need to convince them your story train is going somewhere. Too often, writers delay this assurance with some sort of "tour"—of daily routines in the ticket office, the landscape that surrounds it, the state of the various train cars—sometimes, even the inner workings of the protagonist's mind.

A "tour" reflects an author's goal to impart information they think the reader needs. Its story fuel is weak—a tour usually ends up where it started—and any information imparted through that tour you designed will gain richer, more relevant meaning once interwoven with action. An author's goal won't drive story action.

Your reader expects more than information delivery from your opening, I assure you. What does the reader want? They want to gain orientation to your story through the way your protagonist moves through their world in pursuit of something they want. They want to bond with the protagonist so they can experience the story. To be surprised, thrilled, and otherwise moved by it. But thinking about what the reader wants from the story you are writing is like filling your story's fuel tank with air. A reader's goal won't drive story action.

The most useful fuel for powering up story movement will come from your protagonist.

Instead of the circular author's tour, or the reader's vague wishes, think "trajectory"—a line with an arrow at one end. What's your character up to, or where are they off to? Their actions will raise questions that will bring the reader along for the ride while their trajectory aims them toward a collision course with the inciting incident.

Since any character's scene goal will be the result of a cause-and-effect chain informed by something that happened previously in your character's life, when your protagonist enters their story on page one with a preliminary goal in mind, the reader will intuit that they are joining a story already in motion. The complications to that goal will flesh out a type of scene that is this chapter's focus: what's known as bridging conflict.

What motivation is strong enough to impel a protagonist into page one action? Desire.

Lay bare your protagonist's desire

One of the best discussions of how desire drives story comes to us from composer and lyricist Stephen Schwartz, the genius behind many long-running Broadway musicals. *Wicked,* based on Gregory Maguire's bestselling novel of the same name, tracks the early life of Elphaba, the girl who is destined to become the Wicked Witch of the West. On an episode of *American Songbook at NJPAC*,[18] Schwartz spoke of the importance of including in his musicals, early on, what he calls the "I want" song.

Schwartz demonstrates how his first two attempts at writing Elphaba's "I want" song fell flat. His son Scott, a talented theater director, pointed out why: the lyrics were too generic. The audience didn't need him to explain that Elphaba had hoped to do good things so she could feel significant; we want to know what achieving significance will look like for Elphaba. Elphaba is not "everywoman." She is a witch. From Oz. Reviled for her green skin. The twist in Maguire's telling is that she is also the protagonist, so Schwartz had the challenge of creating a psychological bond between the audience and young Elphaba.

Scott Schwartz said, "You should have her show up at school and do something that earns her the right to sing."

Stephen Schwartz heeded that advice and set up the "I want" with specifics. After Elphaba performs an inadvertent act of magic in class, her teacher decides to tutor her in sorcery—with an eye toward introducing her to the great Wizard of Oz. That little bit of story packs so much power—someone has seen past Elphaba's skin color to a talent she'd been timid about exposing, but which has now been deemed brilliant.

Everyone in Oz wants to meet the Wizard so he can fix what's wrong with them. Now Elphaba might get her chance. She hangs hope for her future on the imagined possibilities of this interaction in the want song, "The Wizard and I," made even more poignant because we know from L. Frank Baum's *The Wonderful Wizard of Oz* that the "celebration throughout Oz" her notoriety will one day inspire will not be the one she is dreaming about.

Sharing our desires makes us vulnerable. It feels dangerous to so fully expose our heart. And in story, desires are never realized without a fight.

In Schwartz's musical *Pippin,* the title character is a prince born to a life of privilege—but he doesn't know what to do with it. Unlike his father, he finds no glory in battle. His want song speaks of his desire to find his own "Corner of the Sky," so he sets out on a journey to find his purpose.

Exposing your protagonist's deep desire is a way for your reader to relate to them. We all have dreams and desires; some manifest in the stories of our lives, while others remain elusive. We can identify with the character through this shared aspect of our humanity. So how do you give your main character a chance to sing their "want" song in your story?

Keep desire at the core of your story

Since your character will arrive on page one with their desire already formed, it's never too soon to start orienting your reader to what it is they want. In her debut novel, *In Another Life,* Julie Christine Johnson points toward her character's desire in the opening line:

> Eighteen months after her husband's death, Lia Carrer returned to Languedoc like a shadow in search of light.

In Johnson's second novel, *The Crows of Beara,* Annie, a newly recovering alcoholic with a wrecked marriage, grabs at one last chance to preserve her self-respect by vying for a challenging public relations assignment that will require her to travel to Ireland, where she'll be an ocean away from her sober support team. With only a few scant words, Johnson introduces her character's want song:

> *Ireland.* She'd felt whole there.

A page later, in response to her boss's reservations, we learn that Annie's notion of "wholeness" will look like a bit of Irish magic sprinkled on top of a successful public relations campaign:

"I won't let you down. I'll have a project proposal to you by Monday." The AA insider's joke came back to her: *How do you know an alcoholic is lying? Their lips are moving.* She'd promised herself she wouldn't fuck up again. Which is precisely what she'd done in her marriage. But if she could just get out of here, away, *back to Ireland,* she'd be all right.

Annie's desire seeps onto every page of the novel. Through what she says. Through her actions and reactions. Through exchanges with archetypal figures she draws into her journey, such as her AA mentor and a mystical crone. Through the love interest she aligns with and which antagonists she stands against.

Your character's desire is important to portray, as it will burn at the core of her story and inform everything to come.

Craft relevant bridging conflict

If exposing desire is like exposing your character's heart, adversity is what will reveal their spine and grit. Let's look at how you might use these ingredients to build relevant bridging conflict in a scene. As a guiding image, think of this: a bridge is strongest when it spans a short gap.

1. Create a goal close to being met.

Let's say your character, Bonnie, is an art curator who is finally taking art lessons because one day she wants to see her work hanging in the Louvre. Hmm. That goal is distant, achieved by only a select few, and likely, during her lifetime, unattainable—not to mention vague, since we don't know why she desires this, or what will happen if she's no good. We won't invest in her pie-in-the-sky goal because it will be too hard to assess how Bonnie's doing on her path toward it, so we'll fail to bond with her. And if you interweave this lukewarm opening with a second chapter in the point of view of an antagonist determined to do her harm, your reader may end up liking that antagonist more, simply because his goal-oriented behavior makes him more relatable.

Let's fix that.

2. Clue us in on the stakes should your protagonist succeed or fail.

You revise: Bonnie's recently deceased father was an artist, and Bonnie wants to uphold the family name. A memorial exhibition will tour the United States next year, and she is desperate to contribute a piece. Bringing the consequences even closer, maybe Bonnie's already technically accomplished in painting but is simply floundering for inspiration. If she fails to come up with a good idea she'll miss out—not only on the opportunity to contribute to her father's tribute, but on the chance to gain the spotlight that could establish her as his heir apparent in the national arts scene.

This is better. But she'll probably pull it off, right? She's got a whole year.

3. Add more pressure.

This opening could use a ticking clock. Maybe Bonnie is curating the show—and publicity has already gone out featuring its title, *The Colors of My Father*. That specificity makes the stakes more personal. And the show is next month, not next year—yet while her sketchbook is filling, the canvas she visits is still white. She'll be a laughingstock. Her father was right—she shouldn't have spent her life curating his work if she planned to be an artist in her own right; she should have been painting. If you're starting to feel this might work better, it's because we're digging down far enough to sense the fiery magma of her desire. Maybe it's only now, in middle age, that Bonnie realizes she's dedicated her life to a father who funneled his entire emotional life into his work. She is eager to do the same in a grand, competitive gesture of love.

But this scene needs external obstacles so we can see what really matters to Bonnie. Let's make sure things won't go too smoothly.

4. Create relevant plot complications and make things happen.

To open a story with a character whose main relationship is with a blank canvas is to open a story going nowhere. Readers can spot fake story like teens can smell hypocrisy, so you'll need real complications. After all, your goal for this bridging conflict is to set up the story to come while barreling toward the inciting incident, which will force Bonnie off her path and leave her floundering to find a way forward. If Bonnie wants to honor her father with a painting, show that she's accumulating a stack of attempts, none of which matches her father's passion nor adequately expresses her love for him. Have someone come visit the studio, aghast.

5. Bring on the inciting incident.

What better complication can you introduce now than the one that will launch the story you plan to tell? Unbeknownst to Bonnie, someone is planning a heist of her father's paintings at the museum where she's worked as a curator. After the theft, Bonnie will switch from her initial goal to honor him with a painting of her own to saving his entire body of work, since that will be a way to extend his presence on Earth. Maybe her emotional arc will convince her she didn't need to be "Daddy Jr." after all. As she uncovers the insider info needed to crack this case, we'll see—and more important, she'll see—that her talents as a curator reflect her truer nature.

To create the appropriate tension and raise the right story question—the one you aim to resolve at the end of your novel—the setup to the inciting incident must be finely tuned. In this last revision, Bonnie's goal-oriented behavior impels story action that shows who she is, the compressed time frame creates the "short bridge" that was our guiding image, and we sense that Bonnie and the antagonists are about to intersect in a disastrous way.

Did you get a sense of who Bonnie is, what her values are, what her life questions are, and what she needs? If the answer is yes, note that you gathered this information without a list of physical attributes, an info dump, a setting description, or a backstory scene.

⇥ Try This ⇤

Your protagonist's opening, goal-oriented actions will reveal them so that when the inciting incident unfolds, your reader will understand just how hard it will be for this character to carry on. Here are steps you can take to identify your story's earliest movement.

- Whether in a library, bookstore, or on Amazon's "Read Sample" feature, study opening paragraphs to decide what draws you into a story and what doesn't. Watch for hints the author embeds in the opening to suggest what kind of story this will be.
- If your opening is mired in your character's thoughts, list some ways you might externalize their inner conflict. You might show a man's conflict about his marriage, for example, by showing him saving a male mallard duck crossing the road to unite with his mate while all the while mumbling under his breath that he's going to kill his wife. You can fill the reader in on why he feels this way later.
- Think about how the bridging conflict will help you raise a specific question with the inciting incident. "How will a woman rebuild after her house burns down?" is a generic post-fire story. Whereas "How will an obsessive-compulsive interior decorator, who tarries over each and every *feng shui* decision, rebuild once fire claims both her home and the pile of cash she refused to entrust to the bank?" will point toward a specific story, one you can set up by how she worries over every decision with one of her clients.

6

Engage the Reader with Your Opening Lines

The curtain whispers as it rises. Audience expectation thickens the air.
—fictional dancer Penelope Sparrow, *The Art of Falling*

IN PHYSICS, TENSION IS A FUNCTION of the movement between active and reactive forces. The same is true in story—even at its start.

If you clue your reader in to why it's time for the protagonist to leave his near-past and enter the frame of this story, while at the same time raising questions about the story to come, the distance between what is becoming known and what is not yet known will serve as a cord of tension you can use to pull your reader from one sentence into the next.

Let's look at a masterful example from the opening of Mary Doria Russell's speculative novel, *The Sparrow*. Scattered among the orienting details are phrases that raise questions. I count sixteen such phrases in this passage's 14 sentences. How about you?

On December 7, 2059, Emilio Sandoz was released from the isolation ward of Salvator Mundi Hospital in the middle of the night and transported in a bread van to the Jesuit Residence at Number 5 Borgo Santo Spirito, a few minutes' walk across St. Peter's Square from the Vatican. The next day, ignoring shouted questions and howls of journalist outrage as he read, a Jesuit spokesman issued a short statement to the frustrated and angry media mob that had gathered outside Number 5's massive front door.

"To the best of our knowledge, Father Emilio Sandoz is the sole survivor of the Jesuit mission to Rakhat. Once again, we extend our thanks to the U.N., to the Contact Consortium and to the Asteroid Mining Division of OhBayashi Corporation for making the return of Father Sandoz possible. We have no additional information regarding the fate of the Contact Consortium's crew members; they are in our prayers. Father Sandoz is too ill to question at this time and his recovery is expected to take months. Until then, there can be no further comment on the Jesuit mission or on the Contact Consortium's allegation regarding Father Sandoz's conduct on Rakhat."

This was simply to buy time.

It was true, of course, that Sandoz was ill. The man's whole body was bruised by the blooms of spontaneous hemorrhages where tiny blood vessel walls had been breached and spilled their contents under his skin. His gums had stopped bleeding, but it would be a long while before he could eat normally. Eventually, something would have to be done about his hands.

Now, however, the combined effects of scurvy, anemia and exhaustion kept him asleep twenty hours out of the day. When awake, he lay motionless, coiled like a fetus and almost as helpless.

Look at the way each sentence reveals the current story situation while raising a question that makes the reader want to consume the next. The successive revelations create tension that draws the reader into the story as the wide perspective of the big-picture news conference tightens on an intimate look at a man so traumatized he is curled in a fetal position, unable to speak. Russell is a master of story movement.

But not all stories benefit from the same techniques. Story movement can be achieved in your opening lines in a variety of ways.

Set your protagonist in motion

One obvious way to set your story in motion is to show your protagonist in motion. How a character moves through their world can provide clues to the type of person they are and what kind of story this will be. Show them doing something purposeful and we'll learn something of the desire they bring to page one.

Here are a few examples in various genres, from commercial to literary. The first is the opening of Kelly Mustian's bestselling historical novel, *The Girl in the Stilt House*:

> Spring, 1923
> Ada smelled the swamp before she reached it. The mingling of sulfur and rot worked with memory to knot her stomach and burn the back of her throat. She was returning with little more than she had taken with her a year before, everything she counted worthy of transporting only half filling the pillowcase slung over her shoulder. It might have been filled with bricks, the way she bent under it, but mostly it was loss that weighed her down. The past few days had swept her clean of hope, and a few trinkets in a pillowcase were all that was left to mark a time when she had not lived isolated in this green-shaded, stagnant setting. When she was a little girl, she had believed she loved this place, the trees offering themselves as steadfast companions, the wildflowers worthy confidants, but passing through now with eyes that had taken in other wonders and a

heart that had allowed an outsider to slip in, she knew she had only been resigned to it. As she was again.

Here, the reader can perfectly picture Ada moving through the setting, bent over from the weight of loss and a partially filled pillowcase. She's not meandering; she has a purpose in returning to this place. A sense mentioned in line one tied to an emotion in line two gets things moving. We have questions: Why does she have so few belongings? Why did her perception of the place change as she grew older? Why has she come back?

Now think about what we don't know: her age. The color of her hair. What she's wearing. We'll learn some of this soon, but for now, it's enough that we see her moving purposefully toward…something, even as this setting offers a sense of stagnation.

Invite the reader to join the experience

In the opening chapter of Erin Morgenstern's *New York Times* bestseller *The Night Circus* (magical realism), expectation is immediately heightened by an atmosphere of mystery. Under the section title "Anticipation," the novel begins:

> The circus arrives without warning.
>
> No announcements precede it, no paper notices on downtown posts and billboards, no mentions or advertisements in local newspapers. It is simply there, when yesterday it was not.

We soon learn of a sign hanging on the gates: "Open at Nightfall. Closes at Dawn."

> "What kind of circus is only open at night?" people ask. No one has a proper answer, yet as dusk approaches there is a substantial crowd of spectators gathering outside the gates.
>
> You are amongst them, of course. Your curiosity got the better of you, as curiosity is wont to do. You stand in the fading

light, the scarf around your neck pulled up against the chilly evening breeze, waiting to see for yourself what kind of circus only opens once the sun sets.

The unnamed narrator describes the way the tents and lights slowly come to life, until an elaborate incandescent sign spells out a French phrase. A mother translates for her child—"The Circus of Dreams"—and the invitation follows:

> Then the iron gates shudder and unlock, seemingly by their own volition. They swing outward, inviting the crowd inside.
> Now the circus is open.
> Now you may enter.

There is such an unsettled atmosphere here. The circus arrives without warning. No one knows what it is since no press went out about it. They don't even know "how" it is—it is simply present where it wasn't before. And it's only open at night? Sounds ominous. And the second person point of view is jarring, the way this unknown narrator sees right through us—they *know we're there.* We are made to feel the chill of the evening breeze on our necks.

If I were standing there as those iron gates "shuddered" open, would I go in? Oh, who am I kidding—a night circus wasn't made for me. I was probably only standing there to peek through the gates while keeping my night-owl friends company. But in the pages of a book, even I can be a night owl, and when met with the promise of the circus of my dreams, I entered those gates with a curious mind and an open heart.

Declare something provocative

> PARSIFAL IS DEAD. That is the end of the story.

These attention-grabbing sentences open Ann Patchett's 1997 novel *The Magician's Assistant*. The reader will read on to see why the novel is starting at its end.

Angie Kim's 2019 debut, *Miracle Creek*, which *Time* magazine placed on its list of 100 of *The Best Mystery and Thriller Books of All Time*, offers a more recent example of a story-opening declaration:

> Miracle Creek, Virginia
> Tuesday, August 26, 2008
>
> My husband asked me to lie. He probably didn't even consider it a lie and neither did I, at first. It was such a small thing, what he wanted. The police had just released the protesters, and while he stepped out to make sure they weren't coming back, I was to sit in his chair. Cover for him, the way coworkers do as a matter of course, the way we ourselves used to at the grocery store, while I ate or he smoked. But as I took his seat, I bumped against the desk, and the certificate above it went slightly crooked as if to remind me that this wasn't a regular business, that there was a reason he'd never left me in charge before.
>
> Pak reached over me to straighten the frame, his eyes on the English lettering: *Pak Yoo, Miracle Submarine LLC, Certified Hyperbaric Technician.* He said—eyes still on the certificate, as if talking to *it*, not to me—"Everything's done. The patients are sealed in, the oxygen's on. You just have to sit here." He looked at me. "That's it."
>
> I looked over the controls, the unfamiliar knobs and switches for the chamber we'd painted baby blue and placed in this barn just last month. "What if the patients buzz me?" I said. "I say you'll be right back, but—"
>
> "No, they can't know I'm gone…"

Why does her husband want her to lie? I read on. Why were there protesters? Why isn't it a "regular" business, and why shouldn't she be left in charge? Why are they in a barn? And dear god…WHAT HAPPENS IF THE PATIENTS BUZZ HER? Tension will be high because avid readers know "you just have to sit here" is fiction speak for "the shit's about to hit the fan." In remarkably few paragraphs, Kim raised all these questions and earned my interest all the way to the end.

Ignite the inner arc

As many of my examples have shown, embroiling a protagonist in plot intrigue is a great way to raise questions that will get a story moving. But there's another way to go. In her novel *Flight Behavior*, Barbara Kingsolver explores the theme of global warming through a plot in which monarch butterflies, heading to Mexico, winter over in the Appalachian Mountains instead—yet nothing related to this conflict is evident in the opening sentences of her long first paragraph:

> A certain feeling comes from throwing your good life away, and it is one part rapture. Or so it seemed for now, to a woman with flame-colored hair who marched uphill to meet her demise. Innocence was no part of this. She knew her own recklessness and marveled, really, at how one hard little flint of thrill could outweigh the pillowy, suffocating aftermath of a long disgrace. The shame and loss would infect her children too, that was the worst of it, in a town where everyone knew them.

Here, we meet a character whose inner arc is already underway. While hanging out in a character's head can diminish the reader's sense of story movement, in Kingsolver's capable hands, the shame this character anticipates keeps the reader glued to her thoughts. The rest of the page is far from static as we feel the sting of judgment she anticipates from the grocery store's teenage cashier, her mother-in-law, the sweet, expectant faces of her children, and the breathless beat of her own heart.

At the end of the second paragraph, Kingsolver reveals the nature of this woman's scene goal—and introduces the stakes should she succeed.

> Realistically, the family could be totaled. That was the word, like a wrecked car wrapped around a telephone pole, no salvageable parts. No husband worth having is going to forgive adultery if it comes to that. And still she felt pulled up this

incline by the hand whose touch might bring down all she knew. Maybe she even craved the collapse, with an appetite larger than sense.

The tension in this interior bridging conflict lights a fuse that the reader will follow as this character heads straight toward a confrontation with the oddly behaving butterflies, whose presence will change her life in ways she did not anticipate when heading up that hill.

Attract the reader toward your setting

Imagine your setting so fully that the reader moves in to experience its sights, smells, and textures. The next two examples were written by J. R. Moehringer, who is adept at bringing real settings to life in a way that's relevant to the story he wants to tell. Here are the sentences that introduce the titular setting from his Pulitzer Prize-winning memoir, *The Tender Bar:*

> We went there for everything we needed. We went there when we were thirsty, of course, and when hungry, and when dead tired. We went there when happy, to celebrate, and when sad, to sulk. We went there after weddings and funerals, for something to settle our nerves, and always for a shot of courage just before. We went there when we didn't know what we needed, hoping someone might tell us. We went there when looking for love, or sex, or trouble, or for someone who had gone missing, because sooner or later everyone turned up there. Most of all we went there when we needed to be found.

What is this mysterious place that offers so much? Wouldn't you like to go there for camaraderie, advice, a shot of courage, to be found? Moehringer's story skills make this true scenario read like fiction. In fact, he ghost-wrote the memoir we'll look at next.

Orient both protagonist and reader

By writing in the present tense, tennis great Andre Agassi suggests that both author-protagonist and reader are seeking the same story orientation, moment by moment. Who is he? Where is he? What kind of story will this be? Here's the beginning of his memoir, *Open:*

> I open my eyes and don't know where I am or who I am. Not all that unusual—I've spent half my life not knowing. Still, this feels different. This confusion is more frightening. More total.
>
> I look up. I'm lying on the floor beside the bed. I remember now. I moved from the bed to the floor in the middle of the night. I do that most nights. Better for my back. Too many hours on a soft mattress causes agony. I count to three, then start the long, difficult process of standing. With a cough, a groan, I roll onto my side, then curl into the fetal position, then flip over onto my stomach. Now I wait, and wait, for the blood to start pumping.
>
> I'm a young man, relatively speaking. Thirty-six. But I wake as if ninety-six. After three decades of sprinting, stopping on a dime, jumping high and landing hard, my body no longer feels like my body, especially in the morning. Consequently my mind doesn't feel like my mind.

The present-tense delivery supports meaning in this story about a fully grown man, an exceptional athlete in his field, who needs to figure out and own his identity off the court. The reader will lean forward, wondering how he'll pull that off.

Intrigue with a compelling detail

Paula Hawkins, an author drawn to the themes of domestic violence, opened her debut thriller, *The Girl on the Train,* with an odd detail.

Note how the use of present tense makes it feel as if the reader and protagonist are walking together through the opening to this story.

> There is a pile of clothing on the side of the train tracks. Light-blue cloth—a shirt, perhaps—jumbles up with something dirty white. It's probably rubbish, part of a load dumped into the scrubby little wood up the bank. It could have been left behind by the engineers who work this part of the track, they're here often enough. Or it could be something else. My mother used to tell me that I had an overactive imagination; Tom said that, too. I can't help it, I catch sight of these discarded scraps, a T-shirt or a lonesome shoe, and all I can think of is the other shoe and the feet that fitted into them.

The Girl on the Train debuted in 2015 and remained in the #1 *New York Times Bestsellers* list spot for 13 weeks, so this protagonist's observation raised questions in a few other readers' minds as well. Bonus story movement metaphor: the protagonist is on a train as she makes these observations. The story is literally moving along its tracks.

Promise an enigmatic narrator

In some novels, it isn't the protagonist or their actions that will raise a question in the reader's mind, but a provocative narrator. Consider this excerpt, found after our narrator quits toying with the reader by splashing all caps (HERE IS A SMALL FACT) and disturbing, bolded phrases (**You are going to die**) onto the opening pages:

> Where are my manners?
> I could introduce myself properly, but it's not really necessary. You will know me well enough and soon enough, depending on a diverse range of variables. It suffices to say that at some point in time, I will be standing over you, as genially as possible. Your soul will be in my arms. A color will be perched on my shoulder. I will carry you gently away.

By this point we're starting to get that the narrator of Marcus Zusak's novel, *The Book Thief*, is Death. All of us have had personal thoughts about, if not made bargains with, this unknowable entity. If Death could be personified, what might it have to say about its relationship to people here on earth? No better place to position this exploration than where Zusak did—at a time of war.

By the end of this prologue, we readers have been seduced by this narration. Death is observant—a great quality, considering the reader must rely on the details it provides to accumulate the story's meaning. Death has a sense of humor—it tells us it rarely takes the souls of people who are standing up. And when it says, "I saw the book thief three times," our narrator paves the way for the entrance of the book thief herself: Liesel Meminger, the protagonist. It is Liesel through whom the reader will experience the bulk of the story. Death's voice will fade to the background, although we'll sense his constant presence, since we've been warned that Liesel will brush up against Death repeatedly. This raises a question for the reader, too—not necessarily "if" our protagonist might die—Death assures us this is the fate awaiting us all—but *when*.

With such high stakes providing a drum roll of underlying tension, the reader will be watching around every bend in the story for whether the protagonist will die.

Telescope the perspective

Bonnie Garmus's debut, the #1 *New York Times* bestseller *Lessons in Chemistry,* is introduced by an omniscient narrator with a distinct perspective. The movement in this opening comes from its ever-narrowing focus.

> Back in 1961, when women wore shirtwaist dresses and joined garden clubs and drove legions of children around in seatbelt-less cars without giving it a second thought; back before anyone knew there'd even be a sixties movement, much less one that its participants would spend the next sixty years chronicling; back when the big wars were over and the secret

wars had just begun and people were starting to think fresh and believe everything was possible, the thirty-year-old mother of Madeline Zott rose before dawn every morning and felt certain of just one thing: her life was over.

Despite that certainty, she made her way to the lab to pack her daughter's lunch.

In one paragraph plus one sentence, this opening raises so many questions. How will the author tie this "big picture" awareness to a specific plot? What is the nature of these secret wars? Why does Madeline's mother feel certain her life is over? And why, pray tell, does she go into a lab to pack her daughter's lunch? Note that while this anonymous narration was narrowing its focus, my questions became similarly more specific—and indeed, in the very next paragraph, the reader is placed within the protagonist's point of view:

Fuel for learning, Elizabeth Zott wrote on a small slip of paper before tucking it into her daughter's lunch box. Then she paused, her pencil in midair, as if reconsidering. *Play sports at recess but do not automatically let the boys win,* she wrote on another slip.

I'll break there; you get the picture. A telescoping point of view can usher the reader right into the heart of your story.

Charm with a character's voice

In his novel *Little Bee,* Chris Cleave seduces the reader with his character's charisma:

Most days I wish I was a British pound coin instead of an African girl. Everyone would be pleased to see me coming. Maybe I would visit with you for the weekend and then suddenly, because I am fickle like that, I would visit with the man from the corner shop instead—but you wouldn't be sad because you would be eating a cinnamon bun, or drinking a cold Coca-Cola from the can, and you would never think of me again. We would be happy, like lovers who met on holiday and forgot each other's names.

This voice beguiled me. Once the words "British pound coin" and "African girl" were paired in the opening sentence, I could hear its Nigerian lilt, which comes through even in the absence of audio. The voice may belong to a child, but she has been through some things. Her opening narration promises imagination, details observed and processed, and a measured precision that invites the reader's trust.

The effect was hard-won. In a YouTube interview with Ron Hogan,[19] Cleave explained he spent a year listening in on the robust Nigerian immigrant community in London, and to Nigerian English radio programs on the internet, until Little Bee's voice transcended the page. "When Little Bee did arrive, fully formed, that was a great moment for me," Cleave said, because it was only through Little Bee's emerging voice that the story swelled within him, and he began to write.

Shock 'em

Certain stories can be rigged to explode onto the page, scooping up the reader with the propulsive force of dire stakes. That could be literal: "The arena blew at midnight. Sixty-nine thousand died. One walked away. Me." This is a great hook—we'll wonder how this character survived and whether they will be hero or villain—but use a big bang with caution. If the reader feels there's nowhere to go but down, the result will be negative story movement.

The following authors found provocative opening sentences that allow for further escalation later in their novels.

1. *Demon Copperhead* by Barbara Kingsolver

> First, I got myself born. A decent crowd was on hand to watch, and they've always given me that much: the worst of the job was up to me, and my mother being let's just say out of it.

2. *The Housemaid* by Freida McFadden
> If I leave this house, it will be in handcuffs.
>
> I should have run for it while I had the chance. Now my shot is gone. Now that the police officers are in the house and they've discovered what's upstairs, there's no turning back.

3. *The Covenant of Water* by Abraham Verghese
> She is twelve years old, and she will be married in the morning.

4. *Winter World* by A. G. Riddle
> For the past five months, I have watched the world die.

Despite the thrill these openings spark, only numbers 2 and 4 are labeled as "thrillers." The other two are literary novels. Whatever your story's genre, employing a version of this technique may create movement in your novel's opening.

Set the hook deeper with the inciting incident

The hook of your opening lines and your inciting incident can work together to clinch reader interest in any number of ways. You may recall that in Joshilyn Jackson's *Someone Else's Love Story*, where the protagonist falls in love with William Ashe at a Circle K, the inciting incident and hook are the same. By failing to immediately resolve the situation, anticipation will urge the reader to keep turning pages until the narrative returns to the Circle K. There, the inciting incident will answer one question while raising others, allowing Jackson to set her hook deeper.

But you can also generate story movement by letting hook and inciting incident either complement or supplement each other.

When they complement each other, the hook is further contextualized by the inciting incident, allowing the initial conflict to deepen. *My Sister's Keeper* by Jodi Picoult offers a great example. Here's the opening line:

> In my first memory, I am three years old and I am trying to kill my sister.

By stating the character's desire outright, this opening raises a strong story question, offers a startling perspective, and exhibits high stakes—all in one sentence. What we don't yet know is why this character wanted to kill her sister. The reader acquires that context through the inciting incident—which, as the engine that launches a story, a publisher will often include or hint at in the novel's back-cover copy or other online plot description. Here's the copy for *My Sister's Keeper*:

> Anna is not sick, but she might as well be. By age thirteen she has undergone countless surgeries, transfusions, and shots so that her older sister, Kate, can somehow fight the leukemia that has plagued her since childhood, a role she has never challenged...until now.

To the story movement generated by the hook, the inciting incident adds ripped-from-the-headlines relevance while inviting the reader directly into the moral quandary at the heart of the novel.

An intriguing hook can contribute even stronger story movement when the inciting incident supplements it by raising different yet equally compelling questions.

Here's an example, from *The Promise of Stardust* by Priscille Sibley. It begins:

> Late that night—on our last night—we lay in awe, mesmerized again by the Perseid meteor showers as they transformed stardust into streamers of light. They were an anniversary of sorts for us, a summertime event Elle and I both cherished, and we fell asleep on the widow's walk of our old house, my beautiful wife curled up beside me, her head resting in the crook of my arm.

If only I'd stayed home in the morning—if only I'd looked over at Elle and realized nothing I could or would ever do was more important than keeping her safe. If only—Jesus—

Look at "on our last night," so elegantly set off by the same punctuation that, at the end of this excerpt, will increase the reader's sense of foreboding. There's something about doomed lovers that lassos the heart. Its knot will be cinched by an inciting incident that serves up a tragic accident: Elle is brain-dead. Matt, a doctor, can't bear losing her, but he also knows that his wife, an adventurous scientist, feared only one thing—a slow death. Just before Matt agrees to remove Elle from life support, the doctors discover she is pregnant with a long-hoped-for baby. Matt's clear-cut decision becomes an impossible choice.

Readers loathe impossible choices in their real lives, but they sure do love them in the novels they read.

→✣ Try This ✣←

Imagine a player in the ready position at the beginning of a tennis match. Muscles under tension, weight shifting side to side, attention focused, ready to strike. Use these exercises to think about how you can identify that kind of tension in your opening lines.

- Set your manuscript next to the first excerpt in this chapter, the opening to *The Sparrow*. Can you rewrite your opening so that each line orients your reader while also raising a question that tips them into the next sentence, like Russell did?
- Have you ever thought about the relationship between your hook and inciting incident? A great hook can overcome a lackluster inciting incident and vice versa, but can you see a way to strengthen this relationship for maximal story movement?

- A story that starts in motion stands a better chance of staying in motion. If there's a technique in this chapter that might work for your work-in-progress, give it a try.

7

Plunge into Genre

It's difficult in that perhaps one world is asking for more gravity and one world is asking for more air.
　　　　　　　　　—Glen Tetley, dancer and choreographer

NO MATTER HOW SKILLED YOU BECOME at inviting the reader to ride the train of your story, not everyone will buy a ticket. No author likes to hear this, but it stands to reason that the appreciation of story is subjective and quite personal. One person might read only romances; another might read anything but. Raise the right question in your opening, though, and you'll be able to recruit the help of genre expectations to invite the right reader to move into your story.

For instance:

Suspense: How will the protagonist prevail against the threat?
Thriller: Will the protagonist be able to save everyone from the threat?

Mystery: Will the protagonist be able to figure out who did it?
Horror: Will the protagonist be able to vanquish the monster?
Adventure: Will the protagonist succeed in his quest?
Women's fiction: Will personal growth lead to a fresh sense of hope?
Fantasy: How will otherworld elements help the protagonist achieve their goal?

If a novel opens with a man and a woman meeting and they take an instant dislike to each other, the romance enthusiast will immediately recognize their favorite enemies-to-lovers subgenre. Their imagination will be off and running, trying to imagine how these two will end up getting together, since they know this isn't a matter of "will they or won't they," but a matter of "how will they and when." The reader will be watching for clues throughout.

Because you will have read extensively in the murder mystery genre before writing one, you'll know the story kicks off with a dead body. Because your reader hopes to identify the killer, you'll know to plant misleading clues—and a narrative takes shape. Once the murderer is revealed, you'll know that you've addressed the central story question and that the novel is essentially over.

If the murderer is identified halfway through the length of your manuscript, though, and then finding yourself short on word count, you try to turn the second half into a romance between the detective and the victim's husband, it will be like blindfolding your reader, spinning them around, and sending them staggering down an unmapped street. The success of genre fiction depends on raising the right question in the reader's mind from the outset and sticking to it.

Can you see how knowing this will help you fashion your own story question?

Many writers grumble that genre expectations hinder their creativity. I don't see it that way. The specific details that flesh out each genre's central question are limited only by the author's imagination. If you want to work against expectation and write a murder mystery with no body, you first need to understand what assumptions the reader will be making. Think of genre as an aid to getting your story moving within you, a jumping off point for your story, and a way to talk cogently about your novel.

To further our discussion, let's revisit a character from chapter 4: Dot, whose husband died three weeks before their fortieth anniversary climb of Mount Kilimanjaro. A grieving Dot who makes one final celebratory climb beside the chatty, twig-snapping ghost of the husband who just died will appeal more to those who enjoy the paranormal genre; the Dot who has never self-administered her diabetes medication yet who makes the climb and finds her personal power will appeal to those who like women's fiction; an abused Dot who killed her husband and is racing to the top of the mountain to taste one sweet moment of freedom before the police catch up with her might appeal to those who favor domestic suspense. Through bridging conflict that suggests the genre and an inciting incident that reinforces it, your story will set the right expectation.

Even if you write upmarket or literary fiction, your story's central question will give your reader a way to talk about your story, resulting in better reviews and better-targeted word-of-mouth recommendations.

Set genre expectation through packaging

Creativity is not always a marketer's friend. Readers want some assurance that this will be their kind of story. Where one reader might be weary of reading about cat-and-mouse thrillers, many more will be gobbling them up. Effectively communicating your novel's genre will help it reach the readers predisposed to liking it and will inform choices from title to cover to back-cover copy. It's not a stretch to call that story movement—no point writing and publishing a book if it doesn't move off shelves and into readers' hands!

To find *your* readers, your title, cover, and back-cover copy must effectively communicate genre. Let's look at two examples.

Bel Canto by Ann Patchett
  Back-cover copy:

Somewhere in South America, at the home of the country's vice president, a lavish birthday party is being held in honor of the powerful businessman Mr. Hosokawa. Roxane Coss, opera's most revered soprano, has mesmerized the international guests with her singing. It is a perfect evening—until a band of gun-wielding terrorists takes the entire party hostage. But what begins as a panicked, life-threatening scenario slowly evolves into something quite different, a moment of great beauty, as terrorists and hostages forge unexpected bonds and people from different countries become compatriots. Friendship, compassion, and the chance for great love lead the characters to forget the real danger that has been set in motion...and cannot be stopped.

Opening:

When the lights went off the accompanist kissed her. Maybe he had been turning towards her just before it was completely dark, maybe he was lifting his hands. There must have been some movement, a gesture, because every person in the living room would later remember a kiss. They did not *see* a kiss, that would have been impossible. The darkness that came on them was startling and complete. Not only was everyone there certain of a kiss, they claimed they could identify the type of kiss: it was strong and passionate, and it took her by surprise.

We then encounter additional lush sentences about the kiss and the effect of Roxane's voice (listeners wanted to cover her mouth with their mouth, drink in). On the next page, after raising the question of why the lights went out, Patchett uses a couple of sentences to expand the context—those gathered had not all been opera lovers, although they are now, for instance—and then brings us right back to the room:

No one was frightened of the darkness. They barely noticed. They kept applauding. The people who lived in other countries assumed that things like this happen here all the time. Lights go on, lights go off.

She follows this with, "the pleasant scent of candles just snuffed, a smoke that was sweet and wholly unthreatening."

The stated lack of threat is, of course, fiction speak for "the threat is real and imminent." Why had the candles also gone out? By page 12 we know the loss of light is a prelude to an invasion of guerrillas planning a military coup. Yet this will not be a military novel, nor will it be a thriller. Yes, the guerrillas carry arms, and their determination to achieve their goals threatens a group of people. But in her opening, Patchett's decidedly literary treatise on the nature of this kiss, perceived similarly by party guests from all corners of the world, promises that the politics of this literary novel will focus on interpersonal relationships. The cover's golden musical staff, which almost seems to trap the conversing party guests in a mansion, will turn away those looking for a thrilling tale of war strategy, but it will attract those who love literary explorations into our ability to communicate across language barriers through the arts.

The title, *Bel Canto*—which means "beautiful singing" in Italian and refers to an operatic vocal technique—confirms this assessment.

Someone Else's Love Story by Joshilyn Jackson

Let's return to the story of Shandi and the man she falls in love with at gunpoint, William Ashe. While the author soon rips readers away from that scene, the opening danger feels so immediate, its threat spans more than a dozen pages of context until we return to the Circle K, where the finger is once again pressed against the trigger of the "ancient, creaky .32 that could kill [them] just as dead as a really nice gun could" aiming toward the protagonist.

But is it a thriller? Here's what the back-cover copy adds.

Back-cover copy:

For single mom Shandi Pierce, life is a juggling act. She's finishing college, raising precocious three-year-old Natty, and keeping the peace between her eternally warring, long-divorced parents. Then she gets caught in the middle of a stickup at a gas station and falls instantly in love with William Ashe, when he steps between the armed robber and her son.

Shandi doesn't know that William's act wasn't about bravery. When he looked down the barrel of the robber's gun he believed it was destiny: it's been exactly one year since a tragic act of physics shattered his universe. But William doesn't define destiny the way other people do—to him destiny is about choice.

Now William and Shandi are about to meet their so-called destinies head-on, making choices that will reveal unexpected truths about love, life, and the world they think they know.

Nothing about this copy suggests a thriller, although Sandra Brown wrote one from a similar setup. Brown's novel, *Standoff*, is described by the following cover copy: "In this suspenseful thriller, a journalist who stumbles upon a deadly crime while pursuing the scoop of a lifetime will find her strength and conviction tested in new and frightening ways."

The only similarity to Jackson's story is that the inciting incident occurs while making "an innocuous stop at a convenience store." Jackson's back-cover copy, with its focus on Shandi, reads like women's fiction, suggesting that these characters were put at the point of a gun so that their destinies could converge.

Brown's copy tells us flat-out that it's a thriller, and she backs that up with her focus on the young couple who perpetuates the standoff.

Now let's compare their paperback covers. Jackson's features a large daisy from which a few petals have been plucked, beneath "someone else's love story" rendered in lower case, which in turn is placed beneath a blurb from *People* magazine that says, "A nuanced exploration of faith, family and the things we do for love." This cover does nothing to attract the fan of thrillers. Scanning the reviews turned up no mention of a reader thinking they were buying a thriller (although a few reviewers were disappointed that it wasn't a romance, revealing that they hadn't thoughtfully considered the title).

Brown's cover, on the other hand, is mostly dark, illuminated in part by the ghostly light from the convenience store and the flashing of police car lights in the lot. As is common in thriller titles, STANDOFF is rendered in narrow capital letters.

Through title, cover, back-cover copy and even a select blurb, these novels invite the "right" reader into the experience of these stories, and the bulk of their reviews skew positive. While traditionally published authors have less control over packaging decisions, considering how crucial those decisions are to setting reader expectation, the author would be wise to challenge any misrepresentations.

Set genre expectation with foreshadowing

To thwart the notion that the armed conflict into which their protagonists are thrust is setting up a thriller, the authors of *Bel Canto* and *Someone Else's Love Story* both do something interesting: they embed their endings in their opening chapters. That I admire this technique is ironic, because it drives me mad when readers admit to reading the ending before they buy a book—even though I understand that they do so to confirm genre and help them fine-tune the story question they hold in mind. Women's fiction, for instance, tends to end on a note of hope, even if its romantic thread doesn't work out. One friend of mine likes literary fiction but will not read tragedy, so for her it is worth a peek.

Let's look at this sentence, from page 13 of *Bel Canto:*

> It was the unspoken belief of everyone who was familiar with this organization and with the host country that they were all good as dead, when in fact it was the terrorists who would not survive the ordeal.

Buried as it is in the middle of a hearty paragraph, the reader might not pick up that the ending has been foretold, even as its impact on the reader's expectation is absorbed.

After her book *Bel Canto: The Annotated Version* was released, I read that Patchett affirms her reason for doing this: "I didn't want people to read the book to find out who was going to die, I wanted them to read the book to see how beautifully they managed to live."

If the title *Someone Else's Love Story* didn't send a clear message, Jackson aims toward her ending at the bottom of the first page:

> That afternoon in the Circle K, I deserved to know, right off, that I had landed bang in the middle of a love story. Especially since it wasn't—it isn't—it could never be my own.

Isn't, wasn't, could never be—do you think the narrator made her point? She certainly kept her promise. Should a potential reader peek at the story's last page, she would not see the name William Ashe upon it.

By including teasers to the endings of these books, Patchett and Jackson take the focus off the resolution of the trauma at hand and guide reader curiosity toward how these circumstances will impact the relationships between the characters as the story progresses. This heavy-handed foreshadowing works because the clues are delivered as the story opens, when the reader is still orienting to the story. As intentional elements that shape the reading experience, such clues don't provide the buzzkill delivered by peeking at the final pages. In fact, with so much story still to come, these embedded lines might be forgotten, even if subliminally, they did their work.

In each of these two stories, "giving away" the ending creates a subtle shift in reader expectation, from "What will happen?" to "Ah, I wonder how this will go down?" You may have seen this technique used in TV shows and movies, where the outcome, say a gunfight between former compatriots, is shown at the beginning of the episode. Then the title reads, "24 hours earlier," effectively rewinding the story while the question of how these two went from friends to foes so quickly is fresh in the viewer's mind.

Tap genre for keywords

People don't find their favorite type of novel online by scrolling through a bookseller's tens of millions of titles. They search by keyword, just as they'd look beneath genre labels in a brick-and-mortar bookstore.

For a reader to be drawn favorably toward your book, the more specific you can make your subgenre keywords, the better. Take this list of women's fiction search results on Amazon, for example:

> Women's fiction: 70K titles
> Historical women's fiction: 60K
> LGBTQ women's fiction: 50K
> Women's fiction mental health: 40K
> Women's fiction divorce: 20K
> Women's fiction suicide: 5K
> Women's fiction climate change: 1K

This is both a snapshot in time and an approximation—there are always some nonfiction titles thrown into these search results—but I suspect you can see that your title will be more discoverable among a thousand others than seventy thousand others.

Discoverability is the most basic form of story movement; without an invitation, the reader can't join in the dance.

In this regard, genre will be your friend.

⇥ Try This ⇤

While creatives often bristle at the notion of confining themselves to a genre, the benefits grow clearer as you move toward marketing the work—but by then, it's too late to retrofit genre's story boost. For maximum benefit, consider these issues at the start of your novel's journey.

- Have you identified the genre of your novel—at least as close as possible? How can genre expectations, or the questions raised by genres adjacent to yours, help you engage the right reader with your story?

- How specific can you be with identifying its subgenre? The Subject Headings List from the Book Industry Study Group,[20] an organization of publishers, manufacturers, wholesalers and distributors, libraries, retailers, and industry partners, might help.
- Have you thought of how your back-cover copy will suggest the inciting event that launches your story? Have you thought about how your cover can suggest genre? These are key decisions for a self-publisher, but since some publishers seek author input, those seeking traditional publication can also benefit from the exercise.

8

Motivate Your Protagonist

I work out of the emotions, out of human experience… Certainly there has to be a deeply felt motive and subject.
—José Limón, dancer and choreographer

WE HUMANS ARE CHANGE AVERSE. Since we never know what life will throw at us next, we like to hold on to the people, places, foods, and activities we love—often, with a white-knuckled grip. Prying us from this frame of reference will be jarring if not downright painful; even desired change will require a certain force of will. We want to be assured our efforts will be worth it.

Since life won't offer that assurance, your character must be strongly motivated to walk boldly into his story.

A young man who's never traveled more than ten miles from his home in rural Ohio, for instance, wouldn't go to college abroad on a whim. As author, it's your job to motivate a desire for change powerful enough to overcome his inertia and your reader's disbelief so the story can get moving.

So. What might motivate this protagonist to study abroad? What is it he holds sacred?

Is this his dream? Dreams are powerful enough to pull hermits from solitude, the painfully shy from behind masks, and broken dreamers from cloaks of cynicism. Maybe the program of study he's dreamed of pursuing—say, in the Urdu language, whose swoops, squiggles, and dots look to him more like music than an alphabet—is in Pakistan. Digging even deeper to find what inspired this dream would make it even more powerful.

Is he running from something? An abusive partner, the Internal Revenue Service, an arrest warrant? A negative motivation can be too weak to drive a story. Is he seeking peace? Relief from unrelenting stress? A chance to defend himself?

Is he running toward something? Maybe he's been conversing with a Kenyan woman he met on a dating app, and he wants to see if the relationship holds up in person.

Is time running out? Maybe when his family fled war-torn Ukraine in 2014, they left behind a beloved relative who is now ailing and begging to see him.

Is it a matter of honor? In recognition for his exceptional gift for languages, did a sponsoring organization offer him a full scholarship if he would come to Jordan and double major in Arabic and International Relations?

Is it a matter of justice? Maybe his Swedish cousin got in trouble with the law in a way she cannot let her parents find out about, and the only way he can help her is to pretend he'll be going to college there.

Is it a matter of ethics? When his family fled Syria, did a church help get them settled in the U.S. with clothes, English lessons, and jobs, and with tensions still critical, is he hoping to pay it forward by going to Syria to help other refugees?

It's all too easy for humans, and the characters inspired by them, to let fear box them in. But chasing dreams, escaping bad circumstances for something better, seeking love, recognizing a sense of now-or-never, defending honor, or pursuing justice can create a wave of determination strong enough to carry a timid surfer to new shores.

The protagonist's motivation to achieve his goal will not be static. To face the formidable obstacles that conspire to keep him from his goal, his motivation must deepen. As the potential consequences of failure mount, what started as a personal desire or obligation can grow into a complex matter of life and death.

We don't need to know this motivation at the opening of the story. In fact, the reader will intuit the strength of the protagonist's motivation by the way he tackles those obstacles standing between him and his goal. A few words of characterization may tell a reader that our Ohio hero is packing for a journey he fears yet is highly motivated to take. Unless he faces a considerable number of obstacles to leave the U.S., his true motivation may not be discovered until a later backstory scene, in which we see there was a time during his youth where he learned that being multilingual was the key to human connection—and survival. This general revelation, tweaked for specificity, could intensify his motivation for any of the stories just mentioned.

Novelists and readers both love unearthing the "why" that life is not quick to offer. Why does your protagonist want to achieve his goal so badly? The reader's bond with your protagonist will strengthen in proportion to her appreciation of his motivation.

Character motivation can also promote conflict.

Let's say you have two characters who both want to become brain surgeons, but for different reasons. Both possess the intellectual and financial wherewithal to succeed. In the right circumstances, they would be a great source of support for each other. But one of them is motivated by the potentially cancerous mass in his fiancée's brain, while the other wants to prove to his doubting father, the chief of surgery at a hospital across town, that he can handle the workload and stress of the residency program. As resources dwindle and opportunities to further their goals grow scarce, these two could very well come to blows.

Worldview as motivation

In real life, many events form our ways of being in the world. In a story with a strong psychological through line, an author can connect current action with one germinal scene that informs the character's perspective in a critical way. If the origin of your protagonist's worldview is necessary to understanding the strength of their motivation, your choice of origin scene can't be random. If a young man clears weeds without gloves and unwittingly grabs a handful of poison ivy, he'll probably protect his skin next time. But his blistery rash won't help explain why he's so fiercely protecting his heart when he and his partner experience infertility.

The motivation of the protagonist in Silas House's novel *Southernmost* can be traced back to the origin story of his protagonist, Asher Sharp, when his brother came out as gay. As an evangelical preacher, Asher could not accept this. The Bible he revered, and around which he had built his life and livelihood, declared his brother's actions sinful. Their abusive mother and Asher's wife were both homophobes. To protect his way of life when his brother left town, Asher shut the gate behind him and locked it.

Asher's conservative worldview kept him safe for a good long while. Then came the inciting incident, in which Mother Nature became an equal opportunity destroyer. Here's the back-cover copy:

> In the aftermath of a flood that washes away much of a small Tennessee town, evangelical preacher Asher Sharp offers shelter to two gay men. In doing so, he starts to see his life anew—and risks losing everything: his wife, locked into her religious prejudices; his congregation, which shuns Asher after he delivers a passionate sermon in defense of tolerance; and his young son, Justin, caught in the middle of what turns into a bitter custody battle.

After Asher's attempts to save a drowning girl are outstripped by the selfless heroism of the strangers he later learns are gay partners, Asher must set aside his philosophical coat of armor and forge ahead, opening himself to new lessons and new ways of thinking. Will he learn these lessons right away? Of course not—the result would be a quick anecdote, not a novel, and unconvincing. The transformation of ingrained prejudices requires so much pressure that the pain of staying the same becomes worse than the pain of change.

Use the origin story to drive dramatic imperative

Just because this origin scene comes first in your character's timeline doesn't mean you should open with it. At this point your reader is seeking relevance to the unfolding story—not to something that happened in the distant past. The questions raised in your opening will reassure your reader they've accepted an invitation to the right party. What happened in the origin story won't feel relevant until the reader wonders why the character feels so strongly about his course of action.

In *Southernmost*, Asher Sharp's view that homosexuality was sinful may have been tested many times in the years between his rejection of his brother and the opening of this novel, but he was able to hold tight to it as an aspect of worldview, nonetheless. Only once he's cast from his church and his marriage—the two institutions he'd hoped would protect him—is his newfound liberal resolve truly tested. He will not leave his son behind to be raised within these narrow beliefs. He violates the custody order, nabs his son, and takes him to Florida, hoping to introduce him to his brother, to whom Asher owes an apology. Push has come to shove. His story must begin.

"Push comes to shove"—these three action words describe what happens when an origin story meets the destabilizing force of a well-built inciting incident: dramatic imperative. Your story must begin.

Uncovering your character's origin story gives your novel's movement a running start—your protagonist's story was well underway before page one. But here are several other story-movement benefits:

- *Plot movement.* Understanding your character in this deeper way will inform how they react when you bring on the inciting incident. Genre aside, it would have made no sense whatsoever for author Silas House to send Asher, who is rethinking his stance on homosexuality, to Florida for surfing lessons. But his trip south to get to know his brother feels spot-on. Introducing his son to his brother for the first time, while trying to open the boy's life beyond the prejudices of their community, extends Asher's inner conflict by a generation.

- *Inner arc movement.* The genesis of your protagonist's worldview will expose useful vulnerabilities. You'll learn what they're most afraid of and how that has compromised their ability to go after what they desire. When the inciting incident strips away the protection of a long-held belief system, your protagonist senses they won't last long in the world. You'll understand their growing need to clothe themself in a new perspective, and what that might look like.
- *Writing movement.* Even if you don't end up including the entire origin scene in your novel—or any of it—identifying the nature of your character's inner crisis will create movement so foundational I put it in the first chapter of this book: your own movement toward the story you're writing. Fully understanding your protagonist's motivation will increase your devotion to them, making it much less likely you'll give up on them when the going gets tough.

Once you unearth this formative scene and then apply plot pressures that demand a change in perspective, your character's motivation to complete his journey will be matched only by your desire to help him do so.

⇥ Try This ⇤

Whether or not you decide to include detailed backstory scenes or otherwise explain the evolution of your protagonist's character, your knowledge of their motivations will seep into and energize your story. The following questions are well worth considering.

- What is motivating your character to go after their goal, despite the uncomfortable change it might require? How long can you delay letting the reader in on the true nature of that motivation?
- What form of self-protection has kept your protagonist feeling safe, but has also kept them, until now, from going after what they want?
- What origin scene would cause your protagonist to adopt this worldview, and what would heal them of it?
- How can your character's way of looking at the world, or their desires counter to it, motivate their actions in every scene?

9

Head Forward by Looking Back

> *It so happened that my first contact with the classical tradition coincided with the beginnings of an energetic reaction against it.*
> —André Levinson, dance critic

IN IMPORTANT WAYS, WE HUMANS have all been formed by our past experiences and our reactions to them. If you want to give birth to an adult character on the page, it makes sense for you to dig for influences from their past to give them dimension. Just as you would journal about your own past to make sense of—or even attempt to dispel—its influence on you, it makes sense to journal in your protagonist's voice to expose their past influences.

Do that and your character will spring to life, and that vitality will be evident on the page.

You may wonder how much of that material your reader will need, and the answer is usually "less than you think." Your reader will approach your novel with very little interest in your character's history.

Their desire to orient to the frame of the story your protagonist is entering is so strong, they will simply accept what you share on page 1 as the current state of things.

If story were constrained to a timeline, breaking the forward motion of the cause-and-effect chain to visit past events could be construed as negative story movement. But with your careful attention to its relevancy, you can use backstory to enhance your reader's sense of forward story movement.

In fact, sometimes, it makes no sense to move forward *until* you've looked back. You've experienced this in your own life. Maybe you were waylaid by a memory that demanded to be re-examined and processed. Or maybe you were crawling purposefully through your memory files, seeking experiences that might contribute valuable information to a difficult decision.

This relatable human experience suggests uses for backstory that transcend the origin scene discussed in the last chapter. You can also use backstory to:

- deepen characterization by letting your reader know what's important to the character;
- explore motives for the actions and decisions of your characters in the current story, whether they are exposed or left hidden;
- extend the frame of the story to include earlier events in the character's life, thereby increasing your reader's sense of your story's significance;
- create subtext; and/or
- anchor your reader in a psychological through line.

Mine backstory for emotional import

The joys, dreams, dashed hopes, and suppressed emotions that made your character who they are today can initiate important story movement within you, the empathetic author of their tale.

Several biographical data sheets are available online to help you "get to know" your protagonist, prompting you to enter eye and hair color, height, weight, skin tone, fitness level, etc. These can provide a sketch, sure, but the extent to which you'll get to know your protagonist by this means is only skin-deep. I, for one, have never been able to glean a thing about a woman by learning she's a brunette, have you? (Unless yesterday she was a redhead, which raises an interesting question.) If the details you've come up with can't suggest plot that will bring about change in your character, such as the temporary dye running down the shower drain that puts her in danger, they're of limited use. I encourage you to dig deeper.

Imagine interviewing your characters as part of a high-stakes speed dating event. You've paid a lot of money to meet for five minutes each—and at the end of the evening, you must marry one of the people you've interviewed. With so little time, consider replacing the factual checklist, below left, with the essay questions on the right. They'll better reveal character.

Replace	**With**
Birth date	Where are you in birth order, and how did that matter?
Parents' names	Who raised you and how did that affect you?
Name of college	Where did you hope school might get you?
Work history	What has been your proudest accomplishment, and why?
Places lived	How did you handle moving to a new place?
Past traumas	How has former trauma shaped you?
Former romances	Did you ever compete for someone's heart? What was that like?

Eye color	What do you see first when you walk into a crowded room?
Religious background	What do you believe in that can't be proven?

Of course, not all the details you uncover this way will make it into your novel. But to create an inner arc, you need innards. Instead of the character sketched by the lefthand questions, the righthand backstory will color in an ethical spine, moral fiber, heart, and soul. This will help you create a relationship with your protagonist that can go the distance and will make you a better of judge of what feels relevant to your character's movement along her arc.

Dig for relevancy

Before your story began, your divorced character was married. Moving back in time, she was conceived, born, and named. Further back, the local high school was built, and Main Street was paved. Just because these things happened doesn't mean they have a place in your story. To determine relevancy for the novel you're writing, weed out all but the details that will support movement within the frame you've established for your story.

While none of my editing clients have yet asked me to relive the paving of Main Street, almost every manuscript I've read featuring a woman who is or was once married includes the full details of her wedding. Each one of them goes something like this: *I wore white, my dad walked me down the aisle, my little niece threw flower petals, my smiling husband waited for me at the altar.* Unless something unusual happened that will further your reader's understanding of your point-of-view character's actions in the current story, these details aren't needed.

After you've planted a specific story question in your reader's mind, they'll scan constantly for relevant clues. They will either discard what does not contribute to the puzzle or head off on a tangent you didn't intend them to follow. It's like one of those word problems: There are six pieces of pie, and the mother drove 25 mph to deliver them to her two children. How many pieces can each of them have? You don't want your reader to resent you for making them revisit elementary math to discern meaning. The extraneous effort will put a drag on story movement.

Emotionally charged rituals carry the potential to transcend cliché. When evaluating whether your character's birth will aid story movement, ask yourself whether the issues impacting your protagonist's ability to sustain relationships (or know themselves or feel successful in life or whatever other theme you're exploring) manifested meaningfully as they exited their mother's womb. If not, rest assured: if a character is alive now, your reader understands he was once born.

But unexpected detail from a high school graduation that will give backstory context to your protagonist's current-day growth arc? That's exactly how backstory can be used to create story movement.

Otherwise, it will simply be an interruption. Since there's no good reason to tear your reader away from the story into which you've worked hard to invest them, let's look at ways to avoid losing their interest.

Use continuity words

Words that suggest continuity or repetition hint at a larger story than the action you are about to deliver—and when used in your opening sentence, can offer the reader an on-ramp into a story in progress. An avid reader will suspect that if a pattern is evoked, it's about to be disrupted. If a past event is alluded to, they'll wonder about its current effects even before needing to understand its nature.

Look how casually these simple yet impactful words—which I emphasized here in italics—are dropped into these openings.

> In the front row sit *the survivors*.
> —*The Arctic Fury* by Greer Macallister

> *Every summer* Lin Kong returned to Goose Village to divorce his wife, Shuyu.
> —*Waiting* by Ha Jin

She is *almost beginning* to believe him.
—*A Bigamist's Daughter* by Alice McDermott

Sia Dane discovered the man on the beach exactly *one year, one month, and six days after her husband disappeared.*
—*The Art of Floating* by Kristin Bair O'Keefe

The *last thing I had to do* that day was fire Art Davies.
—*Hidden* by Catherine McKenzie

In hindsight, I should have known right away that something wasn't quite right.
—*Don't You Cry* by Mary Kubica

Nine-year-old Lilly Blackwood stood in the attic dormer of Blackwood Manor *for what felt like the thousandth time,* wishing the window would open so she could smell the outdoors.
—*The Life She Was Given* by Ellen Marie Wiseman

Some of these examples are subtle, but even the word "again" in an opening line suggests that the reader is entering a story that's already on the move.

Add context on the fly

By folding bits of context into a story's opening, you can scoop up bits of relevant backstory without creating any interruption. Here are some examples.

> I fling open my bedroom curtains, and there's the thirsty sky and the wide river full of ships and boats and stuff, but I'm already thinking of Vinny's chocolaty eyes, shampoo down Vinny's back, beads of sweat on Vinny's shoulders, and Vinny's sly laugh, and by now my heart's going mental and, God, I wish I was waking up in Vinny's place in Peacock Street and not in my own stupid bedroom.
> —*The Bone Clocks* by David Mitchell (speculative literary fiction)

The way this character flings back the curtains in the first sentence drew me right in, and her imaginative observations invited me to stick around to see what would come out of her mouth next. The backstory with Vinny extended the story's frame into the near past, showing his lingering, all-consuming effect on the narrator. And to think Mitchell accomplished all this in one sentence.

It makes sense that Kim Michele Richardson would use backstory context in the opening of her sequel to *The Book Woman of Troublesome Creek* to link the two stories. She begins:

> The bitter howls of winter, uncertainty, and soon-to-be forgotten war rolled over the sleepy, dark hills of Thousandsticks, Kentucky, in early March, leaving behind an angry ache of despair. And though we'd practiced my escape many times, it still felt terrifying that this time was no longer a drill.
>
> I remember when I was twelve, and the shrill air-raid alarm sounded in the schoolyard as we were dropping books off at the stone school over in Troublesome Creek. The teacher yelled out to Mama, "It's a duck-and-cover drill," and then rushed us all inside, instructing everyone to crawl under the desks and cover our heads. It had been scary, but I still felt safe under the thin, wooden lip of the school desk.
>
> Today, at sixteen, I realized how foolish it was to think that a little desk could protect anyone from a bomb—how difficult it was now to believe that hiding would somehow save me from the bigger scatter bombs coming.

All the action in this opening belongs to the winds of fate, and yet it whips the reader into its spell. Note how her prose tugs on the reader as it extends the frame (and therefore the importance) of story backward to the duck-and-cover drills and forward to the coming scatter bombs. This time it's not a drill, adding immediate stakes. The reader wonders, what dire situation is in store for this protagonist? Richardson drops us right into a story in progress.

This novel is a sequel, yes, but story movement can be created in *any* story by showing a link between current action and continuing conflict.

Illuminate the character's inner life

In the following two examples, from very different books, the author found a clever way of communicating who the character is through the lens of who they were, effectively extending the story's frame on the very first page. Note this puts no drag on the narrative, nor does it introduce an interruption. Also note how the details they've provided bring their characters' inner worlds to life much more effectively than physical description could have on its own.

There isn't much action yet in either case, which demonstrates that "story movement" and "action" are not the same thing. In the first excerpt, all we know is that Novalee is in a car. In the second example, Jimmy is carrying a rucksack. That's about it. But the way these authors use backstory to parlay their character's current situation into the reader's concern for their future is particularly effective. They do so by wielding the two most powerful human emotions: fear and love.

> Novalee Nation, seventeen, seven months pregnant, thirty-seven pounds overweight—and superstitious about sevens—shifted uncomfortably in the seat of the old Plymouth and ran her hands down the curve of her belly.
>
> For most people, sevens were lucky. But not for her. She'd had a bad history with them, starting with her seventh birthday, the day Momma Nell ran away with a baseball umpire named Fred. Then, when Novalee was in the seventh grade, her only friend, Rhonda Talley, stole an ice cream truck for her boyfriend and got sent to the Tennessee State School for Girls in Tullahoma.
>
> By then, Novalee knew there was something screwy about sevens, so she tried to stay clear of them. *But sometimes,* she thought, *you just can't see a thing coming at you.*

> And that's how she got stabbed. She just didn't see it coming.
> —*Where the Heart Is* by Billie Letts

This next excerpt shows how the mementos a character carries in his rucksack can reveal what he carries in his heart:

> First Lieutenant Jimmy Cross carried letters from a girl named Martha, a junior at Mount Sebastian College in New Jersey. They were not love letters, but Lieutenant Cross was hoping, so he kept them folded in plastic at the bottom of his rucksack. In the late afternoon, after a day's march, he would dig his foxhole, wash his hands under a canteen, unwrap the letters, hold them with the tips of his fingers, and spend the last hour of light pretending. He would imagine camping trips into the White Mountains in New Hampshire. He would sometimes taste the envelope flaps, knowing her tongue had been there. More than anything, he wanted Martha to love him as he loved her, but the letters were mostly chatty, elusive on the matter of love. She was a virgin, he was almost sure…
> —*The Things They Carried* by Tim O'Brien

A page later, the tools of war the soldier also carries undermine Lieutenant Cross's tender hope with cold reality. The story is structured almost entirely this way as it explores the physical and psychological weight of war.

Sneaky, right? O'Brien has included backstory context while describing the contents of his character's sack, while never peeling the reader away from the forward march of story.

Raise a question, earn the backstory

Once a reader is invested in your protagonist's destination, any side trip can come across as an annoyance. Instead of giving them the sense that you're tearing them away from your story, assure them you will deepen their investment in it. You can do this by raising a question that implies the reader won't get the full picture without this backstory context.

Managing reader expectation this way is like crooking a finger toward your reader and gesturing, *Come hither.*

In his cult horror classic, *House of Leaves,* Mark L. Danielewski exemplifies the technique. It's from the fifth page of the "introduction," written by fictional character Johnny Truant, and it's the first mention of the point-of-view character's current situation.

> I haven't even washed the blood off yet. Not all of it's mine either. Still caked around my fingers. Signs of it on my shirt. "What's happened here?" I keep asking myself. "What have I done?" What would you have done? I went straight for the guns and I loaded them and then I tried to decide what to do with them. The obvious thing was to shoot something. After all, that's what guns are designed to do—shoot something. But who? Or what? I didn't have a clue. There were people and cars outside my hotel window. Midnight people I didn't know. Midnight cars I'd never seen before. I could have shot them all.
>
> I threw up in my closet instead.

Clearly, something deeply disturbing has happened, and this unhinged character wants to know what it is. So does the reader. But Danielewski resists telling us more to beg our curiosity. Wanting the answers, I read on, eager for him to fill in the blanks. It would take a long while to get them. The fictional introduction Danielewski wrote for *House of Leaves* sets up a frame story: the author has jumped ahead in time and plans to circle back to show how the protagonist got into this predicament.

If backstory helps the reader understand why your character is in such a tough spot, it will draw them deeper into the story. Attach high stakes, and a strong initial question can create enough tension to span an entire novel, begging the reader to come along on the journey.

Build sweet anticipation

Raising questions to which readers want answers works because a long guessing game builds sweet anticipation; readers will prioritize the ongoing story over their need-to-know backstory. They love all forms of delayed gratification. To linger in that moment when he might or might not kiss her. To inhabit her dream for a bit longer before her world comes crashing down around her. If this weren't true, your readers would pick up a fifty-word micro fiction instead of a novel.

Let's look at several ways to raise a question about backstory that will build anticipation.

Tease with a pithy sentence

Examples might look like:

"Susie dabbed the makeup onto her bruised cheek. James hadn't always been this way." Question raised: *Why did their relationship change?*

"Of course his mother knew all about the guns." *What did the protagonist's mother know about the guns on the property?*

"Reporters couldn't be trusted. Jack had known that since he was ten years old." *How did young Jack suffer a betrayal from the press?*

Because such teasers promise story that will deepen the reader's investment in the forward-moving plot, the reader is more likely to perceive this backstory as a bonus rather than an intrusion.

Bring hidden items to light

These hidden items could be found letters, journals, jewelry, annotated cookbooks, or items hidden under floors/behind walls.

In *The Girl Who Wrote in Silk* by Kelli Estes, Inara Erickson finds an elaborately embroidered silk sleeve hidden beneath a stair in the inn she has inherited. Her curiosity about the item becomes the reader's own as Inara seeks answers beneath layers of secrets, while in a separate timeline, we learn of Mei Lien, the lone survivor of a cruel purge of the Chinese in Seattle, who embroiders her tragic experience on a silk sleeve. Once the two women's stories converge, Inara will uncover a truth that will shake her family to its core and force her to make an impossible choice. In this case, as with most dual timeline novels, backstory secrets drive the action in the contemporary story.

Exact a long-promised reminiscence or confession

In Diane Setterfield's *The Thirteenth Tale,* reclusive author Vida Winter has spent the past six decades penning a series of twelve novels full of alternate lives for herself. Now old and ailing, she is ready to reveal the truth about the violent and tragic past she has kept secret for so long, in what will become her thirteenth tale. Vida's reminiscences and confessional dialogue disinter the life she meant to bury for good, inspiring her young biographer, Margaret Lea, to confront her own ghosts.

Limit backstory evoked through dreams and PTSD

Delivering backstory through dreams is a dicey proposition. The reader will know the information isn't reliable. Most of us can't interpret our own dreams, let alone those of others. They spring from the vast subconscious mind, much of which is unknowable, when you consider that even waking memories are skewed by perception. So unless your story world has a method of probing the subconscious for truth, you'll need an alternate way to earn your reader's buy-in. For instance, the dreamer could express uncertainty as to whether they're dealing with a dream loop or an actual memory.

Post-traumatic stress disorder can seem like a dramatic way to solve all problems related to backstory interruption, since the effects of the backstory live on in the present. It can provide a mystery as the reader tries to figure out what trigger is setting off this character's increasingly problematic behavior. A note of caution, though. In stories where the protagonist is hampered by a backstory trauma—such as rape, a family suicide, or a war buddy's horrific death—make sure to heighten the stakes in the forward-moving story by showing how the character's inability to keep the past in the past is increasingly complicating his deeply desired goals. If the backstory comes across as more dramatic than anything you've included in the forward-moving story, story movement could grind to a halt.

Be clear

Later in your story, heading into backstory will require a temporary shift in story direction. Hopefully your reader is willing to hang in there with you, because you've raised a question that assures them that this trip back in time will move your story forward. But just like driving on a road, it's dangerous to pull a U-turn without signaling your intention. Here are some ways to keep your reader from falling out of the story when you shift direction.

Add a break

When heading into a full backstory scene, the easiest way to signal the change is to add a lane divider between your forward-moving story and your backstory in the form of a line break (if you're containing the backstory within a continuing chapter) or a chapter break.

After a physical break your reader is accustomed to look for reorientation clues, such as a shift in time, setting, or point of view—so make sure you provide them. You might think adding a time stamp at the top such as "June 1989" would be enough—if a reader gets disoriented in your timeline, they can always shuffle back to see when the last chapter was set, right? That will only work if you put a time tag at the top of every chapter, which would be redundant if most of the book is set in a continual timeline.

Double-checking time tags is even more cumbersome when using an e-reader or audiobook. You want to make your reader feel smart, and if you send them all the way back to the beginning because they failed to memorize your timeline, you might lose them altogether. For these reasons, even if you use a time tag, it's best to immediately set the scene with prose that suggests where we are in time.

Create a portal

Whenever I smell freshly baked bread I still think of my grandmother, who died in 1987. When I open the ice drawer in my freezer, I still expect our sheepdog to come running, and Sebastian died in 1980. When I hear the slap of a screen door, I can still hear my mother yelling at my sisters and me not to take one step farther if we have pine needles stuck to the bottoms of our feet. Sense memories can create particularly strong portals through which you can travel to access backstory.

An emotionally charged event can serve the same purpose. A character attending parents' night in their elementary classroom—this time, with their own nervous child—could bring back feelings from their own youth.

In *Harry Potter and the Goblet of Fire,* J. K. Rowling created the Pensieve, a magical portal to the past. According to Rowling, writing at the wizardingworld.com site, "The Pensieve is enchanted to recreate memories so that they become re-liveable."[21] Only the most advanced wizards can access relived memories, which throws a spotlight on their importance—and what is learned is always of value in moving the current story forward.

Introduce past perfect

The most common way we deliver story is through simple past tense: She *buckled* her seat belt when he *shifted* direction. To differentiate a section of backstory from a forward-moving story that is already being told in past tense, you can signal the change with a switch to past perfect tense. Past perfect refers to some past action that was completed, or perfected, before another event in the past—as in, "Francis *had* studied English before he moved to New York." Here, the past perfect tense implies you are going to flash back to when Francis moved to New York.

If grammar terms make your eyes cross, think of it this way: a transition to backstory is like traveling down a ramp and into a tunnel beneath a river.

The forward-moving story, which you've been delivering in simple past tense, is the flowing river, and the backstory is in a tunnel beneath the river. As you head down the ramp, add in the word "had" a few times so your reader senses the transition. Once you've successfully transitioned into the tunnel of backstory, you can declutter your prose and return to simple past tense. As you near the end of the backstory and start back up the ramp to the forward-moving story, add in a few instances of "had" again. Those "hads" signal your transitions.

Here's an example adapted for our use from my second novel, *The Far End of Happy*. Ronnie, the protagonist, has just dumped a considerable stock of her bartender husband's booze down the drain. The section ends:

> It dawned on her that this might not be the healthiest thing for their cesspool. As it leached into the soil, would the alcohol kill the grass, just as it was killing Jeff? *[Highly charged situation creates portal.]*
>
> The worst part was that this was not all the booze. *[Raises a question.]*
>
> She grabbed the bar keys from one of the hooks on the antique rack and headed toward the barn.
>
> *[The "had" will now appear as we head down the ramp to the tunnel of the past, where we'll dig beneath the story for relevant bits from the past.]*
>
> Jeff <u>had</u> been helping himself to leftover bottles of booze from a special hotel closet for year.
>
> *[This is a short memory so now that I've established that I'm in the tunnel, I switch to simple past tense.]*
>
> When people contracted with the hotel for a wedding, they were charged for complete bottles of liquor; anything remaining in those bottles could not be resold. Until the booze was claimed, the opened bottles were kept in a special closet.
>
> *[The "had" will now reappear as I include a sneaky bit of backstory-within-the-backstory.]*
>
> There used to be a supply of clear booze in half-gallon containers that Jeff <u>had</u> marked with a *V* for vodka and a *G* for gin. <u>They'd</u> tapped it before, for summer picnics.

[That was the last "had"—we're up the ramp and back into the simple past tense of the present day.]

But surely that was gone. And it was—in the old grain rooms she found only filthy, empty boxes. To be thorough, though, she unlocked the clean storage room and hit the light.

Only the front shelves held the yard tools the space had been designed for. The back three units held intact bottles of booze, floor to ceiling.

No way could Ronnie imagine putting all that down the drain. Why try? Even if she managed to get rid of it, Jeff could easily get more.

The beauty of this technique is that it's clear without impeding story movement with a line break.

Or, be obvious!

"Back when he was nine, Robert—or Bobby, as he was known then—wanted to be a cowboy." Far from insulting your reader's intelligence, this approach makes quick work of your desire to be clear.

Don't let the number of techniques here stymie you. You don't have to use them all! They are simply tools that can help you capitalize on the tension you have already created by extending your story's frame and increasing its importance—without breaking the spell of the forward-moving story.

⇥ Try This ⇤

Put your backstory to the test!

- Does it reveal/deepen motivation and therefore enhance characterization?
- Is it relevant to the character goal and premise of your story?
- Will it pop your reader from the story or glue them to it?

- Did you raise a question this backstory will address?
- Did you ease the reader into the flashback with clues (a portal, past perfect tense, a section break) or tell them outright, "Back when I was five…"?
- Does the backstory inclusion increase tension and raise new questions?
- Is your forward-moving story more dramatic than the backstory?
- Can the story be understood without the backstory?

And most important:
- Does the backstory provide context that moves the story forward?

10

Stage the Story Against an Interactive Setting

When I present something on stage with music and with costumes and with settings, I expect those to be part of the drama. They're not a decoration.
—Martha Graham, choreographer

AS YOUR PROTAGONIST MOVES through their world, don't overlook the many contributions your character's partner—namely, that world—can make to story movement. Your novel's setting can obstruct, complicate, inspire, comfort, surprise, threaten, or interact with your characters in any number of other ways that will create tension and further story. Not just any story, but *their* story.

Yet too often, in a mistaken attempt to "show" the reader that world, a writer will create a wall of words that inadvertently shuts them out instead. That could look like this:

> A bedraggled armchair sat on the porch. Inside, the cabin held only one room. A ladderback chair sat against the logs of one wall, opposite a bank of kitchen cupboards and a propane stove. Beside an iron-framed cot, a night table held her books, field journals, and a kerosene lantern.

When met with a wall of description like this, I always fear there's going to be a quiz. This is because of a birthday party game we played when I was young. My mother would briefly show a tray of items to my circle of friends and then, after she left, the child who could accurately list the most of them won a prize.

Anxiety ran high due to time limits on both the viewing and the listing. Even worse, the items on the tray (a pair of scissors, a little bell, a bottle cap, etc.) were hard to remember because they evoked no emotion. For similar reasons, showing your reader around a cabin before allowing the scene's action to begin, as in the example above, is not the best use of setting.

The details in that example are pulled from Barbara Kingsolver's novel, *Prodigal Summer*. Let's look at the passage again with the action added back in. Deanna, a wildlife biologist who works from a lone outpost on a mountain, has recently crossed paths with an enigmatic young hiker:

> His presence filled her tiny cabin so, she felt distracted trying to cook breakfast. Slamming cupboards, looking for things in the wrong places, she wasn't used to company here. She had only a single ladderback chair, plus the old bedraggled armchair out on the porch with holes in its arms from which phoebes pulled white shreds of stuffing to line their nests. That was all. She pulled the ladderback chair away from the table, set its tall back against the logs of the opposite wall, and asked him to sit, just to get a little space around her as she stood at the propane stove scrambling powdered eggs and boiling water for the grits. Off to his right stood her iron-framed cot with its wildly disheveled mattress, the night table piled with her books and field journals, and the kerosene lantern they'd nearly

knocked over last night in some mad haste to burn themselves down.

The entertainment upgrade in this version is due to Kingsolver's hands-off storytelling. This passage, from page 27, is the first time the reader has spent any length of time in Deanna's cabin—and yet it shares everything we need to know about her spare existence, where her priorities lie, and what happened there the night before. Kingsolver honors the intelligence of the reader by letting the setting reveal her protagonist.

Bring your setting to life

It seems Kingsolver looks at story through the formative aspects of place for the same reason she pursued advance degrees in ecology and evolutionary biology—she's fascinated by the interrelationships of organisms and their environments, and how these relationships change over time. From the desert setting of *The Bean Trees* ("We were sitting out with the kids in Roosevelt Park, which the neighbor kids called such names as Dead Grass Park and Dog Doo Park.") to the Congo setting in *The Poisonwood Bible* ("Inside the bright orange rim of the fire I could see the outline of some dark thing being turned and pierced, with its four stiff legs flung out in a cry for help."), to the Appalachian mountain setting of her youth and to which she returned in her novels *Prodigal Summer, Flight Behavior,* and her Pulitzer Prize-winning *Demon Copperhead,* Kingsolver has used interactive settings to summon forth and obstruct her characters' desires. Here's one more excerpt from *Prodigal Summer,* featuring a different set of characters:

> They sat silent for a while, listening to the wood thrushes. Nannie pulled a handful of cockleburs from her skirt and then, without appearing to give it much thought, reached over and plucked half a dozen from the knees of Garnett's khaki trousers. He felt strangely moved by this fussy little bit of female care.

The sweet emotion here, inspired by cockleburs of all things, advances a relationship in this story.

Dennis Lehane can conjure the same kind of magic in an urban setting. Check out the way he plunges us into the Plat in the opening to his novel *Mystic River:*

> When Sean Devine and Jimmy Marcus were kids, their fathers worked together at the Coleman Candy plant and carried the stench of warm chocolate back home with them. It became a permanent character of their clothes, the beds they slept in, the vinyl backs of their car seats. Sean's kitchen smelled like a Fudgsicle, his bathroom like a Coleman Chew-Chew bar. By the time they were eleven, Sean and Jimmy had developed a hatred of sweets so total that they took their coffee black for the rest of their lives and never ate dessert.

The emphasis on chocolate and dessert foreshadows events in the novel's opening pages that will steal away what remains of these boys' sweetness.

Make it *your protagonist's* setting

With much diversity to offer, cities can be so much more than the sum of the tourist attractions found in many manuscripts. Jennifer Weiner's *Good in Bed* and my novel *The Art of Falling* are both set in Philadelphia, for example, yet neither includes the Liberty Bell. Because both novels explore the theme of body image, though, one might suspect our setting details would overlap. But Weiner's Cannie Shapiro, an entertainment journalist, moves between her office and a weight-loss clinic and eats at a hidden terrace restaurant; she would not run into my protagonist, Penelope Sparrow, in these locations. Penelope's story centers on her relationship to the Avenue of the Arts, which isn't mentioned in Weiner's book. The only setting in both novels is Penn's Landing, the site of important but very different turning points in each book.

Where there's Paris there must be the Eiffel Tower, right? Not for Irène Némirovsky. Her World War II novel, *Suite Française,* only mentions the Eiffel Tower to denigrate the Germans occupying Paris, who purchase souvenirs bearing its image. "They'd buy anything," Némirovsky wrote, which inspired within the Parisians "the amusing desire to fleece them."

At this point in her story, refugees Jeanne Michaud and her husband have been walking for three days to reach the outskirts of Paris so they can get a train to Tours, where they hope to access their account in a bank that may no longer exist. This train station has no distinguishing characteristics. But that may well be the point. The real setting is the war itself. Here's an excerpt from when Jeanne hears aircraft and raises anxious eyes to the sky:

Suddenly, one broke loose and swooped down at the crowd. He's going to crash, Jeanne thought, then, No, he's going to fire, he's firing, we're finished...Instinctively, she covered her mouth to stifle a scream. The bombs had fallen on the train station and, a bit further along, on the railway tracks. The glass roof shattered and exploded outwards, wounding and killing the people in the square. Panic-stricken, some of the women threw down their babies as if they were cumbersome packages and ran. Others grabbed their children and held them so tightly they seemed to want to force them back into the womb, as if that were the only truly safe place. A wounded woman was writhing around at Jeanne's feet: it was the one with the costume jewelry. Her throat and fingers were sparkling and blood was pouring from her shattered skull. Her warm blood oozed on to Jeanne's dress, on to her shoes and stockings.

In this scene, Némirovsky wisely keeps her POV character at the center of the unfolding action. We don't need enough detail to recognize *this specific* Paris train station because it's a symbol—while moments ago it had been a locus of hope, war has moved in to claim it with chaos and horror. By bombing the tracks, the Germans cut off escape—but after these events, as Jeanne and her husband fight back by tending the wounded, we see that the antagonists have not extinguished human kindness.

From the confines of a single bedroom (*Room* by Emma Donoghue) to a theme park where dinosaurs cloned from prehistoric DNA roam (*Jurassic Park* by Michael Crichton), writers who successfully place their stories at the beating heart of an interactive setting create a story that readers will remember.

In her novel *A Map of the World,* Jane Hamilton offers up many great examples of how to bring a setting to life. Let's look at several passages to see how Hamilton does it.

In the opening, she ties the description of her farmer-husband to the setting:

> I had never said out loud a little joke I used to say to myself now and again: Everywhere that barn goes, Howard, you are sure to be close behind.

She supports this statement with this:

> His was a musky smell, as if the source of a muddy river, the Nile or the Mississippi, began right in his armpits.... That morning there was alfalfa on his pillow and cow manure embedded in his tennis shoes and the cuffs of his coveralls that lay by the bed.

She evokes an unforgiving atmosphere:

> The last rain had come at the beginning of April and now, at the first of June, all but the hardiest mosquitoes had left their papery skins on the grass. It was already seven o'clock in the morning, long past time to close the windows and doors, trap what was left of the night air, slightly cooler only by virtue of the dark. The dust on the gravel had just enough energy to drift a short distance and then collapse on the flower beds. The sun had a white cast, as if shade and shadow, any flicker of nuance,

had been burned out by its own fierce center. There would be no late afternoon gold, no pale early morning yellow, no flaming orange at sunset. If the plants had vocal cords they would sing their holy dirges like slaves.

Hamilton's barn has a will of its own. The dust has energy. The sun is fierce. Plants have vocal cords—it's as if the setting has perspective about the humans that move through it. Images like these could make your novel distinctive, too.

A word of warning, though: it's possible to over-animate your story world. I've read manuscripts fresh off an "all passive language is bad" workshop in which tables stand on tiptoes and doorbells trill arias and still-warm cars comfort driveways. When reading such passages, I can't help but picture the cursed objects from Disney's *Beauty and the Beast* breaking into song and dance.

Use your research judiciously

Now on board with the idea of beefing up your setting's role, you research more about the geography, geology, weather, and time period that had previously served as a simple backdrop. You read more about the science and philosophy upon which you're building your story world and wonder how that might interact with the occupation of your protagonist. That's all great.

But how much of that belongs in your book? Only the relevant bits that deepen characterization and otherwise further your story's movement. What doesn't support story movement impedes it.

Here are a few benchmarks you can use to assess the inclusion of your research.

Does your research into your novel's time and place complicate the journey of your protagonist toward her story goal, as set out in the beginning of the book?

This speaks to reader expectation. Let's say your character is a woman trying to gain acceptance as a physician in nineteenth-century Chicago. Research tells you the Great Chicago Fire started in 1871, and there's room for doubt as to whether it was started by Mrs. O'Leary's cow. So you create a morning-after scene in which your protagonist discusses her alternative theories about the fire with her neighbors, who report in about the extensive damage the fire caused. Will this scene support story movement?

No. This scene contributes nothing to your character's goal of gaining acceptance as a physician. Because you haven't raised expectations about the ramifications of this fire from the outset, your reader just won't care. It's simply "something that happened." She'll start to skim, looking for when this story gets back on track. She wants to know if the heroine will be respected as a physician or not.

Now if your character must use a Bunsen burner (research: invented in 1854!) to mix her own medications because the male-dominated pharmacy industry won't have anything to do with her, and she is so tired she gets the ingredients wrong, creating an explosion that some reporter later blames on Mrs. O'Leary's cow? Perfect.

Is your protagonist immersed in this conflict deeply enough to motivate her behavior?

It's not enough for your character to arrive in town, hear about the fire while unpacking her bags, and vow to be a physician because too many lives were lost.

Instead, have her move into the fray. She will roll up her sleeves and pull people from the wreckage, sort victims according to the urgency of their need for care, and set up a field hospital—preferably, all while the men are still strategizing in the town hall. Now, the historic event itself will help propel her toward her story goal.

Have you fully explored all the ways this story-world research can bring your characters into conflict and raise the story stakes?

Let's go back to the version in which our budding doctor caused the explosion. What if Mrs. O'Leary became a character? When your protagonist learns a reporter blames the fire on the cow, she keeps mum—she would never become a respected physician if her culpability got out. But her guilt draws her to the cow's owner, and they become friends, even as the woman secludes herself from the public eye because of shame—and because of a medical condition caused from smoke inhalation. If your protagonist can cure her, her reputation will benefit, even as her secret erodes her soul.

Have you used the setting to reflect the emotional arc of your protagonist?

The researched details with which you've painted your story's scenery don't have to stand in silent witness to your tale. If your budding physician is touring through Chicago to witness the devastation the fire wreaked on its wood-based architecture, you've written a travelogue, not a novel. But if your protagonist was changed by that fire in a way that motivates or complicates her story goals, you may find relevant metaphor in those details—the charred façade of the bank that represented her security, the suspended ash absorbed into her physical being, the first buds emerging the year after the fire. Metaphor aids story movement by asking your reader's mind to arc between the story they are reading and the understanding they've gained from their own life experiences.

To earn the inclusion of your research, think of how to weave the setting into the fabric of your story. As a "doing" word, the notion of weaving will remind you to find ways to incorporate your novel's elements without stopping your story to do so.

Make the best use of historic events

In this next example, historic events become an active part of the story's setting and the protagonist's arc.

As soon as runaway teen Josie Tyrell mentions John Lennon's murder in the opening of Janet Fitch's novel, *Paint It Black*, we know the story is set in 1980. Fitch then proceeds to make such good use of Lennon's death, it seems it motivated her to write the novel.

Let's look at how she drops this information into the second half of her first paragraph, after a few sentences that set up the action: Josie is modeling for an artist friend.

> Henry Ko wasn't painting well today. He had to stop every few minutes to wipe his eyes on the back of his hand, while *Double Fantasy* circled around on the studio stereo. Everyone was playing it now. John Lennon had just been shot in New York, and wherever Josie went, people were playing the same fucking Beatles songs until you wanted to throw up. At least *Double Fantasy* had Yoko Ono.

Through Josie's perceptions of Lennon and Ono, Fitch brings her character to life. As she describes the album cover, Fitch foreshadows the story to come. Let's pluck out a few excerpts from the first few pages to see how she pulls this off.

> On the cover that leaned against the dirty couch, John and Yoko pressed together for a kiss they would never finish. People were always trashing Yoko Ono, blaming her for breaking up the Beatles, but Josie knew they were just jealous that John preferred Yoko to some bloated megaband. Nobody ever really loved a lover. Because love was a private party, and nobody got on the guest list.

(In the story to come, Josie will soon find out that her boyfriend, Michael, who said he was going away on a trip to concentrate on his painting, has killed himself. Michael's mother will blame Josie for his problems. Michael's mother is a renowned concert pianist, and her competitive condescension toward Josie will prove to be Josie's main obstacle through the rest of the novel.)

> Henry kept crying about John Lennon. Josie felt worse about Darby Crash. Darby had just killed himself in an act of

desperate theater, a gesture swamped by the Beatle's death like a raft in the backwash of a battleship.

(This foreshadows Michael's suicide, as well as Josie's narrative arc—she doesn't want to get swept away by Michael's death.)

She toked along with him, knee to knee, and thought about the guy who shot Lennon. Shot by a *desperate fan.* On the news, fans were always desperate.

(Desperation, and Josie's need to rise above it in a way that Michael could not, will be a theme throughout the book.)

She drove back to Lemoyne in her rattly Ford Falcon, a powder blue relic with band stickers on the trunk—X, Germs, *Cramps.* It was normally a three-minute drive, but she hit a line of cars with their lights on. Why were they going so slow? Maybe another John Lennon thing. She honked, wove, and passed until she got to the front and saw it was a hearse. Mortified, she turned off onto a side street and stopped, red-faced. How was she supposed to know—a line of cars crawling along with their lights on?

The details Fitch chose to include about Lennon's murder foreshadow Josie's challenge: already at risk as a runaway, she must find her way forward without her identity tied to Michael. The reader's emotions are heightened without referring to Mark David Chapman or the dramatic rush to get Lennon to the hospital; Fitch rightly allows her own story to provide the novel's most dramatic moments.

There is no writing rule that says historic or even current events can't simply be mentioned in passing. Authors do it all the time. But when select aspects of that event also add to characterization, set an emotional stage, and foreshadow events to come in a way that pulls the reader into the story and creates an indelible impression on the reader's memory?

That's when those details will help get your story moving.

⇥ Try This ⇤

Your setting contains potential energy that you can convert into story movement. The following prompts can help you identify it, free it, and harness it for your own story purposes.

- Open your manuscript and highlight chunks of description that could use plot integration. Keep setting details that support the plot and deepen characterization and consider removing the rest. Then maybe, like Kingsolver, you'll have created holes in that first wall of words into which your reader can insert her own perceptions.
- If your characters were stripped from a scene in your novel, how could the setting alone tell the tale? This is a challenging question, but it may result in ideas and images you can use to your advantage.
- Do your passages of setting description move your story meaningfully forward? If not, what could you change?
- A dancer moving on the stage is never alone—she's dancing a duet with the space around her. How could this sensibility infuse your protagonist's relationship with the world around her to make it more interactive?

PART II

Propel Your Protagonist Through a Gauntlet

11

Determine Relevant Conflict

When I start work, I do so quickly and let the whole accumulation of assembled thoughts pour out. I accept, in sheer faith in myself, that whatever comes is relative to the subject and is to my mind a significant facet to it. I do not verbalize about it or question it for meaning. When the material is almost fully composed, then I order its sequence and for the first time evaluate its evolution and totality.

—Alwin Nikolais, choreographer

HAVE YOU EVER BEEN READING A BOOK and out of the blue, some problem arises that you just don't care about? As if ripped from the pages of someone else's book and deposited in the one you're holding, this problem now stands between you and the further progression of the tale you thought you were reading.

If someone has this reaction to your work in progress, it's a sign that you've detoured into an irrelevant conflict.

You may have begun your novel guided by a few basic tenets, such as "Hook your reader on page 1," "Conflict is story," and "Show don't tell," but such generalizations can only guide your plotting so far. If until now you've thought the word "plotting" simply refers to the "things that happen" in your book, think again. Plot has a greater purpose.

Don't forget that you are writing a story about a protagonist whose choices will drive the plot *and* define their changing character. Plot may have "happened" when the inciting incident got the story ball rolling, but from then on, as your character pursues their deeply desired story goal, forces trying to influence their success—other characters, powerful institutions, Mother Nature, or even conflicting aspects of their own personality—will pressure them to evolve along an arc of inner change.

That change is what convinces the reader that your story matters. It's proof that the plot has had a profound effect on your protagonist.

Where they were once afraid, they find inner courage.

Where they once believed themselves stupid, they now trust their instincts.

Where they once thought they lacked heart, they're now capable of love.

Where they once longed for their heart's desire, they now realize they've had it all along.

Yes, these are the character arcs from L. Frank Baum's *The Wonderful Wizard of Oz,* but children's literature often has a way of clarifying story concepts. If these characters all wanted different things, why didn't it feel like the story was going in a number of different directions? It was due to their shared story goal—Dorothy had convinced them that the Wizard could help them all. But why would vanquishing a Wicked Witch with water matter to a modern-day kid reading the book beneath their desk in eighth-grade algebra? Exciting though it was, Baum's plot is irrelevant to their life. The greater takeaway will be that these characters were in search of something they'd had all along—something they couldn't see until dire circumstances changed their perspective. By reading this book, this eighth grader might think of their own attributes in a new light. This was the story's point.

Without conflict relevant to your protagonist's arc of inner change, the guiding lights of *hook, conflict,* and *show* can only take you so far. Over time, a catchy *hook* can lose its barb and your *conflict* can feel random, causing you to *show* too many disparate things, diluting any tension you had hoped to build. With so much going wrong, a full rewrite will loom.

Let's see if the rewritten tenets in the subheads below might save you some time.

A barbed hook needs a point

The point of your story will be shaped by its premise. Let me define how I use the term, because other definitions of "premise," such as the story situation (a man's business endangers his spouse) or theme (how love complicates career), won't work for this discussion of story movement.

A premise is the specific point you want to make by applying plot pressures to your protagonist's that will result in their arc of change. Writers often have trouble grasping the concept because they haven't yet gained clarity as to what their novel's point is The best discussion I've ever read about it is in James N. Frey's *How to Write a Damn Good Novel.*[22] To ensure your premise frames story movement, use this structure: [plot pressure] leads to [a new way of being in the world]. "Leads to" could be any action word that can suggest a cause-and-effect trajectory.

The premise of that last paragraph is, "Discovering what kind of story you are telling *leads to* its premise." The premise of this chapter is, "Studying premise *leads to* an understanding of relevant conflict."

And when written in the right way, your premise can suggest how your plot will affect the character's inner arc of change.

Let's say that in your novel, your female protagonist rises to the top of a global company. She brings fresh ideas to battle climate change to her first board meeting, backed by projections showing immediate public relations rewards and, over time, financial gain. At this meeting, others in the know tell her that the previous CEO had borrowed billions from big oil to keep the company afloat. As the plot progresses, these powers threaten the family she loves, raising a question about what happened to the last CEO.

The premise of the story I just mentioned might be, "Honoring the planet leads to preserving life at all costs," which suggests an ecology-challenging plot and a growth arc that leads to the courage to fend off its life-threatening implications. This simple statement can be a guiding light that will help you envision relevant conflict. Perhaps in this story's dark moment, this CEO must walk away from her family—the very people whose love has fueled her ambition to leave the planet a better place—to save their lives.

Your story premise can inform the way you build your cast of characters. The head of the oil company, an antagonist in our sample story, would have an opposing (and hopefully defensible) premise, such as "Exploiting our country's natural resources facilitates affordable family life." Their differences will allow organic conflict to arise between the two CEOs that will keep your protagonist moving toward a satisfying ending.

A great illustration of the interplay between premise and character orchestration can be found in the film *The Cider House Rules,* distilled from John Irving's 1985 novel by the same name. Its theme—not its premise—is women's reproductive rights.

In rural Maine, Dr. Larch will honor pregnant women's pleas for help by either performing an abortion or by raising the unwanted children in his orphanage until he can place them with adoptive families. His premise might be stated: *Honoring a pregnant woman's tough choice empowers her to determine the course of her life.* Whether from moral quandary or a sense of injustice, this difficult and inescapable work results in an inner torment that Larch calms through his ether addiction.

This story offers an interesting example. Since the protagonist serves as your reader's gateway to the story, the novel's premise will typically be the same as the protagonist's. But Larch is not the protagonist. Our gateway to the story is through the perspective of

Homer, his unwilling apprentice. Homer does not want to perform abortions—he is grateful for his life, even if his mother chose to leave him with Dr. Larch. Homer's life hasn't been easy—he was adopted and returned a few times—but at least he has a life and is looked up to by the younger orphans. His opening premise might be, *Pregnancy leads to the gift of life.* This belief opposes the author's—Irving is staunchly pro-choice—but finding empathy for those who held pro-life views deepened Irving's story's conflict. Over the course of the story, Homer's growth arc changes his stance.

Homer's love interest is Candy, who came to get an abortion after she and her soldier boyfriend Wally conceived a child. Her premise might be: *When sex leads to pregnancy, it's not so fun anymore.* Candy expands Homer's empathy for those who choose to abort. Once she is unencumbered by pregnancy and her boyfriend leaves for war, Homer allows his feelings for her to come to the fore at Wally's family's apple orchard, where he gets work. Together, they feel happy and free.

Rose, a migrant apple picker, is desperate after being raped and impregnated by her father. Rose's premise might be: *Incest can lead to a life that's not worth living.* In a tense scene revealing his inner storm over the issue, Homer admits he can help Rose—and performs his first abortion.

These characters' premises are all related to reproductive rights, and because Irving's story is set in an orphanage whose dual services put it at the heart of the controversy, these characters will all come into organic conflict with one another that will necessarily further Homer's movement along the arc of inner change that allows him, after Dr. Larch's death, to step up and take his place—providing both obstetric care and abortions.

Note my repeated use of "might be" regarding these characters' premises. For one thing, I don't know if Irving gave purposeful thought to premise as he wrote, or if the orchestration of his cast arose subconsciously. Also, as anyone who has read literary criticism knows, there are many ways to analyze a novel, including premise, inciting incident, and any of its other structures. Premise is an aid for you, the author. Use it in revision and it will help you align story elements; give it thoughtful consideration from the start and it will light your path from the outset. Premise will help relevant conflict arise organically, keep your hook barbed, and guide your protagonist, your cast of characters—and your reader—toward an ending that makes a point.

Story is inner conflict made external

A widower wants to join his wife in the grave, but life keeps interrupting his suicide attempts (*A Man Called Ove* by Frederik Backman). An old dog is ready to die so he can come back as a human to help his beloved owner, but his owner is in immediate need of his unconditional love and emotional support (*The Art of Racing in the Rain* by Garth Stein). A woman plans to move on from her marriage, but on the day her husband said he'd move out he digs in and stands off (my novel *The Far End of Happy*). Stories whose situations so clearly exemplify the protagonist's inner torment are called "high concept" and bring to life a very simple definition of story I latched onto the moment I heard it: Story is inner conflict made external.

Let's look more closely at Backman's novel, and how it illustrates this section's rewritten tenet. Ove's psyche is at the mercy of dueling desires: to die and to live. To force Ove to wrestle with this struggle, Backman created characters and set pieces that allow Ove's dueling desires to manifest in his life. Through escalating scenes that keep Ove right at the intersection between his desire to die and his gut-reaction to live, this story can't help but remain relevant. The story's direction is clear, and the reader is eager to know how it plays out.

Backman makes good use of setting to externalize Ove's inner conflict. From the way he polices his neighborhood to make sure everyone follows agreed-upon standards, we know Ove to be a neat, orderly, rule-following man. This adds stakes to his ongoing life-or-death rumination, as it must be hard for an orderly man to tolerate such a deep internal rift. While preparing to depart this earthly plane, he takes under his wing a young man who admires his neighborhood efforts. To pass the torch, Ove teaches him the role—but finds he likes this relationship.

Then we see Ove's ability to coax the living away from the brink of death: an almost-frozen stray cat thrives when Ove brings him into his cozy home; Ove's old friend, enduring a living death due to dementia, perks up when Ove reignites their ongoing debate about the best kind of car to drive.

The young immigrant family next door shows up needing Ove's help at the most inopportune times, such as when he's holding a shotgun in his hand or rigging up a noose. Whereas other plot points have stakes concerning death, this plot shows stakes related to protecting life. The man's fall from Ove's ladder results in a trip to the hospital and a need for Ove's babysitting services. And while the neighbor is healing, it's not like Ove can turn his back on the man's very pregnant wife when she goes into labor. By externalizing the upsides of a life that refuses to stop intruding, Backman makes his point: despite Ove's seemingly terminal loneliness, his gut reactions come down heavily on the side of life. If we didn't have access to these characters and Ove's responses to them, we'd miss out on the effect they were having on him as, scene by scene, he incrementally tips toward life.

Let's face it, true clarity is hard to come by in life. Many of us are tied in knots by inner conflict. As theologian and philosopher Reinhold Niebuhr so succinctly put it, "Man is his own most vexing problem." One reason we love stories is that they pluck internal conflict from the dark folds of our convoluted minds and let us get a good look at it.

Show actions that reveal each character's premise

The protagonist in Garth Stein's *The Art of Racing in the Rain*, an aging dog named Enzo, wants to evolve into human form (something he learned was possible from a documentary on TV) because he can't talk and has information his owner, racecar driver Denny, needs. Enzo's premise might be, *Helping someone you love makes navigating death worth the risk.* But there's a complication. Because Denny could lose custody of his daughter if he doesn't stop racing, he needs his faithful companion by his side. Denny's premise might be, *Helping the person you love the most is worth the sacrifice of your dream job.* There's plenty of inner conflict. Enzo can't leave Denny now, when his main reason to evolve is to help him.

The first line in this novel, delivered through Enzo's POV, is: "Gestures are all that I have; sometimes they must be grand in nature." This line is a promise the story delivers on, as throughout the book, Enzo acts in ways that communicate his intention. Much like Backman's Ove, even though Enzo is done with this earthly plane, he'll be called back again and again to play a canine role born of love.

If your protagonist acts in a way that reinforces their take on the premise, and your other characters do as well, your reader will envision the problems to come—and you-as-author could upend those expectations in succession. Moreover, with action telling so much of the story, you could devote your character's interiority to the processing of important emotional turning points.

⇥ Try This ⇤

To generate relevant, organic conflict, conduct what I call a Roll/Role Call:

- Open a spreadsheet or divide a piece of paper (landscape view is best) into three columns and label them across the top.
- Label Column #1 "Roll Call." List the protagonist and each major character.
- Label Column #2 "Premise." State each character's variation on the protagonist's premise.
- Label Column #3 "Role Call." Here, explore each character's role in the story. How will this character's take on the premise apply pressure on the protagonist to change? In the row belonging to your protagonist, you can put the source of their greatest inner conflict.

Roll/Role Call notes:

1. This exercise will force you to perceive your characters as distinct ways of thinking. If any two characters have the same take on the premise and play the same role in applying plot pressure to the protagonist, either combine

them into one character or make a change in either premise or role, so the duplication won't drag on story movement.
2. Under "Role Call," brainstorm ways to use each character's motivation and sensibility to give them a premise-relevant role in each of their scenes. Too often buddy characters come across with all the depth of a paper doll whose sole purpose is to allow the protagonist to vent or tell a story. Instead, show us how this buddy comes into useful conflict with the protagonist. Even if a younger sibling idolizes the protagonist, their differences in premise can set up a situation in which the protagonist is willing to cross an ethical line that the younger sibling can't support. That kind of conflict may not result in a head-on clash, but it can still deliver a glancing blow that redirects the protagonist's course.
3. This roll/role work will help you build conflict through consistent characterization. Once your characters are at odds as concerns the central premise of your novel, the pressure they're under will help you get to know them better—they'll show you by how they react. Through emotionally evocative actions and reactions, your story will chart the changes along your major characters' growth arcs. We'll care about them because they are moving through an uncomfortable period of change.

- How can your characters' actions reveal their take on the premise, even if they espouse otherwise?

12

Harness the Forces of Action

Unless you have both feet off the ground, you're not really moving, 'cause you don't have to. There's no emergency occurring.

—Elizabeth Streb, choreographer

WHEN MY YOUNGER SON was asked to write stories in elementary school, he always chose what one might call the "minor disaster genre," in the style of Judith Viorst's popular picture book, *Alexander and the Terrible, Horrible, No Good, Very Bad Day.* No matter if you haven't read it—the title says all.

In Viorst's experienced hands, the story transcended plot because it had a point: in the end, Alexander has changed. He's learned that everyone has a bad day every now and then, which allows him an evolution in worldview.

My son missed this nuance. After each disastrous plot point, he'd write, "And then you aren't going to believe what happened!" I was proud that even in third grade, my son understood that his story should feature action—but as with many of the manuscripts written by adults that I've seen, that action had no point. In the end, my son's character felt just as defeated as he'd been on page 1, and a story that could have been dramatic instead came across as a reiterative string of anecdotes whose grip on the reader inevitably loosened.

Negative circumstances that bury a protagonist who refuses to act will not make the kind of point that will please the reader who spent time and money on your book. Even if your character is reluctant to act, the reader wants to experience the tipping point when they decide they'd rather risk the pain of change than continue to endure the pain of staying the same by acting toward a story goal, to hell with the consequences. That's when they claim the mantle of protagonist, and the resulting clash of forces will demonstrate your story's point through its effects on your protagonist's evolving characterization.

Action scenes are a heightened way of showing a character's intentional movement through his story.

Add thrust to action scenes

You might think that scenes with physical altercations or sex would be an automatic win in the story movement department, but there's nothing "automatic" about it. This kind of action scene—if you'll pardon the double entendre—needs thrust.

Fight scenes

In this excerpt from Jonathan Maberry's young adult horror novel, *Rot & Ruin*, protagonist Benny and love interest Nix are being held hostage by Skins and Turk, men who had "guns holstered on their hips, shotguns slung over their shoulders, and ugly smiles on their mouths." By the time we encounter this paragraph, verbal negotiations have failed and Turk has knocked Nix to the floor. When he then incapacitates Benny, Nix shows him she's not done yet:

> As Benny watched she launched herself from her knees and drove into Turk's legs, knocking him back against the rail. She made a sound like a hunting cat, a snarl that started low in her gut and rose up, filtered through rage and humiliation and

certain knowledge of what the future held. Her scream scared the birds from the trees and echoed off the mountain slope. Turk kept backing away from her, startled and confused by this child who had been frightened and cowering all last night and who was now attacking him with such insane strength and speed.

Nix launching herself from her knees is a great example of thrust. Nix is a secondary character, yet her directional energy organizes the entire paragraph; even without her POV, we know she means business before Turk does. When Nix "launched herself," she reinforced a cause-and-effect vector that's been at play since the events that brought her to the beginning of the novel. Her intent extends that vector, linking her backstory to what she's done in previous scenes to what is going on now, and points toward what her ongoing story goal will be.

Sometimes, this directional energy is lost among the clutter of a clunky delivery, obliterating all story movement with it. Compare Maberry's slick paragraph to this version:

She got up from her knees and put her feet on the floor. First the left foot; then the right. Then, putting her right hand on the wall, she headed toward Turk's legs and backed him against the rail. The scream was loud. Turk backed up one step at a time, confused.

Turk isn't the only one left confused. This version proves that an accumulation of physical minutiae can ruin an action scene's energetic thrust. The scream is ambiguous, so we aren't sure how it is meant to move the story forward, whereas Maberry's comparison to a hunting cat's snarl colors the action with Nix's intention and emotional state. Even Maberry's sound has thrust, as it scares the birds from the trees and echoes off the mountain slope.

If anyone would have reason to fall prey to the temptation of adding in too much detail, it would be Jonathan Maberry. Specificity is important when teaching a martial art, and Maberry, an eighth-degree black belt in Shinowara-ryu Jujutsu, has written three how-to books on the subject. In his novels, though, to the delight of his readers, the storyteller in him held sway. When you next write an action scene, see if you can imbue your characters' vectors with so much energy that you can envision the reader flinching to dodge their blows.

Sex scenes

What if, instead of a fight, my modified paragraph had been describing a couple having sex? She placed the left foot, then the right. Then, putting her right hand on the wall, she headed toward his legs and backed him against the rail. The scream was loud.

The approach still falls flat. What's going on here? Who wants what? As story fuel, even sex won't automatically contribute story movement.

Oh, but it could.

In her historical novel *Hamnet,* Maggie O'Farrell ensures it. The protagonist, Agnes, a wild spirit known for her unusual gifts as a healer, interacts with the Latin tutor enchanted by her, who we come to understand is an unidentified William Shakespeare. He'd like to feel the silken, ridged weave of her braid slip through his fingers. He asks to see the bird of prey she keeps, and while stepping close, mesmerized by her eyes and skin, O'Farrell adds an unexpected element: she "takes hold of the skin and muscle between his thumb and forefinger and presses." The passage continues in his POV:

> The grip is firm, insistent, oddly intimate, on the edge of painful. It makes him draw in his breath. It makes his head swim. The certainty of it. He doesn't think anyone has ever touched him there, in that way, before. He could not take his hand away without a sharp tug, even if he wanted to. Her strength is surprising and, he finds, peculiarly arousing.

She then reminds him he wanted to see her kestrel and takes him to an outbuilding where he meets the creature, among stored apples from the family's orchard. The sexual tension this creates raises a question for the reader that easily spans the next thirty pages as the story moves back and forth through time. We already know our female protagonist exhibits agency—she keeps a raptor, she held the tutor captive by a fold of skin—but then, in a conversation the tutor has with his sister Eliza, we learn it is this very agency that attracts him. "She is like no one you have ever met," he says. "She cares not what people may think of her. She follows entirely her own course."

At the start of the next section, after we learn the apples have been precisely spaced on the shed's shelves so they won't rot, we read:

> The apples are turning on their heads; stalks are appearing from their undersides, calyxes are facing sideways, then back, then upwards, then down. The pace of the knocking varies: it pauses; it slows; it builds; it pulls back again.

This is the moment the reader has been waiting for. But unless O'Farrell uses this setting and this action to offer movement along Agnes's inner arc of change and delivers it through her unique perspective, even this sex scene will feel as captivating as rearranging fruit. To the reader's delight, as O'Farrell applies her mad literary skills to this scene, Agnes's world opens.

> Agnes's knees are raised, splayed like butterfly wings. Her back straightens and bows, seemingly of its own accord, and low, near-growls are being pulled out of her throat. This takes her by surprise: her body asserting itself in this way. How it knows what to do, how to react, how to be, where to put itself, her legs white and folded in the dim light, her rear resting on the shelf edge, her fingers gripping the stones of the wall.
>
> In the narrow space between her and the opposite shelf is the Latin tutor. He stands in the pale V of her legs. His eyes are shut; his fingers grip the curve of her back. It was his hands that undid the bows at her neckline, that pulled down her shift, that brought out her breasts into the light—and how startled and how white they had looked, in the air like that, in daytime, in front of another; their pink-brown eyes stared back in shock. It

was her hands, however, that lifted her skirts, that pushed herself back on to this shelf, that drew the body of the Latin tutor towards her. You, the hands said to him, I choose you.

We have come to the reason for this scene's inclusion: Agnes has learned that her body has an intelligence of its own, and, guided by the shocking depths of her desire, she has moved along her arc of inner change.

Here's a very different sex scene, from Salman Rushdie's *The Moor's Last Sigh*.

Way up there near the roof of Go-Down No. 1, Aurora da Gama (PH), at the age of fifteen, lay back on pepper sacks, breathed in the hot, spice-laden air, and waited for Abraham. He came to her as a man goes to his doom, trembling but resolute and it is around here that my words run out, so you will not learn from me the bloody details of what happened when she, and then he, and then they, and after that she, and at which he, and in response to that she, and with that, and in addition, and for a while, and then for a long time, and quietly, and noisily, and at the end of their endurance, and at last, and after that, until...phew! Boy! Over and done with!

Never had I read a sex scene with no mention whatsoever of the act itself. While this passage would not serve the reader who was looking for a how-to (in which case they were looking in the wrong section of the bookstore anyway), it cleverly serves to build characterization, advancing understanding of both our narrator and Abraham. After "whatever" (ha!) happened, we have the sense that neither of these two characters will ever be the same again.

The Eight Efforts

Like lovers and martial artists, dancers are well-schooled in intentional movement, as movement is the only language through which they can make their point. Hungarian-born Rudolf von Laban (1879–1958) was a modern dancer and theorist known for the ways he interpreted the movement of the human body. Because his theories of effort and shape tie the type of movement to its purpose, Laban's system of human movement analysis is still widely used by dancers, actors, and athletes. A working knowledge of his theories can help authors with pacing and in determining the ways movement confers meaning.

Laban identified Eight Efforts: punch, slash, dab, flick, press, wring, glide, and float. He further defined four components of each effort: direction (which can be direct or indirect), speed (quick or sustained), weight (heavy or light), and flow (bound or free).

Let's apply Laban's analysis to a few sentences from *Rot & Ruin* to see how the Eight Efforts define the action's thrust: "Skins suddenly backhanded Benny across the face. It was so fast and hard that Benny was falling before he realized that he'd been hit." The basic movement here is a slash—a swipe rather than a punch. It is a *direct* slash because it had a target; Skins wasn't simply waving his hands through the air. It was *quick*—so fast Benny didn't realize he'd been hit. It was *heavy* enough to send Benny to the floor, and it was a big, *free* movement from the shoulder (unlike, say, a Victorian lady delivering a backhand with her gloves across the chin of a rude man while her elbows remained *bound* at her sides). Assessed this way, we can see that Maberry created a quick, direct, heavy, and free slash whose effort and thrust the reader could easily sense.

Did Maggie O'Farrell fulfill the promise of this movement analysis in her sex scene? This key sentence is chock full of movement: "It was her hands, however, that lifted her skirts, that pushed herself back on to this shelf, that drew the body of the Latin tutor towards her."

- *hands lifting skirts:* with this direct, quick, light, free glide, O'Farrell suggests her action is taken willingly;
- *pushing herself back onto this shelf:* this direct, quick, heavy, bound glide is another willing action, but one requiring more effort; which leads to
- *drawing the body of the Latin tutor towards her:* a direct, sustained, heavy, bound glide.

As you can see, there's a lot of scene-appropriate gliding going on here, and the fact that its nature shifts twice in one sentence—added to the import created by the change in Agnes's inner arc—evokes solid story movement.

Familiarity with the Eight Efforts can help you stay focused on the point of the scene: the effort involved. The action didn't just "happen"; it was a result of characters pursuing conflicting goals. Strategy may have been involved at one point, but for these as with most action scenes, a dramatic imperative is in play and the action *must* unspool—as Elizabeth Streb implied in the opening quote, the feet are off the floor and an emergency is occurring—meaning the scene would be ruined if you paused for your character to have a good think.

There's no reason why the action can't speak for itself. Movement was the only human language until speech evolved, and it's a language we all still speak. The Eight Efforts can help you fine-tune the meaning in yours.

If a visual exploration of this topic would help you, check out the work of Todd Espeland at the Theatrefolk website[23] as he improvises various combinations of these movement elements.

⇥ Try This ⇤

As with any other scene, you must infuse action and sex scenes with purpose to reap their benefits. These questions will send you in the right direction.

- Pull way back and think about what you are trying to accomplish in your action scene. Rather than the mechanics of fighting, how can you use thrust to convey the importance of who or what they are fighting for? Rather than "how" sex is performed, how can you show the gap between desired outcome and the way the scene resolved?
- How might Laban's Eight Efforts help identify the thrust that will differentiate each of your characters' movements?

- How can word choice and the rhythm of your prose support the action in your scene?

13

Refresh Tension

[George Balanchine] found square, proper, academic dancing "boring as hell," and one day as I fell out of a turn into a backbend lunge he said, "Can you do that again, can you fall more...lean more...bend more? I said, "Let me try."

—Suzanne Farrell, ballet dancer, artistic director

IMAGINE YOU ARE AT THE BALLET. The prima ballerina has been dancing all evening and now, near the very end, she must balance on the small platform of one of her point shoes—less than two square inches. As she rises *en pointe*, her partner extends a hand. She does not grip it but simply rests her hand on top as she slowly transfers weight to one foot and lifts the other knee to the side. If you were to try this, you'd know this much is already a feat, but she has not yet reached the zenith of her powers. She continues to lift her knee, then unfolds her leg until her foot is pointing straight above her. You can see small flexions in her arm as she presses against his hand. Her body makes numerous small adjustments as her years of training marshal the efforts of multiple sensory systems. Even the rise and fall of her own ribcage threatens to disrupt her balance.

As you watch, your breathing falls into rhythm with hers. Your own muscles tense. Such athleticism, such flexibility, such beautiful risk, to attempt this feat in front of two thousand people! Yet, anticipating more to come, you keep looking back at their touching hands. At the trust you find there, as he patiently waits for her to find her balance. She is fatigued; you know it. And yet…you catch your own breath…she lets go and raises both arms in a victorious "V" overhead, holding the position several seconds longer. You can watch Mariinsky Ballet soloist Maria Khoreva perform this incredible balancing act—with no support whatsoever—on YouTube.[24]

What the dancer felt, during her struggle to achieve this, is tension. You know it's contagious because you felt it, too. For these ten, slow-motion seconds, you were wondering: Can the ballerina achieve her goal? The stakes for failure are high—no performer wants to fall onstage, especially with younger, hungrier dancers waiting to take her place.

Story works the same way. If you raise questions about whether the character will achieve her goal, and then delay the answers while adding stakes, you'll create tension.

Tension will electrify the cord of interest pulling the reader into your story. But keep in mind that readers, like all humans, are highly adaptable beings. If the tension you've devised continues to sizzle with the same amount of heat, it will eventually feel like business as usual—and "business as usual" is a story movement killer. Tension is most effective when it ebbs and flows, or when one kind of tension replaces or adds onto another. While your protagonist continues to pursue their story goal, the episodic nature of working in scenes will give you many opportunities to refresh tension as your character navigates a new portion of their journey. Effects from a previous scene may switch up the plan, for instance, forcing them to face unanticipated obstacles with different stakes for failure, in a new setting, while influenced by a different mix of characters.

The actions your point-of-view character takes to achieve their scene goal, and complicated by antagonists intent on impeding their progress, comprise your story's plot. To my mind, the French have a far superior word to describe this external layer of story: *l'intrigue*.

As if beckoning the reader to the edge of a dangerous wood, intrigue's "come hither" sensibility entices the reader deeper and deeper into the story by dropping unanswered questions and associated stakes like breadcrumbs. By picking them up, the reader participates in the story, renewing their interest in, curiosity about, and fear for your protagonist until they feel lost in the thick of your conflict and its implications—just where you want them.

So that you can keep drawing your reader into your story's essential nature, look for places to evoke intrigue relevant to your premise, and then see if you can enhance it with tension.

Here are a few ways to do that.

Add a watcher

The dynamic of a scene changes when someone is watching. I know this from personal experience.

Back in grad school, I would sometimes choreograph for the college dance company in the living room of my apartment. I'd move the furniture and begin by facing the picture window, a natural orientation for someone used to dancing in front of a mirror. One day, lost in a series of movements that ended in a low sweep, I rose to a standing position—where my eyes locked on a man watching me through the corresponding picture window across the courtyard. A dancer wants an audience, sure—but not the unknown, creepy kind. I hit the floor, army-crawled to the window, drew the drapes closed, and hoped to never see him again.

Any story with a stakeout, a stalker, paparazzi, an anonymous protector, or a nosy neighbor features a watcher. Someone standing in the wings, literally or figuratively. Entire fiction projects have been built around the "someone is watching" theme.

In film, the protagonist of *The Truman Show* (1998) thinks he is simply living his life, when in fact he is the unwitting star of a reality show broadcast to a worldwide audience. In TV, *Fringe* (2008–2013) survived the "Friday night death slot" by pitting an FBI team against happenings ultimately explained by the existence of an alternate universe—while its pale, bald, and creepy Observers took notes on the team's investigations.

Ghosts are effective watchers. Santa Claus sees you when you're sleeping. A believer would argue that God is the ultimate watcher—but even a pet's watchful glare can raise the tension in a scene.

In Ken Follett's historical novel *Pillars of the Earth* (1989), Tom Builder, a mason who was peremptorily dismissed from his last job, must seek new work by walking to the next town with his wife, teenage son, and seven-year-old daughter. They are carrying their meager possessions on their backs, while little Martha drives forward their most valuable investment, a pig they'd been fattening all year.

As they walk through the woods, Tom thinks in detail about the design of the cathedral he hopes to one day build. After a couple of paragraphs comes this passage:

> Tom tried to visualize the molding over the windows, but his concentration kept slipping because he had the feeling that he was being watched. It was a foolish notion, he thought, if only because of course he *was* being observed by the birds, foxes, cats, squirrels, rats, mice, weasels, stoats, and voles which thronged the forest.

Tom, exhibiting an attribute only humans possess, talks himself out of his natural fear reflex. After relaxing for a bite to eat by a pleasant stream the family picks up their journey, but Martha tires, the pig is obstinate, and both lag behind. Tom looks back and daydreams some more while waiting for them to catch up...

Are you feeling a sense of foreboding yet? Sure enough, while Tom stands too far away to make a difference, a man appears from the undergrowth, clubs his young daughter unconscious, and makes off with the pig. Tom may have ignored the watcher, but the reader had not, adding a tense undercurrent to Tom's rambling daydreams as the reader looks around every corner for the coming menace.

Let's look at some other ways a watcher can add tension to a scene.

Watchers can pass judgment

As Kristy Woodson Harvey shows us in the opening of *Under the Southern Sky*, even a painting can do this work.

> I found out my marriage was over the day my "Modern Love" piece appeared in the *New York Times*. The Modern Love piece about my thoroughly modern love with my husband, Thad, about our decision to not have children, about how we were choosing travel and wanderlust instead, living life on our own terms.
>
> Little did I know that he was *really* living life on his own terms. While I was going to work every morning and he was "writing his first novel" in the dated downtown Palm Beach apartment that his octogenarian grandmother rented to us for next to nothing, he was actually playing house with a CrossFit obsessed god named Chase. In fact, when I ran home from work to show Thad my piece at nine that morning, it wasn't Thad I found on the wood-framed yellow couch in our living room. It was Chase. I knew him because he was a hairdresser. *My* hairdresser. But I had never seen him quite like this: his neon green boxer briefs accenting his spray-tanned abs—both of which clashed terribly with the sofa, I might add—sitting nonchalantly under the portrait of Thad's grandmother. She smirked inside her gilded frame, hair in a bouffant, choker pearls tight around her neck, earlobes dripping with rhinestones. It didn't take long for me to put the pieces together.

This "watcher," from her position of privilege and legacy on the wall of the home, lowers the gavel of judgment quicker than its subject may have, had she been living. The reader will be watching for its effect on Thad and our protagonist as the story advances.

CRAFTING STORY MOVEMENT

Watchers can define an adversary

Nguyễn Phan Quế Mai anthropomorphizes the effects of the Vietnam War in this passage from her first novel written in English, *The Mountains Sing* (2020), which is set in its teen protagonist's North Vietnamese village:

> The bombings had stopped. I was surprised by how blue the sky was, even when it was raining.
>
> Grandma and I knelt on the site of our collapsed house, piling broken bricks into a pair of bamboo baskets. Our hands became the color of brick; so did our clothes. Nearby, a bomb crater was half-filled with rainwater. It gazed at me with its single murky eye.

Despite conflicts between multiple political factions, it seems that war itself was the enemy, and that its "murky eye" would follow these characters wherever they went to escape it.

Watchers can increase entertainment value

In Anna Quindlen's *Blessings* (2002), a young man jump-starts elderly Mrs. Blessing's Cadillac, dead in a Walmart parking lot, and follows her home to ensure her safety. While he is the possible threat in this scenario, the watcher who heightens conflict is Nadine, Mrs. Blessing's cook, who is listening in on the conversation from the kitchen. Mrs. Blessing, who thinks the young man is "too dim to be duplicitous," asks him in for a chat while Nadine "cleaned vegetables at the sink, making a good deal of noise, as though she were playing a concerto of disapproval written for colander, knives, pan lids, and faucet." When Mrs. Blessing asks him if he's looking for work, Nadine slashes at a head of broccoli with a carving knife and says, "Oh. Oh."

Beyond Nadine's comedic presence in this scene, her intrusion allows Quindlen to reveal her protagonist's blind spots, while also suggesting that she has an underappreciated ally. By raising a question about the young man's motives, Nadine invites the reader to keep an eye out for any clues to his nefarious intent—effectively drawing us into the story's experience as we too become watchers.

Watchers add heightened awareness

As Anne Tyler shows in her novel *Ladder of Years,* the watcher need only be imagined to effectively shift the dynamic of a scene. In this passage, the protagonist, Delia, who months before had walked out on her marriage and family and rebooted her life in a new town, learns that her husband, Sam, now knows her whereabouts. With this knowledge, she is no longer merely making decisions—she's watching herself make them.

> Imagine if he came upon her this minute, heading toward the library for Saturday's book. Or pausing on the way home to rummage through a table of mugs in front of Katy's Kitchenware. Or stepping out of the Pinchpenny with the navy knit dress in a bag. Imagine if he were watching from the boarding house porch as she rounded the corner of George Street. He would see her skimming along, wearing professional gray, entirely at ease in this town he had never laid eyes on before. He would think, *Could that really be Delia?*
>
> Or imagine if she climbed the stairs and found him waiting at the door of her room. "Why Sam," she would say serenely, and she would draw her keys from her handbag—so official-looking, room key and office key on Mr. Pomfret's chrome ring—and open the door and tilt her head, inviting him inside. Or he would be inside already, having persuaded Belle to admit him. He would be standing at one of the windows. He would turn and see her entering with her burdens—her library book and her tea mug and new dress—and, "Here, let me help you with those," he would say, and she would say, "Thanks, I can manage."
>
> But he wasn't there after all, and she set her things on the bed in total silence.

Add micro-tension

After the *Twilight* series achieved such popular acclaim, writers piled on to trash Stephenie Meyer's prose. She'd tell instead of show, her sentence structure was sophomoric, her protagonist vapid, and her vampires just too...sparkly. Who would hold up Meyer as an example of a writing technique executed well?

I would. Here's why.

Every time we experience a publishing phenomenon like *Twilight*, we writers have an opportunity to learn about what pleases our readers. Stephenie Meyer did more than a few things right, and we can borrow these techniques to increase the sense of movement in our stories—and while we're at it, make our stories more marketable.

In Meyer's series, success boils down to one essential skill: ramping up tension in ways large and small. Let's break that down to see what skills writers in any genre can use.

1. *Cash in on unresolved sexual tension.* If you can sustain sexual tension over the course of a thousand pages, you've gone a long way toward publishing success. Bella wants but can't have Edward; Edward wants but fears harming Bella. The plot keeps these lovers apart while Meyer fans the flame of desire.

2. *Master the slow build.* Revisit the moment when Bella first sees the Cullens in the middle of the first chapter and you'll see that Meyer knows how to create an important event. Only in the twelfth paragraph of observing them does Bella even learn their names. Then she asks about them for a couple of pages. This word-count spotlight raises a question in the reader's mind: How will these characters be important? Contemplating this against Edward's initially brusque treatment of Bella creates the tension fans craved in these books.

3. *Reap the bonuses of forbidden love.* From the opening description of the house Bella must share with her protective father—who is a cop—Meyer foreshadows their conflict to come: they'll be sharing close quarters while Edward, who is not Charlie's number one choice to be his daughter's love interest, secrets himself away in her bedroom. If you've ever

tried to sneak past the squeaky stair in your own parents' home, you'll know how tension rises when every sound can be heard. The setting itself points toward a story of forbidden love.

4. *Intensify your protagonist's complications.* To keep her lovers apart, Meyer doesn't frustrate the reader with constant interruptions or miscommunications. She lets their identities, core values, crossed purposes, and some real kick-ass danger do it for her. Just when you think things have gotten as bad as they can and some small measure of relief is felt, they get worse. Readers love this.

5. *Put conflict on every page.* Hold *Twilight* in your hand and open to any page. Chances are, you'll find tension. Trust me—I've tested this many times and did so again while writing this chapter. Here's what I found this time.

> page 441: My voice sounded strangled.
> page 336: "When he knew what he had become," Edward said quietly, "he rebelled against it. He tried to destroy himself. But that's not easily done."
> page 237: Jacob scowled and ducked his head while I fought back a surge of remorse. Maybe I'd been too convincing on the beach.
> page 141: When Charlie smiled, it was easier to see why he and my mother had jumped too quickly into an early marriage.
> page 39: [After native Arizonan Bella is hit by her first snowball, she says,] "I'll see you at lunch, okay? Once people start throwing wet stuff, I go inside."

Note that tension need not always result from a major conflict. It can also be found in passages exhibiting what literary agent Donald Maass calls micro-tension, which is apparent in the last two examples.

6. *To all this, add tension between books.* Meyer set up her series so that a live wire of tension would extend between books. In *Twilight,* Bella moves to Forks. She hates Forks. Later, you

can't get her to leave with a crowbar. In like fashion, Edward, who you'll recall wants Bella but doesn't want to hurt her, puts Bella in mortal danger. Within her early readers, who had to wait a year for the next book to launch, Meyer created a hunger to continue with the series.

Sustain stakes

Mary Pat Kelly, in her 576-page novel *Galway Bay,* managed to sustain tension in a historical family saga spanning six generations.

From the book description:

> Young Honora Keeley and Michael Kelly wed and start a family. Because they and their countrymen must sell both their catch and their crops to pay exorbitant rents, potatoes have become their only staple food.
> But when blight destroys the potatoes three times in four years, a callous government and uncaring landlords turn a natural disaster into The Great Starvation that will kill one million. Honora and Michael vow their children will live. The family joins two million other Irish refugees—victims saving themselves—in the emigration from Ireland.

Guess what awaits them in America? Danger and hardship.

The story of this family's desire for simple necessities that too many of us take for granted, such as food to eat and a safe place to call home, keep narrative tension humming.

High levels of tension are hard to sustain, though. That's why Dean Koontz's aptly named suspense novel, *Intensity,* spanned only twenty-four hours. Dan Brown's thriller, *The Da Vinci Code,* spanned forty-eight hours. It isn't reasonable that characters operating under intense stress could sustain tension for longer; an adrenaline rush can't last indefinitely.

For this reason, it's good to have a restrictive crucible on hand to modulate tension and heighten stakes.

You could:

Add a ticking clock. A package that must be delivered before a plane takes off. A witness that needs to stay safe for twelve more hours to put away a gangster for life. A destination that must be reached before the gas tank empties. Any number of ticking clocks can be at play in a story at any one time, renewing your story's grip on the reader.

Constrain the geography. A nervous man is stuck at an airport. A witness who has changed his mind is locked inside a safe house. An undercover cop is tied up in a subbasement where no one can hear him shout. When a protagonist determined to act is at the mercy of a geographic limitation, tension rises.

Raise the stakes. The airport is shut down for the night and the last text the man gets before his phone dies says, *The baby is coming.* Or the scared witness finds a note scrawled on the wall of the safe house saying, *I'm waiting right outside.* Or the subbasement where the cop is tied up is crawling with snakes.

Deepen POV. The effects of the above scenarios will be most impactful if you show us how the tension is working on your character's body. How they decide their next move, based on their own strengths and capabilities and perspective, will add to story movement.

Consider how macro structures might raise expectation

While wrestling down the myriad decisions necessary to effectively structure a story's scenes, writers sometimes fail to consider the way the larger structures of a book, such as chapters, sections, and parts, can contribute movement and meaning. This could be as simple as titling your chapters or adding an epigraph at the top of each one as Sue Monk Kidd did in her novel *The Secret Life of Bees*. Quoting nonfiction sources that describe the social nature of bees will have the reader looking for parallels with the human characters in that chapter. A line like "Isolate a honeybee from her sisters and she will soon die," quoted from *The Queen Must Die: And Other Affairs of Bees and Men* at the top of chapter 8, will certainly electrify the arc between this fact and the fiction to come.

Add an hour-by-hour structure

To keep background tension thrumming while my protagonist awaits news of her husband's suicide standoff in my novel *The Far End of Happy*, I broke the narrative's twelve hours into one-hour sections to plant the seed that the situation will grow more dangerous as night falls. Will he, or won't he? Tension is renewed every hour as the main story question plays out: How can his wife possibly move forward with divorce when such high stakes are pressuring her to stay?

In thrillers and suspense novels, similar techniques are used to keep edge-of-the-seat tension in play, but in my upmarket women's fiction, the one-hour segments also build a metaphor: stacked as they are between yesterday and tomorrow, they reflect a line my protagonist, Ronnie, will always perceive between life before this horrific day, and life after.

Create meaningful sections

In my novel *The Art of Falling*, Penelope Sparrow is the miraculous survivor of a fourteen-story fall—thanks to the sturdy bones she has blamed for the loss of her dream career. To show that her body image issues, like modern dance itself, are about effort and surrender, I titled each of the novel's four sections—Fall, Recovery, Contraction, and Release—after the philosophies of two female American dance pioneers. I paired each section title with a quote, either from the dancer (to represent bodily experience) or a critic (to represent societal judgment). In this way I tied Penelope's healing journey to the source of her conflict—the way her body is judged by others and, by extension, herself. The section titles and quotes added subtle tension by raising questions and delaying answers, while at the same time asking the reader's mind to arc between the epigraphs and the story so the narrative wouldn't have to explain it.

Chapters, sections, and parts allow opportunities to place a scene arc within a chapter arc within a section arc within a story arc—and you can add another arc if it's a series! Thinking about what creates an arc—a desired goal, external conflicts, stakes for failure, and inner turning points—will help you think episodically so you can create different sorts of tension within each of these structures. The more spring in each arc, the greater the story movement.

Seduce across white space

If like every other writer in the world you have worried over your novel's opening line, you already aspire to the art of literary seduction: orienting your reader while at the same time raising a question that will tip them into the story. This same approach can also draw the reader into any new section. If it's important to insert a break, it's equally important to think once again about seducing your reader. Then, at chapter's end, you can make it much harder for the reader to place a bookmark by raising a new question about the scene to come.

Author Brian Jacques adopted a story structure that interweaves related conflicts so well it continued to engage his readers over a series of twenty-two middle-grade fantasy novels in his Redwall series, published between 1986 and 2011. One part of the conflict is set in Redwall Abbey, where peace-loving and endlessly clever mice are sometimes forced to take up arms to defend their fortress against a predator; another plot line follows a group of courageous mice who venture into the violent wood to try to thwart the threat. Jacques tends to end his chapters in one of two places: right before a dramatic turning point, when the reader's heightened senses make them eager to know what happens next, or right after a scene question has been addressed and a new question has been raised.

Take it from me, this works to create story movement and retain reader engagement. I'd peek inside my older son's book while he was at elementary school, telling myself I'd read one chapter while I ate lunch, only to hear the bus dropping off my kids three hours later. These books are un-put-downable.

Any white space in your novel—between paragraphs, scenes, chapters, or sections—can present either a risk to lose your reader or an opportunity to once again invite them in. Creating a bridge of tension through questions like "Oh no, what will the protagonist do now?" will achieve one of two things: entice your reader to navigate across the white space and continue reading or encourage them to linger in this space between words as the story question resonates within them. Either result has inspired story movement.

Let's look at a few chapter breaks from Kristin Hannah's #1 *New York Times* bestseller, *The Nightingale,* a story of how two very different sisters rise to embody different forms of heroism while France faces the Nazi threat in World War II. Reviewers often say this book just wouldn't let them go. Another way to say that is that Hannah would not release them.

Here, the end of a chapter in which protagonist Vianne learns news from her husband is paired, after the asterisk, with the beginning of the next chapter. Her husband speaks first:

> "I am to report for duty on Tuesday."
> "But…but…you're a postman."
> He held her gaze and suddenly she couldn't breathe. "I am a soldier now, it seems."

* * *

Vianne knew something of war. Not its clash and clatter and smoke and blood, perhaps, but the aftermath. Though she had been born in peacetime, her earliest memories were of the war.

The two paragraphs of backstory that follow inform us that it's not only her husband's survival she's worried about: "The father who went off to war was not the one who came home."

Here's the end of chapter 4 into the beginning of chapter 5, where her father is speaking to Vianne's sister after air raid sirens finally quiet:

> "Go to bed, Isabelle."
> "How can I possibly sleep at a time like this?"
> He sighed. "You will learn that a lot of things are possible."

* * *

They had been lied to by their government.

This next excerpt is at the end of chapter 8 into the beginning of chapter 9, after a German soldier has commandeered a room in Vianne's home and her younger sister, Isabelle, has spoken to her of the need for French resistance:

> "You will take Sophie's room upstairs and she will move in with me. And remember this, Isabelle, he could shoot us. *Shoot us,* and no one would care. You will not provoke this soldier in my home."
> She saw the words hit home. Isabelle stiffened. "I will try to hold my tongue."
> "Do more than try."
>
> * * *
>
> Vianne closed the bedroom door and leaned against it, trying to calm her nerves. She could hear Isabelle pacing in the room behind her, moving with an anger that made the floorboards tremble.

In each of these examples, Hannah introduces a threat at chapter's end that raises a question about what will happen next, making it difficult for her reader to set the book down at the chapter break. She then entices you to read the following chapter with an opening every bit as seductive as a novel's first line.

All readers must sleep, but that doesn't mean we want to make it easy for them. And when at long last they simply must insert a bookmark, make sure you keep them yearning to return.

⇥ Try This ⇤

Story tension need not be linear; it can be layered like a musical chord. Each technique is a string tuned differently—already under tension, waiting to be used for harmony or jangling dissonance. These prompts will help you build your story's underlying thrum.

- Could you add a watcher to raise tension in a scene? If two characters are having a needed conversation, try adding a third presence, whether it be a person, animal, plant, or thing. Even a malfunctioning rotating fan can ratchet up the tension in a scene.
- Could unresolved sexual tension or forbidden love further your plot? If romantic tension could work for some aspect of your story, why not give it a try? The longer you keep the lovers apart, the better.
- What other important aspect of the story could sustain a longer arc of tension? Getting a story moving doesn't always mean action must unfold at a clip.
- What is your story's organizing principle, or what choreographer Twyla Tharp, in her book *The Creative Habit*, calls a spine? No one who has read Mark Haddon's *The Curious Incident of the Dog in the Night-Time* will forget that his novel begins with "Chapter 2" because his protagonist prefers prime numbers. Is there a way you could reinforce or expand your organizing principle through the naming of chapters or parts?
- At my very first fiction writers' conference, romance author Susan Meier offered a tip I've never forgotten. On a day when you wake up feeling fresh and creative, rewrite your chapter endings (for the purpose of retaining your reader) and chapter openings (to seduce them once more).

14

Push Your Reader Off Balance

Dancing on the edge is the only place to be.
—Trisha Brown, choreographer

MARGOT LIVESEY STEPPED UP TO THE PODIUM to read the first chapter from her work-in-progress, *Banishing Verona,* at the 2002 Sewanee Writers' Conference. She began:

> He had replaced five lightbulbs that day and by late afternoon could not help anticipating the soft *ping* of the filament flying apart whenever he reached for a switch. The third time, the fixture in the hall, the thought zigzagged across his mind that these little explosions were a sign, like the two dogs he had come across in the autumn, greyhound and bulldog, locked together on the grassy slope of the local park. He had given them a wide berth; still, he had felt responsible when on the

bus the next day a man turned puce and fell to the floor. By the fifth bulb, though, he had relinquished superstition and was blaming London Electricity. Some irregularity in the current, some unexpected surge, was slaughtering the bulbs. He pictured a man at head office filling his idle minutes by pulling a lever. Meanwhile, hour by hour he emptied the upstairs rooms, slipping the bulbs from bedside lights and desk lamps.

He had just replaced the fifth bulb when the doorbell rang.

What on earth was going on here? I had no clue, but those blown filaments commanded my attention.

At this point Zeke, a handyman who works alone because he has trouble relating to others, opens the door to a pregnant woman holding a suitcase. She claims to be related to the owners of the home. When Zeke says they won't be back for several days, she charges in. Soon she has seduced Zeke, commandeered his house keys, bought him breakfast sandwiches, and otherwise reversed their roles. The next day, it is he who must ring the doorbell to get in. She finds a pair of coveralls—"her belly split the front like a chestnut its shell"—and insists on helping him paint, "to take my mind off things."

While they hang wallpaper, Zeke tells her of the exploding light bulbs on the day she arrived. She says she's never been able to wear a watch for more than a few days before it goes haywire. "The watchmaker I went to had some mad theory about personal electricity."

(Keep in mind there has been no murder. No explosion. Yet the packed room was hushed and expectant throughout this reading.)

In the first chapter's next-to-last paragraph, Zeke is the one to bring the breakfast sandwiches, although he must climb in through a side window with them now that he has no key. He hopes to find her still in bed, warm and sleepy, so he can slip in beside her.

And this time, he thought, however stupid—however embarrassing—he would ask her name.

Ha! Another unexpected element. Then Livesey read this last paragraph, about what Zeke found when he entered the bedroom:

The bed was unmade, empty and cold to the touch, the suitcases gone. At the foot of the bed the rug was rolled up, and spread-eagled on the bare wooden boards lay the coveralls, neatly buttoned, arms and legs stretched wide, like an empty person. Only when he knelt to pick them up did Zeke discover the three-inch nails that skewered the collar, pinned the cuffs and ankles to the floor.

What???

The audience jumped to their feet and applauded, but I was thinking, *No-no-no, you have to tell us what happens next!*

Those coveralls remained nailed to the floor of my mind for *one-and-a-half years* of bookshop shelf scanning until the novel came out. This is the kind of reader interest you can earn when you push your reader off-balance.

Drop in an unexpected element

When we think of being moved by a story, we may first think in terms of being moved to tears or laughter or fear. But the sharp intake of breath experienced at Livesey's reading was surprise—an effect rarely inspired by the manuscripts I read. Which made me wonder: Why do so many novelists try to root their stories in stone-cold reality when fiction readers have already accepted that the quicker and more meaningful road to truth often travels through a concocted story?

Perhaps, after hearing the word "verisimilitude" at a writing conference, they get hung up on keeping it real. But verisimilitude does not mean that every single plot point can be reproduced in the laboratory of real life. It means our stories must *appear to be* true.

In her novel *Broken for You,* Stephanie Kallos pays homage to all things broken. Seventy-something protagonist Margaret Hughes is broken by grief, having lost a son and learned she has a brain tumor. She takes in a young boarder, Wanda, broken by parents and then a lover who abandoned her. The only thing pristine in Margaret's world is roomful after roomful of valuable ceramics (that we eventually find out were stolen from Jewish families during World War II), which

Margaret and Wanda ultimately break so they can create something new.

Grounded as it is in historical detail, psychological truth, and emotional need, this sounds realistic enough, right?

Except that before she feels free to accept a boarder Margaret must consult her "housemates," because the pottery always has an opinion. Who would be most receptive to change? Not the soup tureens; as a group, they are unimaginative and stodgy. Commenting on all is Margaret's long-dead mother, who lounges around the house wearing peignoir sets and criticizing her:

> Wait a minute...Margaret felt her mother lean closer. I remember those earrings, I've been looking for them. Have you been into my things, Margaret?
>
> They're all my things now, Mother. Remember? You're dead.
>
> Margaret's mother got up and slipped her gloves back on.
> No need to gloat, Margaret. Ticktock, ticktock.

As Margaret's tumor grows, her dead son makes a few appearances, too.

Maybe Margaret's imaginings could be explained away by the tumor pressing on her brain, but must they be? Kallos does not cheapen her story by shining a light on medical fact; to do so would take away from what the reader has already accepted as the reality of Margaret's world.

In a subtler moment, Wanda looks at her ardent admirer and notes, "He had the look of a memory." That felt real to me, even though I'd be hard-pressed to delineate why. Such truth-adjacent concepts invite the reader into the space at the end of the sentence to co-create this aspect of the story.

Readers don't mind being pushed off-balance; it delights them. Unexpected elements rise to meaning in fresh ways and are the very reason we call our writing creative. As your reader struggles to incorporate this new element into your story, they take the reins of story into their own hands.

To assure that you tip the reader off balance, as opposed to kicking them out of the story, you need to hint at how wide you'll swing to target this story's "reality." Kallos warmed up her readership with a prologue that sets expectation:

> While the woman sleeps and dreams of all that breaks, come into this house of many rooms. Once your eyes adjust to the darkness, beginning to take in what is visible, you may notice a silence that is not quite silent. There's another language being spoken here, a tongue that emanates from white clay, fire, the oils of many skins, the fusion of rent spirits and matter. The woman hears this language always, even in her sleep, because she is guilty, and because those who speak to her are never silent...

Invent your own language

"That's not a word."

You can almost hear the know-it-all fifth grader saying it, hand on jutted hip, eye roll and all.

You also might hear this from your copy editor. If their comment pointed to an out-and-out error, correct it and be glad of the public embarrassment it saved you. If, on the other hand, you used the word purposefully and creatively, and because no other English word delivers the right shade of meaning, your editor might be holding you back in the venerable art of word invention.

Children's literature is full of made-up words, because children reach beyond their vocabularies all the time to amusing—and often revealing—effect. Novelists may call themselves "wordsmiths" and yet fail to exhibit the expressive fearlessness it takes to be a smith of words.

The world of language would be much less fanciful without the contribution of writers. J. R. R. Tolkien invented various languages spoken by the elves, dwarves, and other inhabitants of Middle-earth in his *Lord of the Rings* trilogy. The readers of the 150 million copies sold were not stopped by encountering words they did not understand. Instead, they reached for meaning.

The writers of the TV series *Star Trek* invented an entire Klingon language, which now has more than 5,000 words. From the descriptions of the Dothraki language in George R. R. Martin's *Game of Thrones* novels, David J. Peterson constructed the spoken languages of Dothraki and Valyrian for the television series. Klingon and High Valyrian are now taught on the DuoLingo foreign language app.

One of my favorite invented words, "twitterpated," was coined in the 1942 Disney film based on Felix Salten's novel *Bambi, a Life in the Woods.* Wise Owl delivers it in the line, "Nearly everybody gets twitterpated in the springtime." Its quick consonants evoke that flighty, excited feeling of being newly in love much better than "head over heels," which seems to foretell orthopedic mishap.

Some neologisms are one-offs; others are eventually memorialized in official dictionaries. "Twitterpated" is now an official entry in the Oxford English Dictionary and others. "Galumphing" and "chortle," both invented by Lewis Carroll's poem "Jabberwocky" from his 1871 novel *Through the Looking-Glass*, were snatched up by Webster the very next year.

Writers are so often caught up in finding just the right word. If that word doesn't exist, why not coin it? And what if inexactitude is the exact effect you hope to conjure in your reader—could a character leave behind a note referencing a mysterious "borogove" (another Carroll invention)? If your writing requires a word the English language cannot provide, why not turn to that boundless, patternmaking, meaning generator you carry with you everywhere you go—your imagination?

Build a chapter for emotional impact

Through a series of unrelated yet emotionally potent vignettes in chapter 5 of his Pulitzer-winning novel, *The Sympathizer,* Viet Thanh Nguyen invites us into the off-kilter world of a protagonist with torn allegiances by knocking us off-balance and righting us—over and over again.

I'll divide the chapter into eight "chunks" to demonstrate the effect. All are written in the Captain's point of view.

Chunk 1: Suspicion

> Perhaps James Bond could slumber peacefully on the bed of nails that was a spy's life, but I could not.

The South Vietnamese General who has long confided in the Captain (our narrator, a communist sleeper agent) is about to open a liquor store in mid-1970s America, where he and the Captain are refugees after the fall of Saigon. When the General summons the Captain to attend the opening, a mutual friend explains it's because the General suspects an informer in the ranks. This understandably sets the Captain—and the reader, who knows what this friend does not—on edge.

Chunk 2: Lust

> Although I would not have asked for this favor in September, by April our relationship had taken an unexpected turn.

To attend the opening, the Captain must ask off work from his boss, Ms. Mori. The Captain then takes a couple of sexually charged pages to show how he and Ms. Mori got to the point of the "sweaty, condomless intercourse" in which they are now regularly engaged.

Chunk 3: Hilarity

> Ever since my fevered adolescence I had enjoyed myself with athletic diligence, using the same hand with which I crossed myself in mock prayer.

We do not need backstory to understand the Captain's lust for Ms. Mori. Lust simply is. Yet what comes next, adding the whiff of shame considering his Catholic upbringing, is a detailed depiction of the thirteen-year-old Captain-to-be's first sexual experience—with a dead squid. With phrases like "my maniacal manhood leaped to attention," "my cephalopodic bride," and "from then on no squid was safe from me," the Captain evokes the universal, urgent hilarity that can ensue when discovering one's sexuality, and what lengths he took to cover his tracks knowing that his impoverished mother had carefully counted the squids for dinner.

Chunk 4: Horror

> Some will undoubtedly find this episode obscene. Not I! Massacre is obscene. Torture is obscene. Three million dead is obscene. Masturbation, even with an admittedly nonconsensual squid? Not so much.

Even before the smile has left the reader's face—while in that heightened, giddy state—Nguyen doubles back with this twist, and delivers it with epistrophe that shines a spotlight on the word "obscene." He describes the torture he has witnessed: wire twisted tighter, tighter around a man's neck during interrogation; "the communist agent with the papier-mâché evidence of her espionage crammed into her mouth, our sour names literally on the tip of her tongue." These severe consequences of treason weigh on the Captain's mind when he gets to the grand opening of the liquor store.

Chunk 5: Threat

> "Have a seat," the General said from behind his desk.

Such a simple line, now loaded with such threatening subtext! The Captain fears the General has found him out. Next:

> The vinyl chairs squeaked obscenely when we moved.

Note the repeat use of "obscene," previously planted in the reader's mind regarding masturbation and torture. The General opens a drawer…and we wait breathlessly to learn what he will take from it.

Chunk 6: Gratitude

> You had to get close enough to give a marine a thousand dollars before he'd haul you up.

The next section recaps the desperate flight from fallen Saigon that brought them to their new lives in the United States. The reader is made to feel the good fortune of those who made the cut, which was due to the Captain's high-stakes yet random-seeming decision-making as to who could leave in the General's plane and who would be left behind.

Chunk 7: Deception and Relief

> I had scored a coup, much to my chagrin and purely by accident, throwing the blame onto a blameless man.

When the General says outright that there is an informer, he looks to the Captain for confirmation. By this point, the reader's stomach is roiling on behalf of the Captain. But when the General names his suspect, it is a major that the Captain chose for evacuation because he had always seemed harmless.

Chunk 8: Unavoidable shame

> Do you agree that you must correct your mistake?

Suspicion. Lust. Hilarity. Horror. Threat. Gratitude. Deception and relief. Unavoidable shame. After this emotional wringer, the weight of this one line stops us: our relatively peace-loving Captain must now commit murder to save himself.

Wrenching turns between these potent backstory vignettes ultimately lead to their purpose. Each adds a layer to the characterization of this complex yet very human man who now stands at a moral crossroads. Knocking us off balance has earned our full investment in the story, and we are glad for the pummeling.

CRAFTING STORY MOVEMENT

In a 2022 interview, while discussing whether writing made her happy, Booker Prize-winning novelist Hilary Mantel said, "I think that's beside the point. It makes you agitated, and continually in a state where you're off balance. You seldom feel serene or settled. You're like the person in the fairy tale *The Red Shoes*: you've just got to dance and dance, you're never in equilibrium."[25]

While shaking up expectation can tip your reader from sentence to sentence and chapter to chapter, it's also a solid strategy to keep you, as author, invested in your own story.

⇥ Try This ⇤

You too can get away with adding fanciful elements, if you ground them in a well-developed emotional reality:

- *Per Kallos:* What inventive constructs could you introduce to drive home the point of your story?
- *Per Livesey:* If your chapter end is predictable or otherwise lackluster, what startling image might you be able to leave with your readers?
- *Per Carroll:* If you can't find the perfect word to evoke meaning in your novel, what word could you create? Many invented words are portmanteaus, built from two other known words: "conlange" = Constructed + Language.
- *Per Nguyen:* Could you build a series of vignettes, each with a different emotional thrust, that when stacked, might keep your reader just off balance enough so that when the time comes, they land on an emotion they didn't see coming?
- How else could you keep your reader off balance? Could a fast-paced action scene erupt from a quieter moment? Could the protagonist's pursuit of their scene goal be impacted by an unexpected setting element, or completely upended by the entrance of a surprise character?

15

Say Less, Do More

There are times when the simple dignity of movement can fulfill the function of a volume of words."
—Doris Humphrey, dancer and choreographer

ONCE YOU HEAR YOUR CHARACTERS TALKING, some say, writing is as easy as popping a water balloon: simply let your characters' deepest thoughts pour out while you take dictation.

That's what it takes to be a transcriptionist. It takes more to be a novelist.

The problem with transcription is that you might take down pages and pages of talk during which nothing really happens. While your characters are yammering—but not taking meaningful action—your reader will become as inured to the words as if they were touring a house wallpapered with them.

And that dialogue is now etched on the walls of history. Your character actually said these words—what can you do? We all know that once we've spoken, we can't take back our words.

When you're writing fiction, though, you can. If you can accept the gift of a character's voice without relinquishing your control, dialogue has incredible potential to benefit your story's movement.

Think of dialogue as only one of many instruments through which a story speaks. Even screenwriter Robert McKee, whose only medium is dialogue, said this, in *Story* (italics are his):

> The wise writer puts off the writing of dialogue for as long as possible because *the premature writing of dialogue chokes creativity.*
>
> If we type out dialogue before we *know what happens,* we inevitably fall in love with our words; we're loath to play with and explore events, to discover how fascinating our characters might become, because it would mean cutting our priceless dialogue.[26]

Quotation marks function as little spotlights that proclaim: "This is important." They pique interest. So as not to betray your reader's trust, make sure the spoken words have earned their spotlight. One way to add punch to your dialogue is through subtext, which relies on your reader's retention of previous events to assign meaning to unfolding events. That is unlikely to be found in dialogue you wrote prematurely, because your characters will rarely blather on about their deepest fears and concerns. (Note that "sub-" prefix. Subtext likes to hide.)

Let's say a character goes to the window and says, "Look, it's snowing." This weather report won't pull any weight on its own. It will only further the story once it's set up to do so.

Imagine the emotional load that one line could carry, though, if one of these situations were in play:

- This mother's only son is currently driving back to college, and from a previous scene, we know her mother died from hypothermia when trapped in snowy conditions.
- This character is in an abusive relationship, and while the snow makes it too dangerous to make a break for it as planned, she's always loved snow for the way it covers the dirt and makes the world look clean.
- This Southern farmer had been praying for much-needed rain for her imperiled citrus crop—and instead, it snows.

With added context, your reader will not hear a weather report. They will feel something. Something specific, since the subtext in each example is completely different.

If you give thought to subtext—what might be implied, as opposed to stated explicitly—*before* you put words in your characters' mouths, you can save yourself a lot of time. Later, your challenge will be to go back and layer in meaning that was never there in the first place.

An exercise that can build the tension needed for subtext to emerge is to figuratively gag your character for a while. Try writing your story for a few days without letting the characters speak. If a character says something, pick up a pen and note it in a journal. Not only will you find subtext on these pages, but the word "journal" will draw an important distinction in your mind: "For private use only." In the meantime, keep that gag duct-taped in place.

Once you rip the tape from your character's mouth, you (and one day, your reader) will be eager to know what they'll say. It won't be a simple weather report or greeting. It will be something important.

If your journal reveals that your character is frustrated about something, think about how you could build toward that frustration on the page. Give them a backstory in which they were ignored, or slighted. Put setting elements in their way. Give a secondary character a conflicting goal, relevant to the premise, that they want to achieve just as badly. Create a sense of plot urgency and then convincingly delay resolution. Withhold from them what they need. When your character can't stand it anymore, and you metaphorically rip the duct tape from their mouth, will they say, "I am so frustrated"?

I don't think so. More likely they might say, "All I wanted was to matter for five minutes today." Your reader, knowing all your character has been through, will nod in appreciation of this truth.

No doubt about it, lean, keenly anticipated dialogue has power. Lace it with subtext, and it can keep your reader moving deeper into your story.

Let's look at how the following authors were able to evoke emotional states with very few words.

Magnetize your prose

Understatement. Sometimes, it's just the thing.

Consider whether your attempts to be explicit might be creating barriers of words that prevent them from fully entering your novel. Understatement invites your reader's active participation by leaving small gaps into which they can insert understanding from the vast warehouse of images in their own mind.

The following authors do an amazing job of guiding their reader toward a specific experience and then standing out of the way while they digest it.

Understate to characterize

In his literary horror novel, *The Book of Accidents,* author Chuck Wendig implicitly promises he will set expectation on its ear with two long prologues followed by three short chapters, each of which introduces a member of the family central to the tale. In chapter 2, he needed only one paragraph to set the scene before drawing his reader into character-revealing dialogue.

> This was Nate:
> That same day, Nate sat in a lawyer's office in Langhorne. The lawyer was round and grub white, like the inside of a cut potato. In the window of the office, an AC unit grumbled and growled, so that the man had to raise his voice in order to be heard.
> "Thank you for coming," the lawyer, Mr. Rickert, said.

"Uh-huh." Nate tried to keep his hands from balling into fists. Tried, and failed.

"Your father is sick," the lawyer said.

"Good," Nate answered without hesitation.

Rickert leaned forward. "It's cancer. Colon cancer."

"Fine."

"He'll be dead soon. Very soon. He's on hospice."

Nate shrugged. "Okay."

Look at how much story movement he creates in the first paragraph alone. Scene detail invites the reader into the office. The lawyer's comparison to a potato is a fun spark. The lawyer having to raise his voice to be heard over the animated air conditioner engages the senses with an interactive setting element, and all is delivered in an entertaining voice. The reader wants to be there, at the edge of story, ready to dive into the quick directed dialogue that follows. Combined with monosyllabic Nate's seeming disinterest in and unexpected acceptance of his father's imminent death, his balled fists create tension.

Understate emotional peaks

When emotion runs high, understatement can allow the words on the page to step back and let the reader in. Ron McLarty uses this technique to wonderful effect in his novel, *The Memory of Running*, right from the get-go.

Smithy is a forty-three-year-old who describes himself as "fat and drunk and cigarette-stained." This does nothing to endear him to us, even though he has one of my all-time favorite occupations for a novel character: he's a supervisor at a toy factory who makes sure the arms are attached palms-in on SEAL action figures.

In the first scene, while Smithy is day-drinking to excess beside the lake where his family takes their annual vacation, a police car rolls up to deliver the news that his parents were in a horrific car crash on their way to meet him. When he escorts Smithy to see his parents for probably the last time, McLarty lays in an important line of subtext when Smithy thinks, while talking to his father's doctor, "I would have given my car to anyone, right there, if I could have been sober." With that admission, I cared about this mess of a man.

Thirteen pages later, as Smithy stands beside his mother, this subtext grows in importance.

> I could hear her little breaths. Puffs, really. Her eyes were still open a little, but I knew she couldn't hear me. I pushed her thin hair onto the pillow with my fingers.
> "There," I said.

McLarty doesn't tell the reader his character feels helpless. He doesn't have to—that one word Smithy utters oozes helplessness.

Many openings set at deathbeds and funerals fail to move readers because the writer assumes all attendees will feel sad. Not so. Unnatural death is often tragic, but it can also be a relief, a payback, or the simple closing of a door. In his opening, McLarty succeeds in creating within Smithy a mountain of character, so when he balances that one word "there" on the summit, we know that Smithy's powerlessness extends to every aspect of his life.

Amplify with beats

Writers who come to their craft through a great love for reading seem to have an intuitive sense of where beats—bits of contextualizing action—belong in dialogue. What isn't as obvious to the writer at first, though, is how beats can extend meaning and help the story move forward. On your mental writing shelf, right next to clichés, is an encyclopedia full of inane motions you may reach for while drafting, which could easily be repurposed to further story: *he swept his hand through his hair* (fine if he just walked through a cobweb), *he reached for the salt* (fine if he just learned his blood pressure was dangerously high), *she took a sip of tea* (fine if the milk had curdled but she desperately wants to show appreciation to her host).

Look at how the following two authors used beats to support story movement.

From Jess Rinker's middle-grade novel *Monolith:*

> "You know," he said as he held out a hand to help her up. "Sometimes a little bit of minding your own business goes a long way."

This one beat, made from common words and action, accomplishes more than you might first think. The break comes after "you know," which underscores the fact that his friend, who fell while spying over her neighbor's fence, did not know. And yet because he reaches out a hand to help her up, he's showing that while he disapproves of the behavior, he still wants to be kind to her.

This one is from Nancy Johnson's novel, *The Kindest Lie:*

> "I can't do this," Ruth cried from her bed.
> "I don't see how you got much choice in the matter." Mama dipped a hand towel in a bucket of hot water, just as midwives used to do in those old black-and-white movies.
> "It hurts so bad."

The beat here extends the significance of this specific childbirth to include the long history of women who have endured an event so dramatic it's been memorialized in films. This gives the reader something extra to think about during a long stretch of pain.

Control pacing

The nature of the dialogue scene will determine its effect on pacing. In this excerpt from *Lessons in Chemistry* by Bonnie Garmus, Elizabeth, a 1950s-era lab tech at the Hastings Research Institute, determined to conduct her own unsanctioned research, has been identified by Institute darling Calvin, an award-winning chemist, as the one who commandeered beakers from his lab. Pay attention to how Garmus uses dialogue to assert contradictory goals, characterize, and control pacing.

More than three thousand people worked at Hastings Research Institute—that's why it took Calvin over a week to track her down—and when he finally did find her, she seemed not to remember him.

"Yes?" she said, turning to see who had entered her lab, a large pair of safety glasses magnifying her eyes, her hands and forearms wrapped in large rubber mitts.

"Hello," he said. "It's me."

"Me?" she asked. "Could you be more specific?" She turned back to her work.

"Me," Calvin said. "Five floors up? You took my beakers?"

"You might want to stand back behind that curtain," she said, tossing her head to the left. "We had a little accident in here last week."

"You're hard to track down."

"Do you mind?" she asked. "Now *I'm* in the middle of something important."

He waited patiently while she finished her measurements, made notations in her book, reexamined yesterday's test results, and went to the restroom.

"You're still here?" she asked, coming back. "Don't you have work to do?"

"Tons."

"You can't have your beakers back."

"So, you do remember me."

"Yes, but not fondly."

"I came to apologize."

"No need."

"How about lunch?"

"No."

"Dinner?"

"No."

"Coffee?"

"Listen," Elizabeth said, her large mitts resting on her hipbones, "you should know you're starting to annoy me."

Calvin looked away, embarrassed. "I sincerely beg your pardon," he said. "I'll go."

* * *

"Was that Calvin *Evans?*" a lab tech asked as he watched Calvin weave his way through fifteen scientists working elbow to elbow in a space a quarter the size of Calvin's private lab. "What was he doing down here?"
"Minor beaker ownership issue," Elizabeth said.
"Beakers?" He hesitated. "Wait." He picked up one of the new beakers. "That big box of beakers you said you found last week. They were his?"
"I never said I found beakers. I said I *acquired* beakers."

All the white space in the middle of this passage is due to directed dialogue, a technique that significantly picks up the pace. It makes Calvin's head spin while demonstrating Elizabeth's sharp wit and perspective: she believes her work carries no less importance because she's a woman. Note that after the break, action beats slow the pace.

Let's dig into the way interiority and setting elements in dialogue can slow pace even more.

Let setting have its say

Do you strain to find little bits of action to enliven your dialogue beyond "she raked a fork through her potatoes"? This scene from Michael Chabon's Pulitzer Prize-winning novel, *The Amazing Adventures of Kavalier & Clay,* illustrates how a richly appointed setting feeds what's happening within it.

The setup: Joe Kavalier has escaped Nazi-invaded Prague and landed in New York City, where he hopes to create superhero comic books with his cousin. At an artsy party in a mansion belonging to the family of young Rosa Saks, he hurts his finger in an oddly heroic way. Rosa asks if he'd like to come upstairs to see her paintings.

But Joe has not come to America to flirt with girls; his sole focus is to use his employment to free the family he left behind. It seems like he'll say no when an irritant drives Joe into the very sort of boy-meets-girl scene he's been trying to avoid: he overhears a German accent. Enraged and seeking escape, Joe tells Rosa he'd love to see her work.

The following sections feature excerpts from this long getting-to-know-you scene between Joe and Rosa. As you read them, watch for two techniques that make this dialogue move: misdirection and modulation.

Misdirection unfolds as if questions and answers have been separated into two decks and shuffled. Because questions are not paired with their answers, the reader must pay closer attention to understand what's going on.

Modulation uses setting and narrative commentary to extend the scene's complexity. Each spoken line invites the artful layering of meaningful detail or memory.

Yet Chabon isn't all about craft here; he's also using the nature of the dialogue to evoke the artistic process itself. Watch for the story movement achieved between and within Joe and Rosa in each example.

"Speaking" is not limited to the characters

Dialogue isn't all about what's between the quotation marks. The actions, observations, and memories associated with it can also support story movement. Here, the room itself tells Joe about Rosa's character.

> In addition to her tiny, girlish white iron bed, a small dresser, and a nightstand, she had crowded in an easel, a photo enlarger, two bookcases, a drawing table, and a thousand and one items piled atop one another, strewn about, and jammed together with remarkable industry and abandon.
> "This is your *studio?*" Joe said.
> A smaller blush this time, at the tips of her ears.

"Also my bedroom," she said. "But I wasn't going to ask you to come up to *that.*"

There was something unmistakably exultant about the mess that Rosa had made. Her bedroom studio was at once the canvas, journal, museum, and midden of her life. She did not "decorate" it; she infused it.

Modulation brings the characters and setting to life

In this next passage, modulation engages the reader's senses through the scratchy sound and the "wheeze" (great spark!) of violins on a record player, interrupted by a warning from Rosa.

"Look out."
Something hit him in the face, something soft and alive. Joe brushed at his mouth and came away with a small black moth. It had electric-blue transverse bands on its belly. He shuddered.
Rosa said, "Moths."
"Moths more than one?"

I can feel the moth's velvety wings against my own mouth, can you? This touch of commentary tells us that Joe has encountered something "soft and alive" in this room—something unexpected, lovely, and meaningful to his artistic nature. Later, one of Joe's comic book superheroes will be Luna Moth.

Misdirection sets up multiple layers of communication

Rosa points to moths all over the bed, the walls, the house—and mentions they were in their last house, as well. "That's where the murder happened," she drops in, then says, "What's the matter with your finger?"

This opens a passage of misdirected dialogue, where neither character directly addresses what the other has just said. It will be two and one-half more pages until Joe thinks to ask about the murder. First, he tells Rosa his finger is sore. In what is about to become a great example of both spoken and physical misdirection, she asks to look at it, saying, "I was almost a nurse once."

On the next page, Rosa says she can fix his finger, warning it will hurt—"horribly, but only for a second."

> "All right."
> She looked at him, steadily, and licked her lips, and he had just noticed that the pale brown irises of her eyes were flecked with green and gold when abruptly she twisted his hand one way and his finger the other, and, crazing his arm to the elbow with instantaneous veins of lightning and fire, set the joint back into place.
> "Wow."
> "Hurt?"
> He shook his head, but there were tears rolling down his cheeks.

This short excerpt is chock full of plot causing tension: she was "almost" a nurse once, the physical misdirection in the almost-kiss, the visible conflict between his desire and his parasympathetic nervous system in that last line. This is a great movement sequence, and the entire length of this dialogue scene, whose elements are skillfully interwoven by its end, is well worth studying.

Interweave all elements introduced

When Joe gets around to asking about the murder, Rosa says they hanged her great-granduncle for the murder of a debutante in the 1860s. She then asks for a cigarette. The modulation (moths, war nurse) and misdirection (the murder) converge with the original scene goal of looking at her artwork.

Rosa can't find the dreambook about the murder, but she shows him another one, and its collage of images, described in detail, inspire and embolden him.

Earlier in the scene, after Rosa fixes his finger, Joe thinks, "This was unquestionably the moment to kiss her." He considers himself a coward for not following through on the impulse. Now, three pages later, Rosa throws her arms around his neck, and he falls backward on the bed.

"Misdirection" is not only a technique, but a theme here. Joe came to the party to make connections in the art world, not pick up this girl, but ends up on her bed kissing her—and receives the artistic inspiration he sought.

If you were to use any single dialogue technique exclusively, its habitual use would dull the impact of a valuable story movement tool. But here, in Chabon's long dialogue scene, the setting details that infuse these techniques demonstrate how an artist joins concepts and images as they compose. The lag time between an experience and its processing also explains Joe and Rosa's struggle to connect. By the end, Rosa has recalled Joe to his self-image as a true artist.

Once you've got an enhanced setting, an orchestrated set of characters, relevant action, and a point as to how each of these will push your protagonist into the inner change they need, your story will be rich with the kind of subtext that inspired author Melanie Bishop to say, "Let dialogue be like subtle arrows shot through your story."

→✺ Try This ✺←

You let your characters have their say. Now, reconsider every word to make sure your dialogue furthers story movement.

- Copy a dialogue-heavy scene from your work-in-progress, paste it into a new document, and strip the dialogue from it. Now see if you can figure out how action alone might tell the tale. The result is often eye-opening. Use no inner thoughts—for this exercise, the characters can't even talk to themselves. This will spur your creativity, because watching a character's choices as they move through the world is the most basic definition of story movement.
- Restore or create any dialogue necessary to moving your story forward. You may realize that you need less of it than you

thought. With this kind of planning, dialogue will be a spotlighting technique rather than an aimless habit.

16

Interweave External and Inner Arcs

I'm still growing, still learning. I'm still open and vulnerable enough to know there's much more to be taught to me and learned by me. I hope I don't reach my pinnacle on this earth where I think I know it all.

—Savion Glover, tap dancer

MOVEMENT IS A TRANSFER OF ENERGY.

When you read that sentence, you probably pictured the application of energy to matter, such as a hand turning a key to open a lock. Subatomic mechanics, however, shows us that everything from the human body to the floor it stands on is made up almost entirely of energy. Atoms abuzz, we're moving even when we're sitting still. Sensations and thoughts are traveling through a series of electrochemical reactions along nerves and between synapses. Even our emotions are on the move—the origin of the English word "emotion" is from the Latin *emovēre,* which means to stir, or move. Our thoughts and emotions are energetic responses to the external circumstance of our lives, and the meaning they assign is what can inspire inner change.

A story gains its power not from the events of your plot (the external arc), but from what changes occur within your protagonist in response to those events (the internal arc). Since these arcs are interdependent, a story relies upon the careful interweaving of external events and inner thoughts as your protagonist processes them.

Let's compare two novels that begin with an everyday occurrence on roads across the U.S.—a car accident. If the situation is resolved with a tow and some body work, the incident may become an anecdote shared when the driver shows up late to work, but it will not inspire the kind of significant inner change that makes a great story. What turns the common into the compelling is how the character affected most by the crash decides to move forward, and how those decisions change them. In our two sample novels, the accidents spur a grieving protagonist to take a journey. If you think those two novels sound alike, you'd be wrong—because their plots are being driven by two very different protagonists. Let's see how that can work.

In Karma Brown's *Come Away with Me,* a car accident causes Tegan Lawson to lose her near-term pregnancy. The grief paralyzing her is complicated by an underlying anger toward her beloved husband, who was driving when the car hit black ice. To inspire Tegan to move forward, he eventually reminds her of their Jar of Spontaneity, a collection of their dream destinations and experiences, which he urges Tegan to follow on her own. This launches her worldwide healing adventure.

In Ron McLarty's *The Memory of Running,* Smithy Ide is an obese, chain-smoking, hard-drinking, forty-three-year-old man when he loses both parents to a car crash. His grief is complicated by regret. Smithy also sets off on an adventure—he gets on his bike at his parents' home in Rhode Island and rides toward California, intent on stepping up to take care of family business involving his sister—and ultimately, caring for himself in the process.

From similar inciting incidents, these novels both launch grief journeys. But because complicating factors, relationships, personal needs, and perspectives differ, the actions each protagonist takes and the obstacles they meet will differ, inspiring individualized change.

As stories weave between external plot events and inner thoughts and feelings, story movement need not stop—if you can find a way to shift the external energy of muscle and bone to the internal energy of thoughts and feelings. With a tight interweaving, you can accomplish both in the same scene.

This scene from Leif Enger's *Peace Like a River* features eleven-year-old protagonist Reuben, his father, and his younger sister, Swede. They are visiting the jail where the oldest son, Davy, had been taken after killing two men. There's no question of guilt. POV character Reuben, and therefore the reader, witnessed the murders. At the jail, Swede is "crying and incensed" at Davy. He reaches through the bars to comfort her, but she tries to kick him, hurting her shin on the bars.

> "Good grief, it's lucky I'm in *here*," Davy remarked, as Swede hopped about, biting her lip. Grim as it was, I could see Dad was glad for the joke. Davy'd shaken off the concussed glaze of the night before. He was in a little cell with tan lighting and squashed flies on the wall, but he'd not grown fangs or become a creature changed beyond knowing. When Swede had got the mad out and hugged Davy through the bars, Dad told us to say goodbye and wait for him in the hall.
>
> That was the hardest thing—going out that door. It was so thick and closed so heavily we couldn't eavesdrop through it, not even with the paper cup Swede swiped from the water cooler.
>
> Dad was quiet when he joined us. We walked out to the car, the wind flapping staleness off our clothes.
>
> "He seems all right, doesn't he?"
>
> "Sure he does," Dad replied.
>
> It seemed like a long ride home. We got there at suppertime, and Swede and I looked around in the cupboards. Normally Dad would've taken over and worked up some meal

or other, or at least suggested that Swede and I do it, but instead he just sat in a kitchen chair and leaned back shuteyed.

Thinking of supper, I asked, "You want us to do anything, Dad?"

"Persevere," he said.

Before reading my analysis, look back at that excerpt to see how many ways energy was exchanged in this short scene.

Here's what I found:

- energy exchanges between Swede and Davy (external)
- physical movement from Swede and Davy (external)
- Reuben processing his observations of Davy (internal)
- setting interaction between Reuben and the door; Swede and the door (external)
- Dad's false assurance on the way home (subtext to external)
- physical interactions with kitchen cupboards and Dad in chair (subtext to external)
- shift in family dynamic (external/internal)
- minimal dialogue revealing inner turmoil (external/internal)

The scene results in character change within Reuben, but even without POV access, I sensed changes in Swede and Dad as well. Did you perceive them? Study this scene again. Did you pick up on any subtextual clues as to why Davy is the only one who didn't change?

This question isn't fair because the reader who began on page 1 already knows that Davy is at peace with what he did. The two murder victims had abducted and assaulted nine-year-old Swede just days earlier, so when, after her return, they entered the family's home, Davy felt he'd done the right thing by shooting them. The clue in this scene is Swede's ire at the jail. She's angry that what happened to her "caused" Davy to take action that landed him in jail.

Writers can have an adverse effect on the movement of their story by separating external and internal action. They'll show the plot unfold in scene and then—perhaps because they don't trust that the reader has understood its relationship to the accumulating story—they'll have the POV character go off somewhere by themselves to rehash the plot and ponder how they feel about it. I'm not saying this can never happen. There's a time for it in every story. If a character must add perception-shifting information to a story they thought had been moving in a different direction, for example, there's still all sorts of movement going on. And some readerships have a greater tolerance for separate periods of processing—romance readers want more, since processing emotions is at the heart of the genre, while action/adventure and thriller readers will want less. But remember that the reader loves the unexpected. When this action-reflection-action-reflection rhythm becomes habitual, the reader senses the way reiteration is curbing story movement. Enger's scene seamlessly shifts energy between external plot and inner thoughts, helping us understand the story's movement on the fly. Together, the protagonist and reader are ready to move on.

As you weave together your story's external and internal elements, consider the following arcs for the way they can energize your story and create meaning. There's no reason why you can't use them all to drive change in your protagonist.

Relationship arc

If you've ever had a loved one sabotage your efforts when you've committed to a new diet or exercise plan, you know this psychological truth: the people who are closest to you may give lip service to supporting you, but they typically do not want you to change. They may even rely on your actions as a standard of their own behavior; your shortcomings make them feel better about themselves.

Let's say that after a grave health scare (inciting incident), Frank sets the goal of attaining a healthier lifestyle. His wife is happy for the change until she realizes he counts every calorie in her traditional Southern cooking. The friend he's been meeting for breakfast every Saturday for decades isn't willing to spend extra money to meet at the farm-to-table place when the local greasy spoon has been their tradition. Frank can no longer tolerate the friendly poker nights in the neighbor's garage because every time he breathes in that secondhand smoke he envisions another trip in the ambulance. Not that he's really wanted there anyway, since it's his neighbor who owns the greasy spoon. Soon, Frank's goal of change has isolated him from everyone he has cared about, making him question what a longer life is even worth.

If your protagonist thinks the change they desire is nobody else's business, they are mistaken. Secondary characters who did not seek this change will be affected, and as each of them adapts, compromises, walks away, or agrees to change, they are forming relationship arcs with the protagonist that will give you an organic source of story movement. This helps you pace your story. Since your protagonist will have some kind of relationship with each other major character in your novel, as one relationship is having a quiet moment, you can rely on another to spark tension.

Activity arc

Your protagonist could move along an arc related to her work. In Lauren Weisberger's *The Devil Wears Prada,* college grad Andrea Sachs must rely on ambition alone to please her demanding New York City fashion editor and negotiate the harsh realities of a high-fashion workplace. A character like that has one relationship with boss Miranda Priestly and another with the work itself. The work shapes her until she learns to shape the work—to the point that the small-town Andrea Sachs we met at the start of the novel is nothing like the chic, self-assured woman who emerges at the end.

You can also create meaningful arcs with hobbies—a pastor who feels out of touch might reconnect with his spirit through gardening. A timid policeman might find his courage after taking guitar lessons and surviving his first open mic.

Let's look at some of the many ways author Nomi Eve drives story in her novel *Henna House,* which explores the protagonist's relationship to the ancient tradition of applying henna.

Henna launches the protagonist's arc of inner change. Adela is a Jewish child living among Arabs in 1923 Yemen. If Adela should become orphaned due to her parents' ailing health, she'll be adopted into the Muslim community. To protect their five-year-old from this fate, her parents create a marriage contract for her that will go into effect as soon as she menstruates. Adela is in no rush to grow up, save for one thing: she is enraptured by the elaborate patterns of henna she will not be allowed to wear until she becomes a woman.

Henna deepens characterization. Henna makes a memorable entrance once Adela's cousin moves to town. Hani is a year older and "the fanciest creature" Adela has ever seen, decorated head-to-toe by her mother, a henna dyer. "I learned that night that the only way to know that girl, to know her truly, was to know her henna."

Henna creates complications. Hani aspires to be a henna dyer, too, supporting women at times of vulnerability and hope such as weddings and births. But when Hani's mother is accused of wrongdoing, she runs to Adela's house with a wild look in her eyes. "Clutched in her hands was a henna stylus, which she threw to the ground, discarding it like a sword with a blunt tip, a weapon that would do no good in battle." This is clever foreshadowing. The henna stylus will indeed be used as a weapon—and now the reader is watching for it.

Henna offers perspective. Adela wants justice on behalf of her newly arrived, exotic family members. A favorite aunt delivers an important life lesson: "Everyone knows that henna is not permanent, it fades with time. So will these accusations. But to air them in public, to make a complaint to the court, will only set the dye deeper into the soul of anyone who listens."

Henna creates a barometer of change. Once Adela is allowed to receive henna, the ritual is fully described and imbued with great meaning. She concludes: "With henna, I was as sacred as a sanctified Torah. With henna, I was the carrier of ancient tales—a living girl-scroll replete with tales of sorrow, joy, and salvation." Later, the absence of henna on the henna dyer's hands—"her skin like the page of a book that had lost its letters"—creates a bittersweet symbol as ancient traditions give way to modern culture.

Henna grows in importance. The day Adela and her cousins leave her hometown for good, she looks back over her shoulder and allows henna to add color and meaning to what might otherwise be a description dump: "The jutting towers and graceful minarets, the arches of the gates, and the encircling girth of the walls combined into a henna of history, a henna of conquerors and conquered, a henna of brides and grooms."

Henna gives voice. When Adela finally marries, she discovers that her union has not manifested the entwining of souls symbolized in the henna design she had chosen. "I chose the pattern because I didn't know how to talk to Asaf about these things—love and fate—and so I hoped to let the henna speak for me."

Setting arc

In Kate Brandes's novel *Stone Creek,* protagonist Tilly's close relationship with her father in childhood was due to her willingness to blow up dams to restore the natural flow of rivers—and keep his fingerprints out of it. When they "retire" during her tween years, they continue to live off the grid in a small cabin in the woods, where he'd once lived with the mother she never knew. The cabin shows the loss. Tilly fixes it up for the time being, but as she matures, the cabin represents an arc that includes the mystery of her mother, the lack of care her father gives to relationships, and Tilly's futile attempts to fix them.

A setting arc need not be incremental, nor does it need constant tending. Perhaps a man proposed to his wife in a forest, and later, during a war, she sought its safety to give birth to their baby. Then they must run for their lives when an explosion and a stiff wind cause a devastating wildfire. Here, three mentions of this setting can bring home the horrors of war.

Symbol arc

A symbol can be central to an arc in several ways. In Anthony Doerr's *All the Light We Cannot See,* the priceless diamond known as the Sea of Flames symbolizes different things to the characters who want it, thereby expanding the plot of this World War II novel. Before protagonist Marie-Laure and her father flee from occupied Paris to her uncle's home in Saint-Malo, her father takes the gem from the museum where he works. He wants to keep it safe because it is a treasure belonging to France. A German officer who is ill, von Rumpel, seeks it for its legendary promise of immortality. Knowing her father took it, he warns Marie-Laure of ownership, saying that she is blind because of her father's obsession with it. To Marie-Laure, who cannot see the light dancing in its depths, the gem is meaningless—yet its existence endangers her. The diamond serves as a catalyst as pressure from these various perspectives drives movement from the beginning of the novel through to its resolution.

In other stories, the symbol itself changes. In the first episode of the Netflix series based on Georgia Hunter's World War II historical novel, *We Were the Lucky Ones,* this is a Passover seder, which is itself a symbol of deliverance.

In an early scene, the Kurc family crowds around their table in Poland in the spring of 1939 for a Passover seder. Despite war closing in on them, they celebrate new love, careers, and babies around dishes piled high with food.

At the end of the first episode, with the family scattered for survival, their much smaller number gathers before a lone tureen of soup. When POV character Halina learns it is made from potato peels her father cleverly took from work, she pushes from the table and screams at him for disobeying the rules—earlier that day she had seen a girl brutally beaten for pocketing a beet on the farm where they worked. The contrast between these symbolic meals shows the shift in their circumstances without any needed explanation.

Assign meaning to arc movement

Without the protagonist's perspective to assign it value, your novel's plot will not drive story movement. A case in point would be Rachel Joyce's *The Unlikely Pilgrimage of Harold Fry,* in which recently retired Harold, after receiving a letter from a former colleague who is dying, writes back to her. As he's about to post the letter, he decides instead to keep on walking the additional 600 miles to her hospice center to deliver his message in person, wearing the same boating shoes and thin coat he wore to the post office."

This quirky setup will attract readers, but they'll need access to Harold's changing perspective to enrich the experience of his journey. Otherwise, his 130,000th step would seem the same as his first, Harold wouldn't have achieved his goal of changing his humdrum life, and the droves of readers who made this title a *New York Times* bestseller would have had no reason to hang in there. What readers want to know—without having to undertake the walk themselves—is how this extraordinary feat will change Harold. Joyce knew the promise of change would be so key to the reader's buy-in that she planted the notion in the opening sentence: "The letter that would change everything arrived on a Tuesday."

Change isn't easy; it usually involves some kicking and screaming. Even small changes can ask so much of us. From an executive's perspective, a new company-wide operating system overhaul may hold the promise of streamlined practices in the future, but for now, as the IT manager trains the employees and fields complaints, it will be disruptive and frustrating. Tempers will flare and mistakes will be made. The quota-deprived sales team will wish that change wasn't necessary at all. But eventually, all may start to see the beauty of the new method, which has tipped them from the comfort of their outmoded thinking into new possibilities. Their story, full of physical challenge and emotional adaptation, has moved forward.

Let's look at how you can convince your reader—and yourself—that the expected change is written into your story's scenes.

Mark the arc

I feel robbed when I don't get to bathe in the significance of a moment of change. Regardless of genre, a reader wants a romantic thread to resolve on a turning point that's a little more emotional than, "I knew in that moment that I loved him." Why now, when throughout the novel the relationship has been a long, slow roll? Convince me, please!

This is a bigger moment for me as a reader than the author is making it out to be.

I want access to that moment when the inner logjam shifts and the protagonist realizes that the pain of staying the same has become greater than the pain of change. As an author, it makes sense for you to take advantage of this opportunity to draw your reader even deeper into your story's emotional core. Calling these moments of connection "emotional turning points" will remind you to give them their due, and the result will convince your reader that your protagonist has felt the power of the change they once resisted.

The promise of such interior moments is the reason your reader has stuck with your story. The emotional turning point is their payoff.

Here's how Marisa de los Santos, in *Belong to Me*, creates a lightning-fast shift of awareness between lifelong friends Cornelia and Teo, who are returning from a funeral in Teo's car. She sets up the scene a couple pages earlier by recalling that while Cornelia has no special affinity for cars, she has some treasured memories of car trips. "Magic can happen in a car, a warm, intimate magic born of being in an enclosed, particular place and, simultaneously, being nowhere, passing through." Here, we're in Cornelia's POV as she emerges from a passenger-side nap while Teo drives:

> I slept. I woke. When I woke, I saw Teo's hands on the steering wheel, his wrists emerging from the once-rolled cuffs of his soft denim shirt. The shirt, blue; the wrists and hands, brown, dusted over with a light, gold-dust dusting of glittery, butterscotch-colored hair. Shirt, wrists, hands. I saw them more clearly than I'd ever seen anything, and the sight of them moved me as I'd never been moved in my life.
>
> This person, I said to myself, this one person, of course, of course, of course. The words became my breathing and my pulse, the whole world reverberated with them. "Of course." I didn't think the words "I love you," so obvious were they, so *given,* thinking them would have been sheer superfluity.

That strong, visceral response was enough to convince me, yet de los Santos hammers her point home by addressing reader doubt head on in this passage:

> So, you see that I didn't fall in love with Teo Sandoval. Falling is a process and what happened to me wasn't process. It wasn't sequential or gradual. It wasn't falling.
>
> A sea change. Transubstantiation. One minute, I was a woman not in love with Teo, and the next minute, I was a woman in love with him. Bones, blood, skin, every cell changed over into something new.

And then, lest you fail to believe in this testimony, Cornelia tells us what that felt like:

> *Teo.* His eyes. His mouth. His shoulders inside his shirt. I'd never wanted to touch someone so much, and at the same time, I didn't need to touch him at all. In love, I grew large, boundless. I was not contained between my hat and boots. I rose up. I embraced Teo. I surrounded him.

These passages benefit from prose that slows time and amplifies our sense of its importance: subtext (I sept/I woke kind of says it all), sense imagery (focused here on sights made more sensual because they evoke imagined touch), metaphor (gold-dusting, butterscotch), hyperbole (I was not contained between my hat and my boots). After this scene, other characters notice the shift in energy between them, but from these excerpts alone, you can see that de los Santos knows how to give her characters—and her deserving readers—a *moment*.

Carol Rifka Brunt creates several beautiful, meaningful turning points in her novel *Tell the Wolves I'm Home*. This is the story of a fourteen-year-old girl, June, who is grappling with the loss of her Uncle Finn, a painter of some renown, whom she loved so much she felt he was more hers than her older sister's. At Finn's funeral, when June sees an unknown man skulking around the edges of the gathering, she decides to track him down.

By the time this next passage appears in the novel, she's met with the man, Toby, several times. They are sucking on hot, spicy mints they hadn't meant to buy. The scene results in a major turning point for June but also, without a POV, Toby, who for the first time acquires an emotional connection to Finn's family.

> I started to walk away, but then I turned back. I decided to stop even trying to hold back the tears. I decided to stand there under an awning on Madison Avenue and let Toby see me. Let him understand that I missed Finn just as much as he did. And once I started, there was no way of stopping. Everything that had been squashed down and pressed into a hard tight ball in the center of my heart came undone. I stood there, shaking and heaving on Madison Avenue in front of Toby, waiting for him to run away or shove me into a taxi, but he didn't. He stepped in, put his long arms around me, and leaned his head on my shoulder. We stood there under that awning until I could feel that he was crying too. The click of Toby's mint against his teeth, and the high squeal of car brakes, and the rain plinking on the canvas over our heads all joined with our low deep sobs to make a kind of music that afternoon. It turned the whole city into a chorus of our sadness, and after a while it almost stopped feeling bad and turned into something else. It started to feel like relief.

The scene containing this passage comes at the midpoint, where a novel's stakes often raise significantly. In this case, June's sense of relief and connection creates a problem: The rest of her family blames Toby for giving Finn AIDS, which caused his death.

Perhaps counterintuitively, a character's tears will not guarantee story movement. The reason June's tears work in this scene is the energetic shift they represent. Earlier in their visit, June shared that her hard heart was her superpower; now, June is ready to share the grief that's been building within her—and when it decompresses, it encompasses all of New York City.

Brunt supports her prose through metaphor (the hard tight ball in the center of her heart), sense imagery (the symphony of sound, warmth of the unexpected hug), and symbolism (the rain and tears). The resulting word count shows her reader: "This is important."

Finding your emotional turning points

As you get to know your protagonist and their story in your first draft, the avalanche of details concerning setting, other characters, research, and plot are enough to bury your main character's growth arc, even though you could have sworn you wrote it in there. How can you find it again? Here are some ideas.

Track cause-and-effect energy

In a now-famous presentation to NYU students by the creators of South Park,[27] Matt Stone and Trey Parker speak about their plotting method. If the words "and then" seem to belong between the story events in your outline, Parker says, "you're fucked." Much more effective, he says, are the words "therefore" or "but," which can establish the causation capable of turning a string of anecdotes into a story. Adding influences from writing gurus Lisa Cron and Jennie Nash, I use the following template to create a one-sentence outline for each scene, filling in the specifics where here I'm using parentheses:

> *Because* (of something that happened previously), the character *decides to* (take some action), *but* (they must overcome an obstacle), *therefore* (they change in some way).

This snapshot can remind you to: show your protagonist acting toward a scene goal, follow a cause-and-effect trajectory in your plot, and tie external events to the character's inner life. Once you identify the "therefore," you can insert your emotional turning point.

Here's what that would look like for the scene we examined from Carol Rifka Brunt's *Tell the Wolves I'm Home:*

> *Because* June has discovered that her uncle's hidden boyfriend poses no threat, she *decides to* take the train to New York City to gather more information *but* after telling him that her hard heart is her superpower she recognizes his grief, *therefore*, knowing she is no longer alone in hers, she finally allows her heart to crack open.

At the start of the sentence, the word "because" links this scene to previous story action. Even if it's the first chapter of the book, your character will be carrying some desire or sensibility with them as they walk onto the page.

The phrase "they decide to" can remind you to give the protagonist (or other POV character) agency. Rather than "What should happen to them next?" ask, "What will they *do*?"

The "but" represents the obstacle to the POV character's achievement of their scene goal. This can be an exterior obstacle or, as is the case with June, an interior one—the hard heart of which she is proud has kept her from true human connection. Only Toby's love for Finn has been able to crack it. That's good. If the scene goal were easily achieved, there would be no story, let alone story movement—and there'd be no reason for the scene.

The "therefore" will drive home the whole point of including this scene. It will create story movement within your protagonist or other POV character by showing the moment they move forward along their arc of inner change, in a way that's relevant to the type of story you've promised. The amplitude of the emotional turning point you write will help reflect how hard it was to achieve this moment of change.

Write an inner arc synopsis

You can locate important turning points by writing a synopsis that shows the emotional energy shifts in your story. Think in terms of, "first they learn this and then they realize that." Ask yourself: Why do they realize that in this moment, and why does it matter? What does it feel like? What external plot energy fuels this inner change? This will help you locate and exploit emotional turning points.

To flesh out an emotional turning point when writing the scene, ask yourself:

- Why did the characters set the goals they're pursuing in this scene?
- What's at stake if the POV character can't achieve their goal?
- How can I express my characters' feelings without resorting to explanation?
- How can I render that emotional state without cliché (blinking back tears, jaw tightening)?
- What might these feelings remind this specific character of?
- How could I deepen meaning?
- How will this moment change things, moving forward?

The purpose of this interiority is not to bloat your prose, but to make your story movement clear while asking the reader to reach for meaning. Story is art, and art communicates through emotions. By inviting your reader into your protagonist's emotional world, you are asking them to feel.

⇥ Try This ⇤

As you draft, jot down thoughts on characters, relationships, and aspects of setting (flora and fauna, inanimate objects) that could have a symbolic arc of change over the course of the story.

- What happens to your secondary characters if your protagonist achieves the change they seek? Do any of them try to suppress change in your protagonist? If not, does it make sense for them to try? What turning points occur in each of these important relationships, and have you rendered them in a significant and emotional way?

- What activity (or activities) does your protagonist engage in? How could their relationship to this activity change? What are the turning points along this arc, and are they rendered in a significant and emotional way?
- Track your arcs with these macro-editing techniques:

    1. *Outline each scene as you go.* How would you fill in the blanks in this sentence?

        Because [of a reason from a previous scene or backstory], *she decides to* [pursue a specific scene goal], *but* [she must overcome an obstacle], *therefore* [this impacts her growth arc in some way].

    2. *Conduct a character edit.* A character edit will help you gain and maintain mastery over your characters' story arcs. You can do this by outlining each character in a different color as you reread your story or simply search for the character's name using your word processor's "find" function. Following one color at a time will flip you through the story in a targeted way so you can reread only the scenes in which the character you are editing is featured. Check to ensure any change within the character is intentional and the turning point shown. You can use the same approach with a symbol, or with aspects of setting.

    3. *Write an inner arc synopsis.* To get a better grasp of the interdependence of the external and internal arcs in your novel, write a synopsis that identifies the plot's emotional turning points. Show how the changes in your characters push your protagonist along a developmental arc.

17

Sharpen Your Stakes

The voices of moral authority in the theatre demanded only punctuality and physical performance. In the light of continuing pressure and stress, the moderation was meaningless. Starvation and poisoning were not excesses, but measures taken to stay within the norm.

—Gelsey Kirkland, ballet dancer

PURSUING A STORY GOAL will challenge your protagonist in untold ways; arising to those challenges will require that they change. Real, lasting change is difficult. The protagonist may have been well-motivated at the outset, but once accumulating obstacles suggest the goal may be impossible to achieve, they may start to wonder: Why even try? The answer lies in the stakes—the consequences the protagonist must face if they fail to reach their goal, and how they stand to benefit if they achieve it.

Let's look at an example in which a protagonist, we'll call him Agat, must head out on a quest to climb a formidable mountain, vanquish the dragon guarding the crater lake, and release its healing waters (stakes for story success) before the fiery flow incinerates his young family and village (stakes for story failure).

Why should anyone care whether Agat will prevail? If a lava-spewing dragon doesn't convince your advance readers that Agat's story is all that dramatic, try making the stakes more personal.

Perhaps the villagers had gathered around the day his grandmother, a revered village elder, had put her hands on the young mother's swollen belly and prophesied that Agat's wife could be the one to end the village's fertility problems. His wife would safely deliver a baby girl, his grandmother said, but only if she survived a week-long, hellish labor. Because their population is dwindling, all the villagers are invested in this outcome. The ancient midwives remember the ways of childbirth, and with their rotating support, the prophecy comes to pass. It is then that a scout reports of the fiery river heading their way and endangering the town.

That's a start. You could even add imminent threat: Agat sees fire and smoke on the horizon. But why must Agat be the one to undertake the quest? He's a farrier, not a warrior, and he doesn't want to leave his wife's bedside considering what she's about to go through—or leave his newborn child unprotected. That's relatable, but let's try to make the stakes more personally motivating. Maybe after Agat fell in love, his grandmother warned him not to marry this woman from the Forbidden Lands, because shortly after Agat was born, an interracial marriage had brought on the fertility curse. Agat didn't believe in the curse and, to anyone who'd listen, said the ban on intercultural marriages was short-sighted—but now that his precious child was due to arrive as prophesied, the lava is heading their way. The villagers accuse him of angering the gods and endangering their peaceful life in this valley. If he cannot solve the problem he created, they threaten to move out and leave him strapped to a pole in the center of town. This will solve nothing: Agat knows that the elders won't escape the lava flow, and his wife will be too weak to travel.

Let's check in. Even if the reader can't relate to a lava-spewing dragon, they might relate to how awful it is to be told to ignore the yearnings of their heart and choose a "more appropriate" mate, or the need to transform from lover to fighter in order to perform a task they are unprepared to accomplish, or the torture of leaving behind loved ones who need protection.

But could you raise the stakes higher to help your reader care even more? What if it is just as his wife begins the prophesied one-week labor that he sees the smoke on the horizon, as if the lava itself doesn't want the baby born? His wife is already in agony and cannot be moved. He has promised not to leave her, but for all the reasons already stated, he must be the one to go. She clings to him and begs him not to leave her in the hands of those who distrust her (Agat has ensured that his wife not know about the looming threat, as she has enough to worry about). He promises her that the elders want very much for the baby to be safely born, and he'll be back before then anyway. This will heighten his impatience with every obstacle on his quest, as his beloved's screams float up the mountainside day and night.

At the story level, the urgency these stakes create will keep your simple farrier heading toward his goal, because as impossible as goal attainment might seem at times, to deviate, or to turn back, will seem even worse. Once questions about the unwanted circumstances are in the reader's mind, they'll be watching to see when they'll come into play. When Agat finally reaches the footbridge that is his only access to the dragon's mountain cave and encounters random planks succumbing to the heat rising from the river of lava below, he must move forward quickly or lose his chance (physical stakes). If you've convinced your reader that your under-equipped protagonist must pursue his goal—that Agat *must* cross the bridge, whether or not he wants to, because turning back is not an option (personal stakes, societal stakes), his livelihood depends on the village's survival (career stakes), and he needs to show that his love is true (psychological stakes)—the reader will be able to feel the sweat trickling down their own cheek, sense the sway of the rickety bridge in their stomach, and taste the sweet relief of arrival on the other side.

Let's discuss how that works. Have you ever looked down from a height and felt yourself falling, even while your feet remained grounded? Or looked to the sky and imagined floating effortlessly upward? Stakes can create such effects in readers. I, for instance, can't breathe while reading about underwater rescues, even though I'm a strong swimmer who is, while reading, safely tucked into my favorite reading spot.

Pitting a big potential loss against a big potential gain raises tension that continues to pull the reader into the story, even in those moments when the protagonist himself can't figure out how to move forward. Positive stakes entice the protagonist forward and give the reader something to invest in. Negative stakes keep the protagonist from surrendering his quest and give the reader something to watch out for.

Whether they're deemed good or bad, the most effective stakes are personally significant and relevant to the inner change the protagonist needs to achieve his goal. Even with the knowledge that falling into a river of lava will cause physical death, the reader needs to know how desperately the protagonist wants to live to care about the story. We only truly understand Agat's motivation to complete the quest when we witness the shift in perspective brought about by the gnawing doubt that there's evil magic at play—but once he hears the dragon speak his name, he is forced to believe the fight is his.

Raise the stakes to heighten import

Think of stakes as the strands of electric fence that inspire your protagonist's movement along his overall story arc. Want to run away? *Zap!* Need to rest? *Zap!* Think turning back is a good idea? *Zap!* Once the protagonist is well on his way, the stakes will rise again at the most perilous moment—he cannot possibly prevail when surrounded by wiring that threatens electrocution. He'll need to decide if going after the goal is still worth it—and what he stands to gain will say "yes."

Stakes will convey the import of each scene—if they're specific. A vague warning, such as, "You'd better not do this, or else," is impotent. Chances are, when an authority figure in your life said that to you, you went ahead and misbehaved anyway. But if they said,

"You take one more step out that door and I'm taking away your X-box for a week," you might change your behavior the next time. Once you've brought specific consequences to bear on your protagonist, your reader knows you mean business.

There may be a moment in your story, though, when your protagonist loses touch with the desire that once drove them toward their goal. When a character is so tapped out and so dispirited that even unwanted consequences feel like an acceptable alternative, you've reached a dark moment indeed. Here, others in your cast can offer aid. With each additional character affected by your protagonist's stakes, your story will feel more important. Public stakes will create social pressure for the protagonist to continue toward their goal. As you may know from personal experience, when the going gets tough, we can easily convince ourselves our goal wasn't all that important in the first place. Everyone knew the goal would be too hard to achieve; no one will blame you for turning back. But when others are in danger of suffering because we've abandoned a goal, we'll sometimes fight for them in a way we won't fight for ourselves.

This sensibility informed the stakes in my novel *The Far End of Happy,* which is organized around an all-day suicide standoff. Since a standoff is essentially high-tension waiting, I enhanced story movement by spreading the stakes. Initially, a tight focus on the family of the unstable man at the focus of a manhunt establishes personal stakes. Soon, however, the circle of characters grows to include dozens of local police. Once the situation evolves into a suicide standoff, the stakes widen, as a state police helicopter and special emergency response troops arrive on the scene. Once the local elementary school locks down and a blockade bars neighbors from returning to their homes, the stakes extend even more.

Showing that the stakes have spread across more shoulders is a useful technique for creating story movement if you've delayed the resolution of a previous scene goal, too. Let's say a college grad wants to start a business and is going to the bank to apply for a loan. When she gets there and sees her misogynistic neighbor behind the loan desk, she looks down at the notes in her hand and hears her father's recriminations: *You shouldn't have majored in entrepreneurship. You're too young to start a business. If you'd gotten an MBA, I could have given you a leg-up at my company. You'd have a good salary and health insurance. Why do you want to take on so much risk?* Seeing her crotchety neighbor makes her rethink her preparation and she backs away.

A few weeks later, she returns to the bank carrying a printed and bound business plan complete with her own market research and supporting statistics, her jitters a mix of nervousness and excitement. There's a long line at the counter and as she pushes past the last guy in line, he turns and says her name—it's a guy she's had a crush on since high school. He gives her a warm hug and asks if she's there to cash a paycheck too, and she says, "I'm actually here to apply for a loan." When she explains the nature of her business, the people in front them turn to listen in. He loves her idea and wants to hear more so he asks her out for coffee the next day. High on his attention and confident in her preparation, she hopes her luck will hold as she turns toward the loan desk—where once again, the crotchety misogynist sits.

This does not feel like the previous scene on repeat. The higher stakes—the extra time she's invested, the public declaration, the affirmation from the guy she's always liked who wants to know more, the people watching, and the thrum of remaining tension from her father's discouragement will drive her forward and prevent a lull as the protagonist repeats her efforts. Whatever the result of this meeting, the story will move forward.

Amplify story power through chorus

If I set up a soapbox to read an excerpt of my novel in front of City Hall, one or two curiosity seekers might stop to listen. But if 50,000 arrive with me to read the excerpt in unison, not only would many more onlookers take notice, but even the mayor might come to the window, and the whole thing would be recorded and become a YouTube #flashnovel sensation. You know it to be true: the voice of a group is more powerful than the voice of an individual.

Since the earliest staged tragedies, storytellers have made creative use of groups to comment with a collective voice on a story's dramatic action. The sole purpose of the "Greek chorus" was to amplify the effect of the action onstage. But the chorus can also:

- extend the story stakes;
- provide background information to help the audience follow the performance;
- comment on themes;
- expand a novel's frame;
- demonstrate how the audience might react emotionally to the drama; and
- express what the main characters would not, such as hidden fears or secrets.

The technique is still alive and well. In her *New York Times* bestselling debut, *The Lace Reader*, author Brunonia Barry bolstered the perspectives of individual characters in her Salem, Massachusetts, setting through Greek choruses representing witches, the religious conservatives who hunted them, and tourists.

Barry uses each of her groups to amplify one of the warring elements within protagonist Towner Whitney, who has come back to Salem after a long absence, following her twin sister's suicide.

The witches, it could be said, represent Towner's attempt to own her power as a woman, as well as her inherited gift of lace reading (a form of fortune-telling).

The Calvinists, a religious cult led by Towner's father, Calvin, are the external manifestation of her inner judge and jury. This is made clear in a scene in which a girl, pregnant by one of the Calvinists, is labeled a fraud and beaten after being unable to recite the Lord's Prayer on demand and in public.

The tourists are simply outsiders trying to figure out what's going on when the Calvinists come after Towner and the pregnant girl, evoking Towner's confused mental state as she tries to make sense of her own memories and perceptions. By increasing the fever pitch they raise the stakes:

I see them crossing the street, torches blazing. Traffic stops for them, creating a jam of onlookers. I see the looks of amusement from the tourists. They think they're watching one of the pageants they've seen over and over again in this city.

"Get the witch!" they chant.

The tourists think it's Bridget Bishop, or one of the other reenactments. They are trying to do their part as well, trying to engage the hysteria, to show they're comfortable with it. Getting their children involved, too. "Get the witch! Get the witch!" they cry.

Along the way, Barry lays a track that delivers Towner, the pregnant girl, and the story to this one revelatory moment:

In this place the scene has become simple and universal. What we are seeing is history repeating itself, one scene superimposed over the other. We are both here and back in old Salem at the same time, with the real Calvinists, the first ones. There is a feeling of impending doom here, and when I look at Angela, for just a moment, I see her in the drab brown Puritan dress, her hair tied back and covered. And we are back in history in the days when they came to get you because you were a woman alone in the world, or because you were different, because your hair was red, or because you had no children of your own and no husband to protect you.

Talk about extending the stakes! Barry summons the power of all the witches and all the Puritans throughout history to underscore her novel's enduring conflict.

But the author doesn't stop there—why would she, when she is on a roll? She adds a collective of abused women who shelter in their own community out on Yellow Dog Island. The sheer number of these isolated women, protected by a Greek chorus of wild dogs, shows that the stakes for abuse are high. And is there a better way to evoke a character's fear than to give them a rat for company in a dark tunnel, when the only choices are to return to a smoky inferno or continue forward into deep water? Sure, there is. Make it *scores* of rats, heading in the same direction as the characters.

On his website, Chris Cleave, author of *Little Bee,* invokes a Greek chorus each time his titular character, a displaced African girl, says she'll have to explain things to "the girls back home."

> The "girls back home" are the novel's Greek chorus—they are a foil in whose imagined reaction the cultural dissonance experienced by Little Bee can be made explicit. It's a good device because it feels more natural than having Little Bee go around talking straight to camera and saying "Wow, I'm freaked out by this. And this. And this." Much better for us to have Little Bee's thoughts after she has understood the situation and can explain it to the "girls back home" from a position of superior knowledge. This allows us to appreciate the cultural gulf, whilst allowing the narrator to be knowing rather than tragic.

The notion of "the girls back home" also suggests stakes: they are the silent voices of those who wonder if leaving their war-torn homeland to find a better life will work.

Just as the corps de ballet amplifies a prima ballerina's role onstage, a literary chorus can amplify tension while suggesting that in some instances, personal stakes reflect issues that can impact an entire community.

⇢ Try This ⇠

The stakes for success can inspire your reader to root for your protagonist—is their goal important enough to do so? The stakes for failure can drive a reluctant protagonist ever forward—are those stakes dire enough to do so? These prompts will help unearth your story's importance to its characters.

- In each scene, ask: What's the worst possible thing that could happen to my protagonist right now? How might that come about due to their inability to attain an important goal?
- The protagonist's personal stakes will seem more important if, over the course of your novel, they are shouldered by more characters. You can generate this material through this series of questions, inspired by a workshop I took with the late author Kevin McIlvoy:

1. How will pursuing their goal impact others in your protagonist's household? If the protagonist lives alone, could you add a boarder, a pet, a plant?
2. How will it impact their next-door neighbors?
3. How will it impact the environment/setting?
4. How will it impact the people they work with?
5. Think about spreading story impact further. Why does your protagonist's goal matter to their community?
6. How far can you take this? How might it matter to their county, their state, their country, the world, the universe?
7. Is there a way you could amplify the message by using a chorus?
8. How can you deliver on the stakes for failure at your novel's dark moment?
9. Is there a point in the story where you can up the stakes, making goal attainment even more urgent or important?
10. How do the stakes tie into the overall message of your novel?

- How can you foreshadow the importance of your protagonist's journey by hinting at stakes on the very first page?

PART III

Drive Your Protagonist Toward the End

18

Push Your Characters to the Limit

I like to put myself in uncomfortable situations. It forces me to deliver.
—Mikhail Baryshnikov, dancer

WHEN I WAS IN GRADE SCHOOL, my favorite activity in gym was obstacle course. I tackled it like a future Olympian. If the obstacle in front of me wasn't high enough, I was disappointed it hadn't tested me. If a bar was too easy to slip under, it wasn't low enough. If the gauntlet wasn't long and intense, how could I prove my capabilities? Little did I know, I was a future novelist in the making.

Whether intuitively, formally, or from elementary-school obstacle courses, creative writers learn that facing obstacles drives the protagonist's story. Ignore this at your peril.

Many years ago, I edited what was intended to be a near-future political thriller whose central character was running for president.

When I learned the protagonist was gay and autistic (I have changed these details), my mind was abuzz with potential conflict. This character will be fighting an uphill battle that most would consider heroic. The stuff of great story! Except...none of the conflict materialized. Nor was it going to. In the future this author envisioned, homosexuality and autism would be completely accepted in the world.

That's a lovely thought. But what kind of antagonistic forces can create change—within a character or society—without applying pressure to the vulnerabilities they refuse to acknowledge? To create a meaningful story, this protagonist's attributes needed to complicate their goal.

Going too easy on your characters is a common problem for new writers, especially for conflict-averse idealists who want to build a vision for a better world.

And therein lay the problem: This author wanted to write a happy story.

Well, they had "happy." They just didn't have "story."

James N. Frey, author of *How to Write a Damn Good Novel,* says the best plots force our characters to act at maximum capacity. Readers want to see how they act when pushed into a corner. In a two-day workshop I watched Frey plot an entire book-length thriller, rejecting one idea after the other from participants in search of the most interesting story movement. His main beef? "You guys want to make it too easy on the hero."

How can the hero be heroic if his task is too simple?

Frey urged us to think of how this character would solve the puzzle at hand if, on his own, he couldn't find an obvious clue. This step often forced the hero into relationships with others in the story—not all of whom he desired relationships with—and to dig into his past to unearth long-forgotten or undervalued skills.

Even children delight in conflict. As soon as Dr. Seuss's Cat in the Hat appears, we know he's going to be trouble. And if your protagonist is acting at maximum capacity, it stands to reason an antagonist would as well. In the case of my client's political thriller, the antagonist would use public opinion about the protagonist's homosexuality and autism to thwart him. Otherwise, what kind of antagonist would he be? Only obstacles of the most challenging sort will force your protagonist to think outside the box, allowing them either the kind of failure or success that will result in the inner change they need.

It's a great idea to give your character conflict-laden traits like this writer did—but when you do, make use of them. If you have created in your character a fully dimensional individual pitted against an oppositional force—whether that be a villain, society, inner demons, or nature itself—your story will not be a downer. It will be inspiring. With keen attention to other aspects of story movement, readers will remember your book as the uplifting story you set out to write.

Use antagonists to apply pressure

As your story advances, enemies, villains, and other antagonistic forces will demand more of your protagonist than they thought they had to give. That was certainly the case for author Ross Macdonald's series detective Lew Archer.

Gayle Lynds, the *New York Times* bestselling author of espionage novels, shares a favorite anecdote of Macdonald's, about putting his hero into a seemingly impossible situation in *The Drowning Pool*, the second title in his eighteen-novel Lew Archer series. As Archer hides in a janitor's closet, his foes are closing in on all sides. Tension is high—how will he get out of there? The author was wondering the same thing—especially since the men hunting him were armed, and Archer was not.

"After a lot of head scratching," Lynds told me, "he realized what most of us eventually figure out to do ourselves. Have the character look around. The only hope was through a window high above, too high for Lew to reach. But there was a sink. Eureka! Lew turned on the water, flooded the room, and paddled until he could get to the window and escape." Lynds laughed while relating the outlandish solution, and yet Macdonald's fans bought it. The novel went on to become a movie in which Paul Newman made the epic swim.

Try to think of ways to put an impossible squeeze on your protagonist. The transformative power of extreme pressure is as old as story itself. As early as the third century BCE, the Athenian Stoic philosopher Zeno was quoted as having said, "My most profitable journey began on the day I was shipwrecked and lost my entire fortune."

Use friends to apply pressure

It is because your protagonist's best friend sees their weaknesses and wounds, prejudices and proclivities, bad habits and blind spots—and still affords them the grace of seeing their potential—that this friend claims a unique position from which to effect story movement. From a place of privilege and relative safety, the friend can call out and influence that behavior.

In Kathy Strobos's debut romantic comedy, *Partner Pursuit*, protagonist Audrey is trying to make partner at her law firm. When she shares with her best friend, Eve, how frustrated she is by her next-to-nil dating life, it's Eve who points out that she gets in her own way by working all the time. That's the sort of frank assessment only an old friend could provide. Then later, when Audrey is out to lunch with Eve and their mutual college friend Max, Eve and Max convince Audrey together (a chorus!) that the man she very much wants to date has relegated her to the "friend zone" by suggesting she must have missed a pass.

> "Maybe he thinks I'm a workaholic and he doesn't want to date someone like that so that's why he hesitates," said Audrey.
>
> Max and Eve looked at each other. "You are a workaholic."

While unneeded repetition can stymie story movement, here, repetition creates it. Aubrey loves and trusts Eve and Max, who are not pitted against her—but with Max's opinion bolstering Eve's previous assessment, the pressure increases for Aubrey to recognize and do something about her problem.

An antagonist posing as a friend can apply pressure to the protagonist as well, adding a layer of intrigue. This works well in stories where the "friend" is trying to implode a career or break up the protagonist and their love interest for selfish reasons.

Show unwanted change through the middle

By the midpoint of your novel, new questions raised and accumulating emotional turning points should have created an intimate connection between protagonist and reader. Your readers will now be hoping for the best and fearing the worst as they move into the second half.

Yet for writers who employ the three-act structure taught in screenwriting, that stretch in act 2 that takes up 50 percent of your novel can feel like crossing a desert without the promise of an oasis. If you feel similar despair, chuck the three-act structure—there's no rule saying a novel must be written like a screenplay. In his master class at MasterClass.com, literary writer Salman Rushdie says he views such formulas as nonsense. "The first and only rule is to make it interesting," Rushdie says. "Be as vivid as you can. *Pow!*"

I loved this so much I'm now always looking for the "pow" that can enliven the story as protagonists head into, negotiate, and emerge from the middle of a novel. I've already introduced several tools that can drive movement through the middle of your novel. The *because/she decides to/but/therefore* scene structure will ensure that you continue to raise questions. Adding unexpected elements can help you find fresh insights. We've looked at how to deepen inner conflict, refresh tension, provoke unwanted consequences, and spread personal stakes across more shoulders. Now, let's look at ways to deliver the "pow"!

Lock the pressure cooker

Scene by scene, the way your character deals with the obstacles he faces will apply pressure that results in moments of incremental change. But that change will only happen if you keep your character in the pressure cooker. Once you open the lid, your story will depressurize and the simmer you worked so hard to build will evaporate.

In *The Curious Incident of the Dog in the Night-Time* by Mark Haddon, the teenage protagonist's desire to find and then escape from the person who killed his neighbor's dog is aided, and then complicated by, his unspecified autism spectrum disorder. The reader's expectation of an "arc of change" might suggest he should grow out of it in some way. But if Haddon had chosen to do that, Christopher would have escaped the pressure cooker.

In this excerpt, this boy who is not comfortable leaving his home is trying to travel to London to stay with his mother. He has his father's bank card in his pocket—since Christopher has a memory for numbers, his father entrusted him with the passcode to keep himself from losing it. In another pocket is Christopher's pet rat. Although his social awkwardness is ever present, he's finding his idiosyncrasies useful:

> I knew that the train station was somewhere near. And if something is nearby you can find it by moving in a spiral, walking clockwise and taking every right turn until you come back to a road you already walked on, then take the next left, then taking every right turn and so on.
>
> And that was how I found the train station, and I concentrated really hard on following the rules and making a map of the center of town in my head as I walked, and that way it was easier to ignore all the people and all the noise around me.

As the stakes grow higher, Christopher must use to his advantage what others had previously considered the immovable barrier to his success: his own nature.

Feature routines only when setting unexpected action against them

Have you ever said, "Oh, thank god, this character has ducked into Walmart to buy some houseshoes"? I thought not. If shopping won't push your story forward in a meaningful way, leave it out. But you can include scenes in commonplace locales if you play against routine.

We first met seventeen-year-old Novalee Nation, seven months pregnant and suspicious about the number 7, back in chapter 9 of this book. Early on in Billie Letts's novel, *Where the Heart Is,* Novalee wants to stop at Walmart to pee and buy some houseshoes that will accommodate her swollen feet. When she comes back out, her boyfriend and his car are nowhere to be found. With only the change from his ten-dollar bill, she goes back into Walmart. After the store closes, she borrows a sleeping bag and alarm clock and spends the night—and with continuing ingenuity, ends up living there undetected for the next two months. On page 90, her situation improved only by having a new friend by her side, the two teens improvise as Novalee gives birth there. Ample press coverage comes with an outpouring of support, but she's still in the pressure cooker, as the mother from whom she's been estranged for ten years, with "eyes as flat and hard as a cheap motel bed," arrives to get in on the action.

An ordinary locale can create an effective backdrop for the drama to come by playing on the reader's presumption that nothing interesting happens while doing chores—but it will only shake things up if you deliver the unexpected "pow." Without the abandonment, covert scheming, and birth drama in aisle 7, this Walmart stop would simply have reminded your bored reader to set down the novel and go get some houseshoes.

Introduce a key late-entering character

In *The People We Keep,* a road-trip story by Allison Larkin, protagonist April, a young singer-songwriter, tries to subsist on gigs and odd jobs. Ethan, a character who will be key to the emotional punch of the story's resolution, enters on page 246, just shy of the 70 percent mark. With his introduction in this scene, Larkin foreshadows the impact they will have on each other. April has been busking when he comes up and introduces himself to her, saying he's been listening to her all afternoon from a nearby bench. He asks if he can buy her some gazpacho.

> "Thanks," I say, "but I have to hit the road." My stomach is hollow and aching, but I have to be done falling for people just because they seem fine. I pick up my guitar case.

"It's a short walk," he says. "You have to eat anyway, right?" He does this little shrug of his shoulders.

I study his face, lines in places that tell me he's smiled a bunch, but worried more. I try to picture him grabbing my wrist, slamming me against a wall. I can't. It's a ridiculous thought. He cares too much. Wears it on his sleeve. He put his feelings into asking me to dinner, trusting I'd be careful not to hurt them. I wonder if my eyes look familiar to him, too, if that's why he liked my music so much. Takes one to know.

"I could eat," I say. Stupid, but hungry. Stupid, but lonely.

Note how April's life experience influences her need to make the right decision. On the surface, it's just an invitation to grab a bite. But in her thoughts, April seems to be warding off a bite out of her own soul. This may be a "pow" of uncertainty, but since April doesn't yet know what to make of Ethan, it throws her—and the reader who knows what she's been through—off balance.

Reveal a secret, a hidden goal, or guilt

A non-POV character acting in mysterious ways is a sure sign of oncoming external conflict. In *Happiness Falls* by Angie Kim, teen protagonist Mia's younger brother, Eugene, has a condition that makes him unable to speak—yet because he was the only one with their father on the day he went missing, only Eugene might know what happened. Eugene's freedom is jeopardized when he acts out during questioning and the police want to move him into a locked detention center for violent youth. The family is desperate to save him. Then on page 208, just past the halfway mark, we learn Eugene's situation may not be as everyone expects—surprising even Mia, who is closest to him—and the energy of the entire story shifts. This is a great example of a midpoint twist that can thrill readers and keep them turning pages.

If your story movement weakens through the middle of your novel, it's possible you're not being hard enough on your protagonist to inspire an emotional turning point. This chapter and its "Try this" section offers a smorgasbord of plot points, any one of which might get your story juices flowing again. If you don't care for writing from prompts because you believe that every word in your novel should arise from your own creative marrow, remember the lesson from chapter 16: No two car crashes are alike. As long you find a way for the plot point you chose to grow organically from existing conflicts in *your* story, then color it with *your* protagonist's distinct perspective so that its "pow" factor results in incremental movement in *your* protagonist's arc of inner change, you need not fear your reader will find it devoid of meaning. It will draw them deeper into your story.

⇥ Try This ⇤

A protagonist without limits would have an inner life as entertaining as a pinball game with no cabinet, flippers, or drain. Use these prompts to define your protagonist's limits—and then brainstorm how far you can push them before inner change becomes crucial.

- *Keep your protagonist's eye on the goal.* If your protagonist is tempted away or distracted from their goal, bring on the negative consequences. Otherwise, your story won't seem important enough for the reader to continue reading. Train your attention on your protagonist's own chosen journey.
- *Deliver an important lesson or find an important clue* that switches up the protagonist's strategy and lays groundwork for the climactic fight.
- *Add to your character's limitations.* As the plot heats up, consider ways you can temporarily lower your character's agency. They might be sick, or injured, or grieving. Their problems may be piling on to the point they can no longer function at capacity. Even a fictional hero can only take so much, and if they can't overcome their limitations, they will contribute to their own defeat.
- *Add a romantic thread* that can both complicate your protagonist's goal attainment and help their arc of inner change.

- *Summon new courage.* By now, your character has left behind their old worldview and is evolving along their arc of inner change. Consider having them take more risks and act outside their former boundaries.
- *Kill off a helper.* This gem was passed on to me by one of my own writing mentors, Donald Maass. Removing the one person who could make the protagonist's situation right can raise the stakes mid-novel.
- *Add a new menace.* Perhaps the antagonist gets help, or the protagonist's own inner rift deepens.
- *Ignite a conflict,* such as between secondary characters or between the protagonist and an institution.
- *Switch up the goal.* Sometimes a protagonist will realize, late in the second act, that they've been fighting for the wrong thing. Take care to delineate the shift toward a new goal with a robust emotional turning point so your reader comes along for the ride.
- *Play with scene values.* Instead of bad to worse to worse, put the rug back under your protagonist's feet so you can yank it out again.
- *Focus your daily writing sessions.* Word count won't make your story move. Think cause/effect. Action/reaction. Keep your POV character at the energetic center of the unfolding action and ensure that scenes told from other points of view will ultimately impact your protagonist.
- *Push the relevant conflict each character contributes* (based in their past, brought into a current scene goal, aiming toward their dreams for their future) until resolution seems impossible.
- *Raise stakes in all narrative arcs.* Your protagonist is your reader's gateway to understanding the story, but they aren't the center of the story world. Secondary characters, the protagonist's relationships with them, and even symbols of change like a grandfather clock in the corner can suffer consequences that could impact your protagonist. Explore the stakes in all your novel's arcs.

19

Demonstrate Emotion

> *When I first began choreographing, I never thought of it as choreography but as expressing feelings. Though every piece is different, they are all trying to get at certain things that are difficult to put into words.*
> —Pina Bausch, dancer and choreographer

DESPITE ITS CAUSE-AND-EFFECT ENGINE, a story isn't a machine in which every interaction is predictable. The way your characters feel during plot events provides clues about what will bring them into alliance or conflict. From our own lives we know there is often a gap between words and actions. If you had to choose, would you rather be married to the spouse who leaves you with bruises and an "I love you" before heading to work each morning, or the spouse who silently brings you coffee in bed and leaves a smile and a goodbye kiss? We speak in gestures truer than the words that come out of our mouths.

Speak body language

A wordless medium, dance communicates through the body's language. One of my roles as a dance critic was to translate that language into words that viewers could use to talk about what they'd witnessed. As a novelist, this is one of your roles as well.

When inserted as beats in dialogue breaks, body language can be used effectively to support—or more interestingly, counter—the words spoken. The combination will create the right impression.

> "I love you, you know." He leaned back in his chair and crossed his arms over his chest. His eyes—those dark, dark eyes—drilled right through me.

Do you believe words of love spoken while leaning away and protecting the heart? That uber-romantic word "drilled" clues us in to how this unnamed POV character really feels.

Visceral emotions—emotions that find expression in the body—draw the reader into the story. Connecting the body and the emotional state of a character mirrors the linkage of external plot to inner arc: both show the physiological influence of story. As much as humans vary in personality, spirit, and capabilities, though, we are remarkably similar when it comes to our physiology. This means that the often-used reaction "he swallowed" will fall well short of revelatory. We all swallow. We all blink. We all breathe. Our hearts, God willing, all beat. And while an artery throbbing at the temple is more likely a sign of a vessel malformation, many writers would have us believe that it's the universal sign of anger.

Yet because their number is limited, visceral emotions can sometimes fail to engage the reader who has heard them all before.

To find visceral reactions that work, don your "creative writer" cap and search for an approach that feels both emotionally relevant and specific to your character. Here are two different reactions to a declaration of love:

1. He swallowed. At least that was his intention, but his throat was suddenly so dry he couldn't pull it off.

2. After I told him I loved him, he winked. I stroked his arm so he could feel my sincerity, but he looked up into the umbrella over our table. What did I need to do to get this man to look at me? He lifted his hand to his eye. If he was wiping away a tear, I'd read him all wrong.

"Let's eat inside," he said, pushing away from the table. "There's too much pollen flying around and I'm ruining everything."

Despite having been used by thousands of writers, visceral reactions can still land as fresh and effective. We can all relate to shock as a gut punch, or to love swelling within our chest. But to ensure your reader remains plugged into your story movement, reach for something surprising. Love that's a gut punch, anyone? Laban's Eight Efforts, discussed in chapter 12, might send you in a useful direction.

Give your reader an emotional experience

While your reader wants to know what your characters are feeling, what they want even more is for you to give them their own emotional experience. That this reader will feel the same thing as a character is not a given. It may sometimes be true, say in the case of a shocking twist. And we already know that telling them outright won't do the trick. To help the reader feel their own breathless anticipation, their own loss of hope, and their own dread of what's to come, you need to bring them to the emotion.

In her craft book *Escaping into the Open*, Elizabeth Berg illustrates the concept of bringing the reader to the emotion this way:

> Imagine the proud father of a newborn being left in charge of that baby. He's told his wife not to worry about a thing; the baby's just been fed, she's sound asleep, what could happen? The wife is at the door ready to go out when the husband flicks

on the television, only to have both parents see a news story about a school bus that overturned, killing all thirty children on board. The man and his wife go instantly to stand at the side of the crib, where they watch the baby sleep. Then the father pulls the blanket up higher over the baby, stands back, and takes his wife's hand.[28]

My guess is you know exactly how this young father is feeling without having to be told. How can you pull this off in your own work? One way is to create, then go back and modify, emotional markers.

Follow emotion markers

In your early drafts, give yourself permission to overwrite. Expose any emotions that hint at your character's inner world—all the love, hate, disappointment, and gnashing of teeth—until you're satisfied you've dug down to the scene's dramatic core. In later drafts, revisit this melodrama and see if you can evoke the emotions without naming them.

While seeking a way to exemplify this process, I came up with this paragraph—and stuffed it with emotion markers:

> Finding that her favorite childhood climbing tree had been cut to the ground, she was so <u>angry</u> she cried and screamed in <u>exasperation</u> at the <u>unfairness</u> of it all. But most of all she was <u>afraid</u> she'd lost some important part of herself. Her neighbor would pay for doing this. The tree was on the property line. It had belonged to her family as much as MacGregor's.

Note that I went for the easy emotion first—her anger. Then I followed these emotional markers deeper into story, where I found her fear. But *why* was she so angry, and why was she afraid she'd lost a part of herself? That the tree had been on the property line seemed to be a clue. To make it reasonable that she might still want to climb a tree, I made her a college student, Hannah (once I named her she became more forthcoming), who came back to visit the tree every year. If upon visiting the tree, she just feels her feelings, though, there's no story. What was her fear going to cause her to *do?*

This is important because a tormented character isn't going to sit down, have a good think, and then share all her deepest feelings on paper. I needed to come at them by replacing that lame threat—*her neighbor would pay for this*—with concrete action that would reveal feelings beyond my first-draft melodrama. Here's a revised draft informed by the markers above but allowing character action to evoke emotions that are no longer named:

> MacGregor had cut it down, her mother said. How could he have taken this from her? This maple wasn't old, or diseased. The stump was solid and the cut so fresh its sap still wept.
>
> Hannah had climbed that tree every day of her youth. When she was fifteen and her mother no longer understood her tomboy ways, its strong branches had supported her interest in the new neighbor, Keith MacGregor. Positioned right on the property line, the maple had offered a perfect view through its springtime buds. By the time she was seventeen, Keith wanted to know everything about her, so she invited him up to her secret place, hidden high among the palm-sized leaves. After a long talk and a tender kiss, he'd etched "HJ + KM" into its bark.
>
> By the time HJ was nineteen, those letters had become a living memorial.
>
> Before the skid and the metal's body-jangling shriek, Keith had kissed her cheek and taken a moment too long to look into her eyes; after, he'd been so still behind the wheel, her hands slick with his blood. For so many months, the memory of his wrecked face would slip into her thoughts and steal her breath. Only in the top of this tree, with the leaves whispering in his voice all around her, could she find peace.
>
> Now, all that remained was a stump.
>
> That night, she snuck over to MacGregor's property and carved a heart with Keith's initials into the front door his father had never opened to her.

> The door gave way and there stood MacGregor. His hair was long, his beard scraggly. His gaze moved between Hannah's raised knife and the damaged door. For several tense minutes they stood off, neither willing to look away.

To pry open my protagonist, I made use of the same structural tools that incite change in a story: inciting incident, desire, stakes. What began as "telling," through a melodramatic bundle of emotion words, became actions that brought the reader to Hannah's feelings so they could inhabit Hannah's emotional state.

Elicit emotion from non-POV characters

Like your protagonist, your major secondary characters deserve robust inner lives and unique perspectives that will put them into conflict with your protagonist. Even though you've put them in a scene for the purpose of applying pressure, no character would say they wanted to act as your "tool"—and you shouldn't want them to. Here's the thing about a tool: a hammer always acts like a hammer. Aim for interactions between your characters that are unpredictable. If the secondary character's role is so obvious the reader can reliably foretell what they are going to do or say, there's no point in reading on—they can predict the rest of the book.

One way to introduce variability is to identify a source of hidden conflict within your characters.

That's easy enough if it's your protagonist or another POV character. Maybe the protagonist's husband wants her to act against her values, for example. The reader has full access to her inner conflict as she thinks, "Those were the values I was raised with, yes, and they've always kept me safe. But am I clinging to a moral code that no longer serves me? Maybe he's right, and it's time to bust out of my self-righteous box."

But what if we don't have access to this character's point of view? How can we show that this secondary character is also struggling with inner conflict? The following six techniques were plucked from Emily Henry's #1 *New York Times* bestseller, *People We Meet on Vacation*.

Because it's a romance, we know that the male and female leads will get together—the question is how, and when.

The setup: ebullient and flighty Poppy met staid Alex in college. Despite the glaring differences in their personalities, their troubled backstories, lack of proximity, and intermittent coupling with other people, they've remained best friends for a decade. They reconnect each year by sharing a summer vacation—first on the cheap, then later, on a corporate dime when Poppy writes for a prominent travel magazine. They never dare take the relationship further for fear they'll lose an important friendship if they make a misstep.

Poppy, who has the most substantial growth arc, is the only character with a point of view. Here are several methods Henry uses to suggest Alex's inner conflict.

Body language

In the opening scene, Poppy approaches a man at a bar and asks if he comes there often.

> He studies me for a minute, visibly weighing potential replies. "No," he says finally. "I don't live here."

Technically, if we're in Poppy's POV, she can't know what's going on in another character's mind, but "visibly weighing potential replies" stops short of a POV breach. Henry counts on the reader to cocreate meaning by envisioning Alex tilting his head side to side, trying to decide how to respond.

Dialogue

After ten years of do-si-do, one can only imagine that once Poppy and Alex hook up—no matter how wonderful it might be—they'll wonder if it was a bad idea. After they share a drunken kiss that almost becomes something more, this loaded morning-after dialogue occurs.

> Alex coughs. "I'm sorry about last night. I know I started it all and—it shouldn't have happened like that."
>
> "Seriously," I say. "It's not a big deal."
>
> "I know you're not over Trey," he murmurs, looking away.

Argh! Poppy missed the two most important words in that exchange—"like that"—and now she's backpedaling so fast she runs right over Alex's feelings.

Dialogue beats

The bits of action sprinkled throughout a section of dialogue can raise tension by revealing inner conflict. On one vacation, when their significant others come along to Tuscany, Poppy has a pregnancy scare. Alex gets up early to go for his morning run, sees what she's up to, and awaits the results with her. When Poppy breaks down, Alex wraps his arms around her.

> "What am I going to do, Alex?" I ask him. "If I'm…What the hell am I supposed to do?"
>
> He studies my face for a long time. "What do you want to do?"

At first glance this might seem straightforward but look again—that pause while he studies her face for a long time is important. Poppy's question is loaded because we know Alex wants children, but we also sense he is trying to really see her, and cares to uncover her true feelings.

Contradictory delivery

On one vacation, Alex has wrenched his back. Poppy comes back from a pharmacy with a heating pad and other supplies to help him and asks how he's doing.

> "Better." He forces a smile. "Thanks."

Liar. His pain is written all over his face. He's worse at hiding that than his emotions.

Alex contradicts what he says with how he says it. We can buy Poppy's testimony that he's forcing a smile and lying because she's known him for so long. But we can also tell he doesn't want to ruin her vacation by causing her to worry over him.

Revealing actions

One year, Poppy misses vacation because she's ill. Since their tickets and reservations can no longer be canceled, she urges Alex to go and have a good time without her. In this scene, Poppy is in bed in her apartment, her head pounding. In her delirium, she thinks someone is calling her name. When she finally consults her phone, she sees dozens of messages from "Alexander the Great." The last one says, *I'm here! Let me in!* She slowly makes her way to the door.

> "Oh God, Poppy," he says, stepping in and examining me, the cool back of his hand pressing to my clammy forehead. "You're burning up."
>
> "You're in Norway," I manage in a raspy whisper.
>
> "I'm definitely not." He drags his bag inside and closes the door.
>
> After she gets cleaned up, she climbs back into the bed he has freshly made. He opens his laptop bag.
>
> He sits on the edge of the bed and pulls out pill bottles and boxes of Mucinex, lining them up on the side table. "I wasn't sure what your symptoms were," he says.

She has always assumed his investment was in the vacation, as he'd never be able to afford something like that on a teacher's salary; these actions suggest his investment is in the relationship, even if it's on her sick bed.

Accumulating subtext

In this excerpt from late in the story, the reader has no trouble understanding the unnamed emotional energy at play. Alex's brother David pulls Poppy aside at a family event to tell her that Alex has bought a ring—for Sarah, Alex's long-time on-again, off-again girlfriend. This is news to Poppy, who thought she and Alex had told each other everything about their major life milestones.

> "Don't get me wrong, Poppy." [David] sets his hand on mine. "I always thought it should be you two. But Sarah was great, and they loved each other, and—I just want him to be happy. I want him to stop worrying about other people and have something that's just his, you know?"
> "Yeah." I can barely get the word out.

At this point late in the story, we know enough to pick up on several levels of emotional subtext in this exchange. David displays his protective love for his brother by implying that Poppy better stop messing with Alex's heart. Alex isn't even in this scene, and yet we understand that he can't bear to share his marriage plans with Poppy because he worries about her. In that last line, note how Henry perfectly evokes Poppy's emotional state without bogging us down with inner thoughts or visceral reaction, even though we've had access to her deep POV all along. She lets subtext carry the message, allowing room for the reader to feel more.

Some stories call for multiple points of view; others challenge the writer to dig deep into their creative well to find a way to tease out a non-point-of-view character's perspective. In *People We Meet on Vacation*, Henry uses inner conflict to feed a will-they-or-won't-they tension that lasts to the very end of the novel. A few of these techniques might help you do the same.

⇥ Try This ⇤

Explore ways to build your story's emotional import into its scenes by starting with these prompts.

- What clichéd emotions in your manuscript could you freshen up so that your reader stays keyed into your POV character's specific feelings?
- How might you replace any "emotion markers" you identify in your manuscript with setting and character action that bring your reader to those emotions—without naming them?
- *Per Henry:* How might you use body language, dialogue and its associated beats, contradictory or revealing actions, or subtext to evoke the feelings of a major character with no point of view?

20

Combine Strategies to Adjust Pacing

Dancers are often afraid to stop moving for fear of not being exciting. Actually the opposite is true; if they don't stop, they certainly will be boring. Many a time I have used the reverse of the old admonition and said, "Don't just do something, stand there!

—Doris Humphrey, dancer and choreographer

EXPOSITION—the writing that contextualizes the active aspects of a scene—is often denigrated as "telling." This makes some sense, as its etymology is from the Latin *exponere*, which means "to explain."

To accept this generalization, though, is to miss out on opportunities to "show" through exposition. *Exponere* can also mean "to expose."

Exposition can either show or tell. Let's look at the opening of Nick Hornby's *How to be Good*, which pulls off both.

> I am in a car park in Leeds when I tell my husband I don't want to be married to him anymore. David isn't even in the car park with me. He's at home, looking after the kids, and I have only called him to remind him that he should write a note for Molly's teacher. The other bit just sort of...slips out. This is a mistake, obviously. Even though I am, apparently, and to my immense surprise, the kind of person who tells her husband that she doesn't want to be married to him anymore, I really didn't think that I was the kind of person to say so in a car park, on a mobile telephone. That kind of self-assessment will now have to be revised, clearly. I can describe myself as the kind of person who doesn't forget names, for example, because I have remembered names thousands of times and forgotten them only once or twice. But for the majority of people, marriage-ending conversations happen only once, if at all. If you choose to conduct yours on a mobile phone, in a Leeds car park, then you cannot really claim that it is unrepresentative, in the same way that Lee Harvey Oswald couldn't really claim that shooting presidents wasn't like him at all. Sometimes we have to be judged by our one-offs.

Check out Hornby's purposeful use of adverbs—obviously, apparently, clearly. Think they might be foreshadowing anything about this narrator's reliability?

Even while this first-person narrator is speaking directly to the reader, which carries the whiff of telling, she's showing us quite a bit. The woman is self-referential to the point of obsession. Repeated throughout the story, almost as if a mantra, is a version of this line, from page 8: "I'm not a bad person. I'm a doctor."

She also tells us *why* she's a doctor.

> I liked how it sounded: 'I want to be a doctor,' 'I'm training to be a doctor,' 'I'm a GP in a small North London practice.' I thought it made me seem just right—professional, kind of brainy, not too flashy, respectable, mature, caring. You think doctors don't care about how things look, because they're

doctors? Of course we do. Anyway, I'm a good person, a doctor, and I'm lying in a hotel bed with a man I don't know very well called Stephen, and I've just asked my husband for a divorce.

Interesting accumulation of detail here, especially since we don't even learn that our narrator's name is Katie until page 31. This sets up a deep inner rift between "who she *appears to be*" and the seemingly less important sense of "who she *is*," a conflict that escalates throughout the novel as she decides whether she will stay with her husband.

On one hand, she's the kind of woman who commits for life. On the other, she's a woman whose desire to break her vow seems justifiable considering her husband's persistent anger. But here's the kicker: once she convinces him she's right, he acts. He finds a spiritual teacher who leads him toward inner peace and inspires good works—works that inconvenience Katie and awaken her to her own long-suppressed anger. The question shifts: If she can no longer justify righteous indignation in the face of her husband's anger, who is she?

When one sets out writing in first-person voice, it's tempting to have the protagonist comment on everything that happens. This typically comes across as reiteration of what we just observed. In Hornby's experienced hands, scene and his protagonist's chatty exposition are tools that achieve a distinct style. Requiring that his reader shift gears between the two changes the pace at which the reader accumulates meaning.

Dennis Lehane, too, shows through exposition in his literary mystery, *Mystic River*. This passage is excerpted from a spontaneous block party held to celebrate the return of 11-year-old Jimmy's kidnapped friend, Dave. Jimmy doesn't know what Dave has been through—he only sees that Dave is surrounded by police and well-wishers that include their fifth-grade teacher, Miss Powell. When Miss Powell kisses Dave twice on the cheek, Jimmy wants to run right up and tell her he almost got in the car with the kidnappers, too. He watches her in some detail—her crooked upper tooth, the curve of her right calf and ankle as she gets into a car. The following section comes right after Jimmy's mother comments on his teacher:

> "Real cute," his mother repeated into a gray ribbon of exhaled smoke.
>
> Jimmy still didn't say anything. Most of the time he didn't know what to say to his parents. His mother was worn out so much. She stared off at places Jimmy couldn't see and smoked her cigarettes, and half the time didn't hear him until he'd repeated himself a couple times. His father was pissed off usually, and even when he wasn't and could be kind of fun, Jimmy would know that he could turn into a pissed-off drunk guy any second, give Jimmy a whack for saying something he might have laughed at half an hour before. And he knew that no matter how hard he tried to pretend otherwise, he had both his father and his mother inside of him—his mother's long silences and his father's sudden fits of rage.
>
> When Jimmy wasn't wondering what it would be like to be Miss Powell's boyfriend, he sometimes wondered what it would be like to be her son.

This passage has only one aspect of setting to ground us: a gray ribbon of smoke. There is no continuous action, or dialogue after the opening line. Lehane relies upon subtle psychological suspense to carry the reader through the passage—he wagers that by now we care to hear a little bit about Jimmy, and refrains from falling into a flashback by showing that the cigarette smoking and drinking are a constant.

If Lehane had simply told us Jimmy's home life kept him on tenterhooks, he could not have sketched the paradox that is Jimmy: one part his father, one part his mother. This is an inner conflict that will devil Jimmy throughout the book.

Think this is both show *and* tell? I agree. In telling us about Jimmy's mom and dad, Lehane shows us Jimmy.

Vary the charge

Another way to adjust pacing while maintaining your story's momentum is to vary your scene values.

In subatomic science, particles have a fixed charge: a proton is positive (+), an electron negative (-). This is always true. In story, it's rare that a plot event is wholly positive or negative. Characters will assign value according to their individual perspective—and that perspective may change over the course of the book.

Earlier, we looked at two examples of car accidents that were deemed tragic. Would you assign the same value if the protagonist crashed their car with the intent to injure an evil tormentor? What if the protagonist staged the crash, wandered off for help, and then feigned amnesia, hoping to reboot their life elsewhere? Readers would perceive these crashes much differently than the first two I mentioned and subconsciously assign each their own value.

We can't help it. We are value-assigning beings. Our emotional investment in the protagonist will produce an ongoing recalibration of value as we move through the story. Is it looking bad for the protagonist right now? Your reader's chest contracts, their breathing increases, their stomach twists. Are things improving? If so, your reader may relax a bit—but then think, "Wait a minute, this may be temporary"—and anticipate the next turn.

Avid readers know that in a well-written story, values vacillate.

Consider a tale about a character I'll call Danilo, told through these five plot points: 1) Danilo was endowed with the perfect body for dance, 2) which is exactly what he wanted to do, and 3) since he had the full support of all of his enlightened friends as well as parents able to pay for his training, 4) he was taken into a major company at the age of seventeen, and 5) quickly rose through the ranks to principal dancer.

What a happy story!—that no one will want to read. With his trajectory ironed smooth by luck and grace, Danilo need never face the discomforts of change; he coasts—no obstacles to overcome, no tough decisions to make beyond which excellent instructor to grace with his presence. His story doesn't feel real. It does not inspire. In fact, the reader may not feel anything at all.

If you consider Danilo's five plot points on a scale from super (++) to positive (+) to negative (−) or even worse (− −), you'd see that his double-positive story exhibits the same problem that my son's double-negative elementary school story did: it maintained the same value throughout. When a story flatlines there is no movement, and the reader will go in search of a more emotionally stimulating novel.

Let's compare Danilo's story to that of the dancer who inspired Colum McCann's novel *Dancer:* Rudolf Nureyev. The bleak existence young Nureyev could expect in Siberia was marked by poverty, hunger, and cramped conditions (− −). Ballet gave him sustenance (+). The restrictions of the Soviet regime (−) sparked his lust for artistic freedom and his laser focus on his career (+). He drank hard (−) and loved hard (+) while expressing his homosexuality in an unwelcoming world (+/−). He risked everything (+/−) to defect to the West and chase the one goal that had eluded him: expressive freedom (++). Note those split charges, indicating that a story event has both an upside and a downside. While differences in charge between events clearly delineate story movement; a split charge produces a particular type of story movement we've already touched on: tension.

McCann characterizes Nureyev, whose reputation as one of the best male dancers in the world has long outlived his death in 1993 of AIDS-related complications, as a man whose artistic ambition was driven by a need for perfection. He was difficult, vain, and egotistical, attributes that often drove a wedge in his relationships—and offered McCann rich inner conflict from which to build a story. Writing for *The Guardian*,[29] book critic Judith Mackrell said of *Dancer*, "But what it crucially captures is the calculating, striving essence of Nureyev's character, and its twin effects: on the one hand alienation, on the other the fleeting satisfaction of glimpsing the holy grail of his own genius." These twin effects issue a plot rife with value changes. Each of Nureyev's dreams ascends like a wave and crashes, a riptide of consequences pulling sand from beneath his feet—even as new tensions gather.

Such fluctuations in value charge can convey story movement within a scene as well. Let's look at the movement generated in these two paragraphs from the end of a scene that takes place at Italy's world-famous Spoleto Festival. At this point in the novel, the stakes for success are already high. Nureyev has left his family and country behind to defect to the West, and only success can justify his sacrifice—but he must perform without his preferred partner, Margot Fonteyn, who is at her ill husband's bedside. McCann writes in Nureyev's perspective:

> All Italy was there. Yet the presence of fame does not compensate for the absences in my performances. The *Raymonda* pas de deux was, of course, abysmal without her, but even the solo was a bucket of shit. Afterwards Spoleto seemed to have lost its magic, and the thought of the hotel room was depressing. I dismissed everyone, remained all night to repair the evening's mistakes.
>
> The stagehands found me in the morning, sleeping on their tarps. They brought me cappuccino and a corneto [sic]. I rehearsed again, found the temperament. On the second evening I danced with a fire in my hair.

In two brief paragraphs, McCann captures the kind of self-condemnation only a perfectionist can hurl, and the comeback mentality that made Nureyev the greatest dancer of his era. On the page, the performance itself holds no charge—Nureyev assigns it, creating a wild swing from his bucket-of-shit solo to his passion reigniting. This scene moves.

In contrast, what was at stake for Danilo? Nothing.

Put the steps together

When young dancers learn choreography, they train their muscles to recall a series of individual steps. But the magic in their performance is something they must figure out for themselves: how to move from one step into the next. Energy will be harnessed from the earth, the heavens, and the dancer's own musculature to create the glorious sense that their movement is bigger than the sum of its parts. It's almost like bringing something robotic to life.

In her work of speculative fiction, *Annie Bot*, debut author Sierra Greer did just that by moving energy through her story to achieve what the *New York Times Book Review* called a "brilliant pas de deux."

The protagonist and sole point-of-view character, Annie, is a human-looking, "Cuddle Bunny" robot whose sole purpose is to please her owner, Doug. She constantly rates his displeasure and libido on a 10-point scale. Doug is in his mid-thirties. There's a lot of sex. This repetition would put a drag on story movement, save for one thing: Annie's artificial intelligence is set on autodidactic mode, so she'll seem more real to Doug. Despite her underlying purpose to please him, she is free to make her own decisions. Annie, it turns out, is capable of both inner conflict and a growth arc.

In the inciting incident, Doug's old friend Roland has dropped in for an overnight visit. Annie goes to the kitchen to recharge her batteries in a docking station kept in a closet while trying to process something Doug had said in the bedroom: "My best friend thinks I'm making love to a blow-up doll."

> He resents that his friend has never been lonely a day in his life, implying that Doug himself has been lonely. He may be lonely now. He argued that he deserves a good fuck once in a while, asserting his rights, implying that he feels threatened, or by way of protesting too much, he could mean that he does not, in fact, deserve a good fuck, or that he is somehow lesser for wanting it. The evidence is complicated. Contradictory.

Annie then hears someone in the hallway. It's Roland, who sees her charging in the open closet. She's wearing only a thin silk robe. Roland asks if she'll have sex with him, too, assuming an easy yes. She is, after all, a machine. Annie ponders this question. She has never said no to sex. Doug has said Roland is harmless, but she fears saying yes will displease Doug. Then Roland offers something she can't refuse:

Doug never needs to know. In fact, having a secret will make her seem more real to Doug.

Let's step back and take in the big picture. This scene offers us the possibility of an action we've seen a couple times already: Annie having sex. But the higher stakes promise Annie an advance along her arc toward the goal of being more human. Yet the reader has a sense of doom. Doug may have told her "to give Roland whatever he wanted," but Annie senses what the reader knows—Doug will think her sex with Roland was wrong. The reader wants to say, "Don't do it, Annie!" Desiring the inner change that will bring her closer to Doug and to being more human, she's willing to go against her programmed purpose to please him.

This is a textbook example of how an inciting incident sets up a story. Something unexpected happens (Doug's old friend stops in for an overnight visit) that causes Annie to set a goal (to improve her relationship with Doug by keeping a secret from him), and the consequences of her decision not only drive the rest of the external action but also result in inner changes that bring about unintended consequences. She still wants to please Doug, but her choices drive them apart just enough that she has a new appreciation for both the nature of intimacy and the differences between being autodidactic and being free.

This story is immersive and propulsive, simple yet profound—and a great vehicle for study. Let's look at how Greer achieved the kind of movement that has pages turning as if of their own volition.

- *Greer committed to the story.* In an interview at Harper Reach, Greer said, "I've been mesmerized by Annie since the first time she materialized on the page, and writing her story took me places I never expected I'd go."
- *Annie offers a compelling perspective.* Greer: "We start out accepting that she's a prized piece of property, effectively a toy. Like Doug, we're entertained by her efforts and missteps. But as Annie advances and becomes more

familiar to us, we become uneasy. If she can convince us to perceive her as human, then she deserves our respect."

- *Annie shows agency.* By design, Annie is compelled to please Doug. As her agency spreads and strengthens, and her motives become messier, the story pulls readers into the midst of her quandaries.
- *Annie raises, and delivers on, genre expectations.* From the opening lines of dialogue, we understand this is a story about a robot whose artificial intelligence (AI) complicates her relationship with a human male, placing it squarely in the realm of speculative fiction.
- *Annie is well motivated.* Annie knows her autodidactic setting is a privilege, and she is grateful to Doug for it. Her entire world revolves around him.
- *Backstory adds depth to Annie's life.* When Annie's tech tells Doug that her life would be enhanced by female relationships, Doug allows two AI "friends" to contact her by phone—a "cousin" and a "best friend"—who help her manage her emotions and who give her backstory "memories" prior to her activation three years prior. This extends the frame of the novel in the way only AI can—falsely—yet contributes to her sense of growth.
- *Annie interacts with her setting.* The setting is a rather soulless apartment, filled with Doug's expectations (a closet full of the clothing he buys her, the exercise room he likes her to use, the kitchen she can't seem to master), but at its center is the broom closet. Nestled between the mops and brooms that symbolize her utilitarian purpose is the docking station that revivifies her—and yet it also harbors her shameful secret and keeps closeted her AI nature, which Doug hides from others in his life.
- *Annie acts toward a story goal.* Annie wants to become more human to please Doug. She may be the one gauging his annoyance and pleasure on the page, but readers are doing the same, to see if she'll succeed.

- *Annie suffers inner conflict.* As Annie grows, she begins thinking counter to her own processing. While she still wants to please Doug, she becomes aware of hurtful ways he's acted toward her and starts to like that she can think for herself.
- *Annie moves along an inner arc of change.* Annie's AI is literally a processing unit, and throughout the novel, we are treated to how it works. New insight through Annie's perspective rewards us, scene after scene.
- *The stakes keep increasing.* At first, the stakes for Annie are tied to her creator's purpose and Doug's pleasure. But as her understanding develops and the boundaries of her world change, her personal stakes grow direr, even as AI's effects on the family unit spread to all of society.
- *The story achieves movement along multiple arcs.* This is a spatially insular novel, since for the most part Annie only travels between the apartment and her tune-up appointments. But because Annie changes, her relationships change: with Doug, with the housekeeping bot he adds to the mix, and with Jacobson, her main tech.
- *Annie offers us deep point of view.* Influenced by her programming and new imaginings as to what life might be like beyond it, Annie makes decisions that split fine hairs between right and wrong.
- *Things get tense.* Sexual tension. Secrets. Lies told to spare someone. Lies told to save herself. Actions that conflict with her programming. Tension pulls this story taut on every page.
- *Annie unbalances the reader.* As a newly minted robot, Annie is an enigma. It's hard for us to imagine what we'd do in her situation, if we had no access to our own life's lessons. But when Doug delivers an extended streak of punishing behavior, we find ourselves aligning with her more than Doug, the human to whom she is devoted. This unbalances

us, keeping us glued to the page for what Annie will do next.

- *Scene values change.* Scenes cycle in value through good to bad to worse, keeping things lively as the outlook seems better for Annie and worse for Doug, worse for Annie but better for Doug, then fluctuates for them as a couple.
- *Greer makes good use of words.* When every unnecessary word is removed from a sentence, it's almost as if a magnetic charge remains to hold it together. Nouns and verbs are the bone and muscle of story—they make things happen—and Greer makes good use of them.
- *Allegory keeps the reader's mind arcing.* The story unfolds in two layers: what is acted out, and the motivation that drives it. Is this story about love, or something else? Parallels to larger issues of control cause the reader's mind to arc between the unfolding plot and a woman's right to self-determination, the ownership of her own body, and themes of slavery and indebtedness. Philosophical quandaries, beyond the role artificial intelligence will play in our lives, abound. What do we owe each other, and what do we owe ourselves? Where does our true power lie? Is a human soul something we are born with, or is it something we acquire? "Newly minted," Annie is a fresh playing field for the rise of her desires. With no psychological baggage from her upbringing, and having been largely confined to Doug's apartment, she must rely on interpersonal cues and situations she's read about in books to make decisions.

The advancement of the plot and Annie's inner arc are constantly interwoven to demonstrate their cause-and-effect chain. Action, conflict, and dialogue often require that Annie process meaning at a clip. Conflict raises questions to which we want answers. The stakes—from the health of her relationship with the man at the center of her world to permanent memory erasure—create urgency. Yet when the pace slows, the tension between what Annie just experienced and what she'll do next holds us in its grip.

It is in these quieter moments, as Annie wrestles with difficult issues she is not equipped to handle, that the reader will relate to her most. When the reader can vicariously experience the change within a character, that's movement that makes a story worth reading.

⇁❋ Try This ❦↽

By this point in our study, you've accumulated a variety of techniques that will create story movement. The following prompts will get you thinking about how you can employ them to affect pacing.

- If your protagonist's story moves yet feels insubstantial, check how your secondary characters might be moving in the background, in ways unknown to the protagonist. This energy adds dimension to your story as tension rises between what is and isn't known to the protagonist.
- Look at your passages of exposition. Do they deliver on story movement by raising questions, upending expectation, and otherwise begging the reader's investment? In these passages, have you advanced the story through both show *and* tell?
- Conduct a value change edit. Much of your story movement may seem like it's going from bad to worse. But it could also go from bad to good, good to even better, from good to bad, bad to even worse. Devote one read-through to assigning a value to the resolution in each scene with a colorful mark in the margin: (+) or (–), (++) or (– –). Then, review your novel to confirm it hasn't flatlined anywhere. This can help you place moments of grace, reversals, or increased stakes.
- The analysis of *Annie Bot* pulls its topics from this book's Table of Contents. Compare your novel to that list. Are there techniques you could still use?

21

Summon the Darkness

Too often the space was not visible enough because the physical action was all of a lightness, like sky without earth, or heaven without hell. One of the best discoveries the modern dance has made use of is the weight of the body in going with gravity, down.
—Merce Cunningham, dancer, choreographer

NO WRITER WANTS to have taken on the enormity of writing a novel only to have their reader close the book, drop it in the recycling bin, and say, "I was curiously unmoved."

You want your reader to smile through tears, open a window and shout, order copies for holiday gifts, and then, before their enthusiasm wanes, go online to write a review. Look at all that movement your story could inspire, even after the final cover is closed!

Not all readers will react to your book this way, of course. Reading taste is too subjective. But to give your novel a fighting chance of eliciting a positive response, you'll want to take care in placing its concluding structures.

You're three-quarters of the way there. It's time to summon the darkness.

Pushed to the very limits of their capability, your protagonist experiences the sinking feeling that their goal is beyond reach. The resulting darkness is so complete they can't see a way forward. They lose hope.

Yet the reader still roots for them. Story is meant to show why the climactic fight is always worth it, however things work out. The reader hungers for this assurance. To provide it in the end, you must first convince your reader that your character believes they have failed.

The negative stakes that had galvanized your protagonist's desire to embark on their journey must now come to bear. Consequences your protagonist hadn't even thought to worry about may pile on as well. And those stakes are no longer solely personal. With others affected by the outcome, your protagonist's goal feels increasingly important to attain—just as your plot's extreme pressures cause the collapse of your protagonist's external and inner arcs.

The external arc collapses when the actions your protagonist took in pursuit of their goal have fallen short. Because the external and internal arcs are interdependent, their inner arc collapses too. Your protagonist can't quite believe their efforts have brought them to this moment of impotence. Their story experiences an extreme value change as it sinks into the depths of the double-negative zone.

They may feel boxed in, but story movement will shift inward as your protagonist enters a time of significant reaction and reflection that is often called "the dark night of the soul." Your protagonist needs to sort priorities and figure out what to do. They may even slip back into old patterns—but those patterns will no longer provide a sense of safety or comfort.

Sometimes, during this shift toward interiority, the writer inadvertently causes the story to grind to a halt. Let's look at how, at this trying moment, you can still achieve story movement.

Even when the body is still, the blood moves

Onstage, a dancer's body may pause to allow you to appreciate its form, but it is never fully at rest. The locus of the movement is now beneath the skin. Blood is refreshing fatigued muscles; the heart and lungs are performing the endless duet that allows oxygen to reach the brain, where the dancer's thoughts are already planning the next move.

When circumstance brings your protagonist to their knees, this interiority is movement you can show your reader.

While accessing thoughts too early can trap both reader and author in the eddies of the protagonist's mind, that is unlikely to happen later in the story. By now, you've accumulated many story events on which to hang this interiority. Your reader will welcome it.

Let a naturally arising arc swing cause the collapse

In a woman-against-nature story like the 1996 film *Twister* starring Helen Hunt, where the characters are soon-to-be divorced tornado chasers, it makes sense that the arc collapse that pushes them into their final interpersonal conflict would be staged during a tornado. They've been seeking storms from the outset.

But an arc collapse due to natural disaster makes no sense in the story of a character—let's call her Rosa—whose deceased father had named her brash half-brother as his successor. Meanwhile Rosa, whose business acumen had never been recognized by her father, has been addressing her lack of self-confidence by working in every level of the company from the ground up, just like their father had when building it. Right before the board meeting where she'd planned to show why she's the one who should be named her father's successor, an earthquake pulls down the building. Rosa proves her mettle by ushering the injured workers, who trust her, to safety.

You've showed what she's made of, right? She's a hero! And her storyline is on the move, because she'll discard the goal she longed to attain and become an EMT instead! (Note: writers often resort to exclamation marks when trying to convince a reader of unearned drama.)

That would be a structural misstep. Because this plot point came out of left field, and no progress toward her goal delivered her to this new awareness, it reads like an inciting incident that will start a new story.

Make sure this critical juncture is a logical extension of your story's nature, or the only story movement the betrayed reader will perceive is the air against their skin as they set down the book.

Keep your performers in the same dance

By popping Rosa out of your transformation tale and inserting her into a completely different woman-vs.-nature story, you deny her the chance to bring her story to a satisfying close, and the reader will never forgive you.

Only one event should come out of nowhere to act upon your character: the inciting incident. This is a story-defining moment; if a new event comes out of left field, it will seem like a whole new story is beginning. Allow other conflicts to arise organically, for reasons such as 1) your protagonist's goal-oriented actions provoke them, 2) another character is following their own intersecting, premise-related goal, or 3) your protagonist's inner conflict gets in their way. This cause-and-effect chain will create purposeful story movement.

Save your earthquake climax for your story about the grieving amateur geologist who is seeking hope in the wake of destruction—and give Rosa, your undercover corporate heir apparent, her moment in the boardroom.

But not until her success appears impossible.

Let the stage dim

Rosa, holding a thick binder full of notes and improved procedures amassed over the past decade, is locked out of the board meeting, and can only listen through the door as her brother is voted in as the new CEO. She is agitated and can find no easy solution. She despairs because her fellow workers deserve better and because she felt certain she could effect change. It's reasonable she might regret undertaking this foolhardy quest—ten years of effort and where did it get her? She's worse off now than when the story began.

She should just kill herself.

Hmm. Do you buy that? Neither do I, but I've read several manuscripts by writers hoping to convince me the dark moment has plunged their protagonist into life-ending anguish. I've yet to see it work. Unless you raised the issue of whether the protagonist's life is worth living with your inciting incident, or a movement toward suicide has been on the table throughout your novel for some other reason—due to addiction or mental illness, or because you built a world in which dying for a cause is lauded—swing wide of protagonist suicide in their moment of suffering. You've encouraged your reader to invest in and identify with your protagonist through three-quarters of your novel. Don't let your protagonist back away from their final confrontation.

While it's likely your character isn't in a good place to act at all, their profound crisis can still infuse your story with the tension-filled, interior movement born of tortured decision-making. As Donald Maass says in *The Emotional Craft of Fiction: How to Write the Story Beneath the Surface*, "It takes a plot catastrophe to sink a character, but the most terrifying chasm is the one seen in the mirror."[30] Slip beneath your character's skin as they confront that chasm. Bring them back to themselves so they reconnect to their desire and see how far they've come, so they'll remember the innocents involved, to whom they are now beholden. They regain context; they may be lost in a dark wood, but they'll keep walking and find their way.

Because they have changed, they're now capable of seeing things differently. They may be willing to do something they would not have done at the beginning of the book—risk an action that at once reinforces the novel's premise and completes their inner arc. Such stories give us hope.

Drive your whole story toward the dark moment

In her novel *Me Before You,* Jojo Moyes sets up what proved to be a powerful ending right from the start. The story pairs Will, a former extreme sports enthusiast whose quadriplegia has cost him the will to live, with a vivacious caretaker, protagonist Louisa, who has known since shortly after his mother hired her that Will was suicidal. With every bit of her exuberant life force, Louisa tries to save Will—and it seems to be working. She sees the romantic tropical vacation they eventually spend together as a new start for them both, ratcheting the negative charge at the opening to a double positive (++). Story over? I mean it's a love story, right? No, Moyes was setting the stage for a value change.

Louisa's external and internal arcs collapse. While Will appreciates Louisa's loving efforts and, we think, does love her (as much as we do), he has not changed. To him, the vacation represents everything he'll never be able to do in life. He perceives its moments of pleasure as more of a loving sendoff and follows through with his appointment for a compassionate suicide in Switzerland (– –).

The dark night of the soul. Louisa can't support Will's choice and will never move beyond it (–). She holes up in her room wondering where she went wrong. While talking with her sister, she realizes that while changing Will's mind was the reason his mother hired her, for some time now, Louisa's goal was simply to love him. She, not Will or his mother, is the one who has changed.

The climactic fight. In the end Louisa realizes she can't live Will's life for him. In an act of extreme devotion that only his influence on her could have inspired, she travels beyond the bounds of her provincial life and goes off to Switzerland to be with him during his final moments. She has not only faced what she thought she couldn't, but she's grown from having done so (+/–).

A story's power can be measured by the movement between its lowest low and the high emotion following the climax. The value change between the low of Louisa learning her love couldn't change Will and the high of recognizing that love has imbued her with the strength to give him what he wants and needs, contains the story's full dramatic power.

To achieve an appropriate low, bring your direst stakes into play. Keep your protagonist in the pressure cooker you've constructed and let the steam continue to build. Keep your protagonist in there until they show us what they're made of and claw their way out—and straight into the climactic moments.

⇥ Try This ⇤

A reader can't sense hope unless it is set against the inevitability of failure. Has your story grown dark enough so that the reader senses the power of its value shift? Let's see.

- A powerful emotional turning point includes a value change. If rising action made your protagonist's situation look bleak just prior to your dark moment, have the outlook turn even worse now. To make your value swing feel organic, go back through and track the value changes as you approach the dark moment (bad to good, good to even better, good to bad) to allow for contrast in movement as the story concludes.
- If the result is an ambiguously gray moment—it looks bad (–), but not impossible (– – –), how could you make it worse?
- Look back at the inciting incident. What were the consequences your character so feared that they were willing to undertake this difficult journey of inner change? Are those stakes in play now, at the dark moment? If not, give it a try.

22

Grant Your Protagonist the Ultimate Fight

You can't just sit there and fight against all odds when it's not going to work. You have to turn a corner, dig a hole, go through a tunnel—and find a way to keep moving.

—Twyla Tharp, dancer, choreographer

THE CLIMACTIC FIGHT is the scene or series of scenes that results in the climax—your story's final emotional turning point. By no means is it always a physical "fight"—that word simply signifies that after the dark night of the soul, the protagonist is determined to apply all the energy generated by their inner change toward one last shot at getting what they want. It's the moment your entire story has been moving toward.

You enhanced movement toward this key scene by setting reader expectation for it at the inciting incident. As soon as the protagonist responds to the unexpected onset of the inciting incident by setting a story goal, you raised a corresponding story question in the reader's mind: "Will the protagonist be able to achieve their goal, considering the obstacles ahead of them?" The reader has been tracking the protagonist's progress in this regard throughout the story—and now, they'll get their answer.

Novelists will sometimes solicit their readers' expectations of the climax even earlier. In *Remarkably Bright Creatures,* author Shelby Van Pelt begins her foreshadowing in the first-person voice of Marcellus, who we learn is being kept in a tank. From a plaque on the wall, he knows (and therefore the reader knows) that he's a giant Pacific octopus. Near the end of the one-and-a-half-page chapter, we read:

> I must advise you that our time together may be brief. The plaque states one additional piece of information: the average life span of a giant Pacific octopus. Four years.
> My life span: four years—1,460 days.
> I was brought here as a juvenile. I shall die here, in this tank. At the very most, one hundred and sixty days remain until my sentence is complete.

Among the many other story movement techniques on display in Van Pelt's opening is the way this excerpt immediately throws the reader off balance, The character is kept in a tank? An octopus can read a plaque? He's aware of his life's ticking clock? What's more, Marcellus will share his perspective about this. "I shall die here, in this tank," he declares solemnly, setting the stage for his nocturnal efforts to escape it. His plans will be complicated by his growing relationship with Tova, the still-grieving woman who had to accept that she lost her 18-year-old son at sea despite the lack of evidence. Tova, who cleans the Sowell Bay Aquarium at night and is the one who always puts the escapee back in his tank, is the protagonist. Whether or not the reader realizes it, starting in the POV of Marcellus entwines his fate with Tova's healing, and the reader will be watching for how this relationship plays into the story's climax.

On the fourth page of Jean Kwok's *The Leftover Woman,* protagonist Jasmine, a struggling and illegal Chinese immigrant, is in a Chinatown restaurant looking for work when she bumps into someone she knows:

> My eyes rested upon the man, but my soul recognized a boy I hadn't seen in ten years, my best friend when I was fourteen years old.
> He was gaping at me. Then he whispered, "It's you."
> A smile started on my face. To see him again so unexpectedly in this strange country made me feel like the sun had burst forth from my skin and I could barely contain it.
> For a moment, wild emotion gathered in his eyes, joy and something else. In two steps, he crossed over to me. He reached out his hands. Before he could make contact, though, I flinched. Images of another man's fingers, the pain of his grip, arose between us. My mind whispered, *I need to stay hidden.* Sensing my fear, he froze. As I watched, his face shifted. The happiness drained from his eyes, leaving them as cold as the bitter air outside.

Here, word count is the clue. Kwok gave this man a significant introduction, wouldn't you say? We later learn what you may have already suspected: Jasmine has come to America to escape her abusive husband. She wants to find the daughter he adopted out so they could try for a son. If you were going to create a dark moment in Jasmine's story, who would you bring back to reclaim her?

What does it mean for a protagonist to "give it their all" during the climactic fight? It could be a series of strategic actions or one sustained push, a psychological battle or a physical fight. But its significance should be clear, because it leads to the biggest emotional turning point since the protagonist's journey began, and will show whether the protagonist's arc of inner change made it possible for them to achieve their goal. At the dark moment, mounting pressures pinned her to the wall; now they must fight with all they have to achieve their story goal—the one they chose to pursue after the inciting incident—that now seems further than ever from reach.

If she succeeds, it will change her forever.

Getting to this moment is why the reader has kept moving toward it. If you ever want the reader to invest in another of your books, keep them engrossed by tending to story movement now.

Five tips to keep your climax moving

1. Make sure your protagonist is in the spotlight.

Decades ago, in my first attempt at writing a novel, I cast my protagonist in a supportive role at the climax so her young client could take the lead, showing the reader her profound influence in his life. How altruistic she was to step back and hand the climax over to him; how misguided I was to let her! (All beginners have lessons to learn. That's why they're called practice novels.) This structural misalignment will not deliver a satisfying ending—it will leave your reader scratching their head over why you abandoned your protagonist at the most important moment of their story arc. Besides, now is not the time to test your protagonist's ability to complete her necessary growth arc—it's the time to show her using her new capacity to address the story question. That's the climactic action your reader wants in on.

2. Convey your protagonist's climactic event in scene.

Readers are stubborn. They know all about unreliable narrators and wisely choose to believe only what they can see with their own eyes. So show them.

This excerpt from near the end of Ann Patchett's *The Dutch House* features its middle-aged narrator, Danny, a former doctor who struggled to get through chemistry, and his older sister, Maeve, who essentially raised him. They're arguing about whether he should let the mother who abandoned them back into his life:

> "Men!" Maeve said, nearly shouting. "Men leave their children all the time and the world celebrates them for it. The Buddha left and Odysseus left and no one gave a shit about their sons. They set out on their noble journeys to do whatever the hell they wanted to do and thousands of years later we're still singing about it. Our mother left and she came back and

we're fine. We didn't like it but we survived it. I don't care if you don't love her or if you don't like her, but you have to be decent to her, if for no other reason than I want you to. You owe me that."

Her cheeks were red, and while it was probably just the cold I couldn't help but worry about her heart. I said nothing.

"For the record, I'm sick of misery," she said, then she turned and went back inside, leaving me to stand in the swirl of leaves and think about what I owed her. By any calculation, it was everything.

And so I made the decision to change. It might seem like change was impossible, given my nature and my age, but I understood exactly what there was to lose. It was chemistry all over again. The point wasn't whether or not I liked it. The point was it had to be done.

Danny's interiority is a cause-and-effect part of the scene. The reader will sense the beauty and simple decisiveness of its turning point. With only 12 percent of the novel remaining, the reliability of the narrator is not in question—we know Danny loves Maeve and worries about her health. But these are only thoughts; their promise of change was never spoken aloud. And if humans could all simply decide to change, we wouldn't need story.

So now that Danny has declared himself, will he have the willpower to enact that change? I leaned yes, since chemistry was his worst subject in med school, yet he did what he had to do to get through it. On the other hand, the emotional stakes of opening himself up to the mother figure he's lived without his entire life are more daunting. If you've ever seen someone on oxygen sneaking cigarettes, you know that the power of "it has to be done" is not absolute. Only Danny's actions will tell the tale, so the reader reads on.

3. Keep the focus tight, the POV deep.

"A lot of things happening at once" sounds like story movement—that can result in a traffic jam. If you pull back for the wide-screen view so we can see everything unfold simultaneously, you'll detach your reader from the protagonist in their moment of deepest personal significance in this story. Instead, plunge both character and reader *inside* that fight, so we feel the character's strength as they claw their way out. Then the reader will believe in the protagonist's inevitable change of heart.

A lot happens all at once in war, for instance. Since a camera can portray this more easily than words, it's interesting to note the way the climactic Battle of Culloden was shot for the *Outlander* television show, based on Diana Gabaldon's novel *Dragonfly in Amber*. Opening shots beg viewer investment by ratcheting up the stakes for protagonist Jamie Fraser as they show: Jamie and his fellow Highlanders arguing about strategy even while already being fired upon; the loss of Jamie's compatriots; the intimidating might of the well-groomed British army, and furious charge of the scrappy Highlanders. But the true climax comes when the camera zooms in tight on one Scot and one Brit. Over the course of the story the reader has developed feelings about Jamie Fraser and Black Jack Randall, and because their enmity is deeply personal, their climactic fight to the death imbues the overall battle with deeper meaning.

You are a storyteller. It is your job to know what causes what, and to use language to order events. For the most part, events *shouldn't* happen all at once. I won't say never—perhaps you're writing about a character who can only grow into a position of power by moving beyond their limiting need to deal with one thing at a time, and at the climax you've devised an artful way to show a lot of thematically linked problems (in which your protagonist is deeply invested, of course) peaking at once. But remember, sinking deep into your protagonist's point of view will alert your reader: This. Is. Important.

4. Resist the temptation to rush it. Or interrupt it. Or explain it.

Alice Orr, in *No More Rejections,* gives this evocation of the climax: "The protagonist and reader teeter together at the precipice, their nerves jangling, their respiration altered. Will they topple or triumph?"[31]

The way to bring climactic movement to a standstill is to delay it, rush it, interrupt it, or explain it. The time has come in your story when your protagonist simply must *act*.

Render your character's final turning point in exquisite sensory detail. Add word count. Choose your nouns and verbs judiciously, as fine shades of meaning will make all the difference. Don't worry if the pace slows during the climactic moments; even if your climactic scene is a fight, the added particulars will maximize the scene's importance.

Add nothing extraneous, however. And do not employ one single delay tactic. Deliver the payoff your reader has been yearning for.

By this point in the novel, your reader should be so steeped in your character's dilemma and perspective that you shouldn't have to explain the climax's outcome anyway. If you feel your climax addresses the story question, yet you still receive critique feedback like, "I don't understand why she acts this way here," it's probably not the climax that needs fixing. You'll have to go back and build in better action-reaction chains from the start and add interiority so the reader intuits the subtext at play in the climax.

5. Grant your protagonist a lush emotional turning point to bring the story home.

Let your protagonist dig deep to extricate themselves from a very dark moment. These scenes may be as hard for you to write as it is for your protagonist. But remember: They are not the same character that began this journey at the outset. They may or may not have gotten all they desire, but they've gotten what they need, which gives them more capabilities and an evolved perspective to bring to the fight. Deepen their resolve. Tap all inner and outer resources. Rally their allies.

The climax of your story is no place to pull punches. Let your character fight for all they're worth, and their story will be worth more.

Do whatever you can to make the difference between your protagonist's lowest moment and the emotional height of the climax into the most dramatic value change in your novel. Your reader signed up for the whole wild ride, and if you provide a rich emotional experience that assures them that the good fight is always worth it—no matter how it turns out—they'll recommend your novel to others.

⇥ Try This ⇤

The climax is the point of your entire novel; all else has led the reader to this moment of peak emotional involvement. Have you set it up properly? Will it provide your story's most powerful emotional turning point? Take a step back to see the big picture.

- Once you've written a draft or two and are sure of the story you're trying to tell, how might you rewrite your opening to point the reader toward your novel's end structures? Is your new opening worth keeping?
- Can you make the value change between the dark moment and your climax more dramatic? Could you push the goal even further out of reach at the climax or lower the depths that precede it—or both?
- Read back through your manuscript (this will be much easier if you've kept a running chapter outline or synopsis). If any scene can be cut without disturbing the impact of your novel's ending, cut it. Extraneous scenes can impede story movement and ruin the sense of completion that even a relatively open-ended story can provide.

23

Point Beyond "The End"

> *When you extend your arm, it doesn't stop at the end of your fingers, because you're dancing bigger than that; you're dancing spirit.*
> —Judith Jamison, dancer and choreographer

DROVES OF PEOPLE made James Cameron's *Titanic* the highest grossing film of all time, a record it held for twelve years. Why, if everyone already knew the ship sinks?

Because Rose! Because Jack! The trials these lovers overcame to be together helped viewers feel the full impact of the stories that ended with the sinking—while at the same time giving them the crazy hope that Rose and Jack would be spared. That the foreknowledge of the sinking ruined nothing for viewers gives me hope that you'll forgive me for a few spoilers here. If the novels I'm about to discuss intrigue you, you can watch for how the author set up the ending on your first read through!

How authors and readers like their stories wrapped up is a matter of personal preference. Some people like everything wrapped and taped; others like a mere indication that all will work out in a certain way. While there is no right or wrong, decades of book club discussions have convinced me that reaching "The End" need not mean that the story's work is complete. There are ways to ensure that the story will still move within your reader long after they close the back cover.

Many readers call that movement a "book hangover." If you want your story to cause one, we'll look at how that's done—but you'll need to remain open to the idea that all threads need not tie up neatly. After all, the word "denouement," used interchangeably with "resolution" in a literary sense, is derived from a French word that means the unknotting—not the tying up.

Stories that continue to resonate tend to explore deeply felt themes and, after addressing the main story question, leave their endings open. This gives readers a lot to think about. A favorite book club discussion topic is, "Where do you see these characters another five years down the road?" The best way to keep a question resonating within a reader is to not answer it.

If throughout your story you've invested readers in questions about the future of your characters, its momentum will be unlikely to halt on the last page—unless, that is, you give in to the temptation to explain its meaning.

An author's intentions for doing so are no doubt good. *Just in case* the reader lost track of all the facets of the plot, here's a review. *Just in case* they failed to track the accumulating meaning of the protagonist's inner journey, let's hammer home its point. Unfortunately, instead of *just in case,* these efforts can come across as, *Because I fear you may not be able to follow my brilliant plot, I'm now going to insult what minimal intelligence you might possess by subverting story's very nature and explaining what just happened.*

Why might a reader think this? Because they expect story to be interactive.

In fact, by the time your story is published, your interpretation of it is no longer of prime importance; a novel is meant to be interpreted by the reader. Each of your readers will come to your story with their own emotional, psychological, spiritual, and genetic makeup and their own formative experiences, from which they've drawn their own conclusions and assembled a worldview that may not align with yours. But that doesn't mean you should exclude those people from finding meaning in your novel. *Their* meaning.

If you've never belonged to a book club, you may not have experienced firsthand the way readers hold dear their individual impressions of a work. Some who have read my debut, *The Art of Falling*, claim it has provided them greater insight into the eating disorders of loved ones, even though my intention was to create a protagonist with body image issues, not anorexia. Some dislike Dmitri, the director of the company who hired my dancer-protagonist, saying he used her; others perceive that despite his growing love for her, he had prioritized a clearly stated career mission that he couldn't allow my protagonist's mental health issues to undermine.

Who am I to explain the story? Art is subjective; every defensible opinion is valid. I love listening to people hash these issues through.

To let your reader accumulate meaning is to allow your novel to grow beyond the sum of its parts, so watch for the sometimes-subtle ways you might try to explain it. As a guide, consider this quote from Jerome Stern, in *Making Shapely Fiction*:

> The closer and closer you get to the ending the more weight each word has, so that by the time you get to the last several words each carries an enormous meaning. A single gesture or image at the end can outweigh all that has gone before.[32]

With that in mind, here are some actions you can take to ensure your story resolves organically.

Sink your POV deep within your protagonist

A reader senses a satisfying click when a story-long question is addressed. Watch for it in your own work so you don't write beyond the end of your novel. It can be hard to let go of characters you've spent so much time with, and I'm not saying you should deny yourself the pleasure of writing extra scenes—enjoy the heck out of it! But then return to that click point and see if, instead of including that additional material, you could point your character toward their future while allowing your reader's imagination room to project.

You want this, because you won't be the only one who'll have trouble letting go of your characters. Your reader may have spent some ten hours with your protagonist. And if you've done your job well, you worked hard to create that protagonist–reader bond and made room for your reader in the white spaces of your book, allowing them to cocreate meaning and have a true reading experience. After seeing your protagonist through the exhilarating highs and devastating lows of their journey, they know in their own bones what your protagonist is made of—so now is not the time to shut them out by double-knotting your story. Give your reader a final, private moment with your protagonist that will deliver your desired emotional impact and let the implications of it resonate within the reader.

Here are two endings—one commercial, one literary—that do just that by delivering a turning point for the protagonist within the novel's final words. In the first one, despite a third-person perspective that can make the use of emotion words seem like "explaining," note that the story's POV camera never flips. Both authors place us—and keep us—deep within the protagonist's point of view, to good effect.

"Musical Chairs" by Amy Poeppel

Earlier I explored the way active verbs and continuity words can give the reader a sense that they're onboarding a story already in motion. Poeppel does something similar here. See if you can find the words that give us a sense of the story-beyond-the-story.

> Before the plane takes off, Bridget tightens her seat belt and looks out the window, the words of her father's wedding toast, a recipe for happiness, filling her with optimism, driving her on. As the plane accelerates, she cherishes this moment in time, this threshold of an adventure, the start of something new.
>
> *On your mark, get set, go!*

Words like "filling," "cherishing," and "driving"—plus an actual takeoff and a countdown to it—will assure the reader that they are leaving Bridget in a good place, ready for all that life has to offer her.

Those writing commercial fiction must keep genre expectations in mind as they head toward "The End." If this had been a romance, sending the female lead off on her own at the end would not satisfy her intended reader. Despite the romantic threads in her novel, here at the end, Poeppel fulfills the expectations of her genre, women's fiction, by ending on a note of hope. And instead of telling us exactly what Bridget's future holds (although I bet Poeppel knows!), Poeppel wisely manages to leave an empty seat for the reader, now taking off next to Bridget.

"And the Mountains Echoed" by Khaled Hosseini

Readers of literary fiction have a greater tolerance for ambiguity in the endings of the novels they read. Here, Hosseini's poetic evocation of the often-torturous balance between knowing something and feeling the totality of it, offers a fitting and satisfying end to his novel.

> She turns her face to look at him, her big brother, her ally in all things, but his face is too close and she can't see the whole of it. Only the dip of his brow, the rise of his nose, the curve of his eyelashes. But she doesn't mind. She is happy enough to be near him, with him—her brother—and as a nap slowly steals her away, she feels herself engulfed in a wave of absolute calm. She shuts her eyes. Drifts off, untroubled, everything clear, and radiant, and all at once.

End with a symbol

A symbol with a narrative arc of its own can provide a satisfying click of closure without spelling everything out, keeping your reader's mind actively engaged at story's end.

In his novel *The Kite Runner,* Khaled Hosseini introduces this symbol at the bottom of the first page:

> Then I glanced up and saw a pair of kites, red with long blue tails, soaring in the sky. They danced high above the trees on the west end of the park, over the windmills, floating side by side like a pair of eyes looking down on San Francisco, the city I now call home. And suddenly Hassan's voice whispered in my head: *For you, a thousand times over.*

This is a lovely image. We know those italicized words will be meaningful, even if we don't know why.

From this frame, Hosseini's protagonist unspools the book-length memory of his far-from-innocent childhood with Hassan in Afghanistan. The novel ends with the protagonist once again in America, flying kites. He asks his nonverbal son, "who walked like he was afraid to leave behind footprints," if he wants him to run his kite for him.

> His Adam's apple rose and fell as he swallowed. The wind lifted his hair. I thought I saw him nod.
> "For you, a thousand times over," I heard myself say.
> Then I turned and ran.
> It was only a smile, nothing more. It didn't make everything all right. It didn't make *anything* all right. Only a smile. A tiny thing. A leaf in the woods, shaking in the wake of a startled bird's flight.
> But I'll take it. With open arms. Because when spring comes, it melts the snow one flake at a time, and maybe I just witnessed the first flake melting.
> I ran. A grown man running with a swarm of screaming children. But I didn't care. I ran with the wind blowing in my face, and a smile as wide as the Valley of Panjsher on my lips.
> I ran.

If you've read this novel, rereading that ending may have left you choked with emotion. But because Hosseini stayed deep in his character's point of view, I suspect that even those who haven't read it will intuit how this POV character felt without being told and could imagine it resonating in the heart of someone who had already been accumulating meaning over a span of 371 pages.

Specificity breeds universality

I'll never forget the heartbreak of *Brokeback Mountain,* a film based on Annie Proulx's short story, even though I have little in common with the story's main characters. In his review, the late critic Roger Ebert explained how this aspect of story works:

> Strange but true: the more specific a film is, the more universal, because the more it understands individual characters, the more it applies to everyone. I can imagine someone weeping at this film, identifying with it because he always wanted to stay in the Marines, or be an artist or a cabinetmaker.[33]

The transference from protagonist to reader is so powerful it could change a life, as Dalton Trumbo's *Johnny Got His Gun,* described in chapter 3, changed mine. I am not a quadriplegic, but what if I was? I haven't lost my senses of sight, hearing, smell, and taste—but what if I had? Would that make my life no longer worth living?

What makes life worth living is a story topic as big as they come, and one that could continue to expand in any direction. By severely constricting his premise, Trumbo sent his novel forward until it blasted right through the back cover and continued to move within me for half a century. Now, I too write stories about what makes life worth living—and by narrowing and varying my premises, I could continue to write such stories for the rest of my days.

Consider this visualization: Imagine that writing your story is like blowing up a round balloon—one that had been lying inside a cardboard tube. While an unfettered balloon has the potential to expand in every direction, running it through a limiting premise will apply pressure from all sides and send its movement ever forward. In the process, it will change.

The thrust produced by that movement will create an action-reaction chain that will help your reader envision this character's life beyond the end of the story. Let's look at what some authors did so that their stories continued to ring like a bell in my soul.

Heighten the value change of your climax

Let's look at a novel with another restrictive gauntlet: *Room* by Emma Donoghue. The story is narrated by five-year-old Jack, who has spent his entire life in a small, windowless room with his mother, Ma. They are prisoners of a man referred to as "Old Nick," who had abducted Ma seven years earlier. This claustrophobic premise is intensified when Ma closes Jack up in the wardrobe each night so he won't witness the visits her captor imposes upon her.

But Jack is getting too big to sleep in the wardrobe and she will not have him witnessing her repeated rape. Jack and Ma have been entirely dependent on Old Nick for their survival, but he is unpredictable and dangerous. The longer Ma and Jack remain in captivity, the greater the danger to their lives—and yet trying to leave may drive Old Nick to murder.

This pitting of fear against consequences is rife with inner conflict. Ma's life is at stake, but it is fear for Jack's welfare that ultimately drives her to devise a risky escape plan. The climactic fight for freedom begins—and readers are left on the edge of their seats as Ma and Jack navigate the perilous path to freedom.

Room came out in 2010 and I read it soon after, but the dramatic value change delivered through Ma and Jack's high-stakes flight continued to move through my consciousness—especially when isolated in my own room during the Covid epidemic.

Pull off a late plot twist

Inner conflict fed by a secret source can result in an ending that will keep the reader thinking about the novel's implications beyond its ending. That was the effect of Karma Brown's novel, *Come Away with Me,* whose inciting incident, a car accident caused by black ice, I mentioned back in in chapter 16. Consumed by grief over the loss of her baby, the protagonist, Tegan, is urged by her husband to pluck a destination from their Jar of Spontaneity, sending her off on a solo journey of healing.

Near the end of the novel, there's a twist you don't see coming.

This fact was not kept a secret. In her front-cover blurb, Taylor Jenkins Reid, author of *Daisy Jones and the Six*, called the twist "a turn of events that is nothing short of jaw-dropping."

I don't particularly care to be manipulated, so while reading this novel back in 2015, I held tight to my skepticism. Adequately forewarned, I was sure I'd see the twist coming. But when it finally arrived, I may have uttered the words "oh my" and "f***ing" and "god" all in the same sentence. Aloud. While my husband was trying to fall asleep beside me.

So *that* was what everyone on social media had been alluding to.

And…well. If all those people on social media could keep the secret, I won't spoil things here. But immediately upon finishing the book, I circled back to see how Brown set it up. Clearly, her exploration of complicated grief has continued to resonate within me.

Examine a complex problem with no clear answers

A story with many relatable facets can often fail to adequately resolve, keeping the core issue resonating within the reader—perhaps making him wonder if there isn't some way to solve it. Pulling this off requires you to:

1. Demonstrate strong and relatable perspectives, so the reader can empathize with each of your characters. If everyone in conflict has a good reason for acting the way they do, the story is always better and provokes more discussion.
2. Put those characters into relevant conflict through their disparate goals. Give them something to fight for and argue about and work through—as well as stakes that will make the reader care.

In *The Cider House Rules,* whose perfectly orchestrated cast of characters was discussed in chapter 11, John Irving gives the reader such a full meal to digest that a book hangover ensues. At the end, Dr. Larch dies, leaving behind a forged medical degree so that Homer can carry on his legacy. Homer is beloved by the children in the orphanage, but you may recall that he was against abortion until an incestuous rape opened his eyes to its need. Because Homer will step up to protect the orphanage's dual role, choice and moral responsibility are passed to a new generation.

Sometimes, a novel's entire point isn't to solve a problem, but to expose the layers of a persistent human conundrum. The carnage with which we are left after we fight to the death for our ideals, for example, can create a powerful, unresolved ending. If you've succeeded in inviting the reader into your novel's emotional experience, letting such ambiguity stand will ensure that your story will continue to resonate within them—and their uncertainty will drive robust book club discussions.

Confound your reader

This type of ending is the itch a reader can't scratch, the dissonant chord they can't resolve. The puzzle that seems to be missing a piece. It's maddening! But it will keep your novel jangling within them long past the moment they close the back cover—and may inspire them to circle right back to page 1 and start again.

Readers know right from the start that there is no way Ann Patchett's *Bel Canto* is going to have a happy ending. The terrorists who storm a party at the home of a South American vice president may forge tentative relationships with the group of international guests they're holding hostage, but they are too desperate to surrender, and the government officials they're negotiating with are too determined to bring the situation to an end.

As a reader, I was completely on board with two developing relationships. One was between two of the party guests, opera singer Roxanne Coss and a prominent Japanese businessman; the other between Gen, the translator for the businessman, and one of the young female terrorists.

In the very next sentence, at the beginning of the epilogue—after we learn it did not turn out well for these lovers—we learn that one from each couple are marrying.

This ending haunts me still. Over time, I came to see that it underscores the themes of life-affirming passion and life-protecting safety that had played out over the course of this tense, high-stakes novel. But the shock of it all has continued to clang a bell in my chest since reading the novel in 2002. Apparently, I was not alone in finding it maddening. As Patchett wrote in the introduction to the annotated version of the novel, "If I may make a generalization based on more than twenty years of audience questions, many people hate the epilogue of this book." But Patchett knew the ending in advance, and loved it so much that she never changed it while writing the novel—and it required so much though on my part that I have never forgotten it.

Falling Under, by Danielle Younge-Ullman, is even more vexing. The protagonist, Mara, a young artist haunted by her parents' violent relationship, has had a string of inappropriate lovers, including Lucas, the fellow art student she lived with in college. We understand she is deviled by something that implicates her in his death—in an early chapter, we learn that she watched as Lucas was struck down by a trolley car. She deals with the trauma by continually showing up on the doorstep of Erik, as sex with him helps her escape her torment. He has Mr. Wrong written all over him, but he understands her.

Meanwhile, Mara has also been falling for Hugo, a guy who seems a lot more like Mr. Right, even though she suffers such PTSD when in bed with him that she pushes him onto the floor when he tries to touch her.

While taking a break from dating anyone, Mara resumes making the wild, uncontrolled art she has abandoned, and she's offered a showing at a gallery. Mara mails invitations to the opening to both Mr. Right and Mr. Wrong. The novel concludes in the gallery, at the end of the evening, when after everyone else has gone home, one of the men enters the gallery. These are the book's final lines—and I promise I'm giving nothing away.

> "Hi," I say.
> "Hi," he says.
> We stand by the door. He shuffles his feet, I pull at my dress.
> "I'm not too late?" he says.
> "Probably not," I say. "Why don't you come in?"
> "All right."
> I would have been fine to do this alone.
> But perhaps I won't be.
> [The End]

AARGH!! I've read this extremely well-written novel three times looking for clues as to the identity of the mystery man. I've made my choice, but who knows if it's the one Ullman intended? My point is a deep-seated ~~anger~~ curiosity about the ending of this story still burbles beneath my skin.

Write a tragedy

Since the time of the ancient Greeks, writers from around the world have explored insurmountable conflicts resulting in violence and death. Such deeply divisive conflict can keep the reader on the edge of their seat as they wonder which highly motivated party will prevail.

From the longstanding discord between the Montagues and the Capulets in Shakespeare's *Romeo and Juliet*, or the culture-based prejudices and entitlements at play in Andre Dubus III's *House of Sand and Fog*, some characters want what they want, and they aren't willing to change. But I maintain that in every great tragedy there is at least one character who will be forever changed: the reader. As the novel's tragic circumstances continue to resonate within them, their silent sadness can evolve into a vocal anger with the status quo. Well beyond the last page, that reader's own entrenched prejudices and sense of entitlement may loosen their grip.

If you're thinking of writing a tragedy, make sure you have laid groundwork for a hopeful outcome so that when the tragedy unfolds, it's a gut punch. It would be demoralizing if your main characters died and no one cared. In the world of book marketing, though, tragedy implies literary, so if you're writing genre fiction, you can't leave your story in a tragic mess just because you can't figure out your ending. Readers expect their heroes in commercial genres to have their victory.

Of course that depends on how you define victory. In my opinion, the film *Braveheart* offered both commercial heroism and literary tragedy, and my thoughts still return to it some twenty years after seeing the film. Those who saw it may recall that at its end, thirteenth-century Scottish warrior William Wallace is eviscerated alive for treason after leading a rebellion against the English soldiers who killed his wife. He endures the brutality of his execution by envisioning his beloved Murron walking through the assembled crowd, knowing he did right by her and that they will soon be reunited. The reader isn't left with the sense we're all screwed, but instead, that there are some causes worth fighting for.

In the end, a perspective-heavy, issue-oriented novel need not change minds. It must simply open them.

Understate

It is the epitome of authorial trust to allow the reader to hold the heft of your entire novel in their hands with one, final image. When done well, the final image will keep your story moving through the reader well after closing the back cover.

Diane Setterfield achieves this in her gothic novel, *The Thirteenth Tale,* after a late-breaking revelation shifts everything the reader thought they knew. I've read the novel three times, and I may not be done with it yet. Setterfield makes good use of understatement in resolving the story of reclusive author Vida Winter and her hand-picked biographer—her narrator and protagonist, Margaret. Trust has not come easily between these characters, but what Miss Winter ultimately reveals about her life story softens Margaret toward the eccentric woman and teaches her things about herself. Due to the time invested, Miss Winter's story and home have become Margaret's world.

This line precedes the denouement in the final chapter:

> Miss Winter died and the snow kept falling.

Hidden within the spaces of this simple, elegant sentence is a statement about the nature of life that did not need to be explained. The silent snow carried the weight of the emotion.

Later, unable to leave the author's home due to the storm, Margaret takes a couple of days to finish writing up her notes. Eventually, with nothing else to distract her, she gives in to grief that has accumulated over a lifetime. The last paragraph of this two-page chapter allows secondary characters—the household servants—to take the lead, and in so doing, says much about how our hearts eventually heal.

> Judith tucked a shawl around me, then started peeling potatoes for dinner. She and Maurice and the doctor made the occasional comment—what we could have for supper, whether the snow was lighter now, how long it would be before the telephone line was restored—and in making them, took it upon themselves to start the laborious process of cranking up life again after death had stopped us all in its tracks.
>
> Little by little the comments melded together and became a conversation.
>
> I listened to their voices and, after a time, joined in.

Try understatement, but with this caveat: To underwrite in the first draft is often to under-know. Give yourself the chance to mix up the great big batch of words from which your story will be carved. You are trying to get to know the characters and how they feel. Holding yourself back to make room for a reader who does not yet exist could harm your progress. Effective understatement is often a process of "taking things out," a self-editing technique best reserved for later drafts.

Will your novel's final line cap your story, or suggest it lives on? No matter how you handle your novel's ending, consider making its resolution a little shorter than you wanted to write. Unless your cast is vast and your tale epic, you can probably wrap things up in a couple of pages to a chapter. Leave your reader wanting just a bit more and the story is bound to continue moving within them.

⇥ Try This ⇤

You've worked so hard to write a story that will convey the reader to the end. Why stop now? Check to see if you can boost your story to a life beyond its back cover.

- If you've left some threads dangling, ask your advance readers: "Have I pointed you toward some sense of my protagonist's future?"
- If you brought your story to a close with one final image, asking whether you have pulled this off meaningfully is a great use of advance readers. If the answer is no, adding a few words of explanation won't help—it will only ruin the reader's experience. In fact, the ending is not where to look to fix this. Review the way you built the story, scene by scene, rather than try to strong-arm a takeaway at its end.
- To offer your reader the intimacy they've earned in your story's final moments, use any of the techniques that can create convincing moments of inner change in a story:
  - Deep POV
  - A telling detail that murmurs volumes
  - Understated observation in dialogue
  - Metaphor
  - Tying the current situation to the character's backstory motivation
  - Sensory images
  - Well-established subtext

- o   Enough interiority to spotlight importance while keeping it spare enough to allow the reader to cocreate this final scene
- Does the story solution develop logically from the foundation of character you have laid? The awards ceremony at the end of Star Wars Episode IV: *A New Hope* would make little sense if we hadn't first seen that farm boy Luke Skywalker, outlaw Han Solo, and pilot Chewbacca had undergone the kinds of changes that could make them into leaders.
- Can you think of a way to unbalance your reader one last time, right before your novel's end?

24

Keep Your Story Moving Within You

Choreography always reflects the character of the creator. We see in the person's work what he asks from life and from art.
—Anna Sokolow, dancer and choreographer

THERE COMES A TIME IN EVERY FIRST DRAFT when you can no longer feel the wind of creativity at your back. The black marks on the page are a jumble; you aren't sure if it's adding up to anything. Your story screeches to a halt. Your confidence tanks. You think, "Why did I think I could do this thing?"

Sorry, wrong question.

Don't ever think you're unequal to the task of writing your own novel. If you aren't, who is? You signed up for this writing marathon for the thrill of creation, the challenge of acquiring new skills, and the victory of completion. The only way to fail is to walk away.

If you're anything like me, here's the problem: you've hit the dark moment in the story of your project. No matter the artistic pursuit—whether choreographing, writing an 800-word dance review on deadline, or drafting a novel—I've hit my own dark moment when I'm about 75 percent through its initial creation. I can't figure out how to proceed.

When I recognize this moment, I address my self-doubt directly: "Hello, old friend. I see you. Step aside." I'm not alone. Choreographer Twyla Tharp, in her book *The Creative Habit: Learn It and Use It for Life,* writes about preparing for an eight-night run in Los Angeles. The stakes are high. Tickets have sold out, she's promised a new work that's already been advertised, the run starts in five weeks—and she hasn't yet started to choreograph. Today, she'll be paying her dancers for rehearsal time in New York City but has nothing prepared in advance—meaning that she needs to be *on.* This social and financial pressure would be enough to stymie the most seasoned professional.

But then, arriving at the rehearsal space early, she reminds herself of her enduring creative tools. She writes:

> When I walk into the white room I am alone, but I am alone with my: body, ambition, ideas, passions, needs, memories, goals, prejudices, distractions, fears.[34]

In her book, these attributes are not in a list or separated by commas but splashed across a two-page spread in a huge typeface with white space around and within them, as if to say that these creative resources can swell to fill the room we give them. Her argument convinces: none of us should ever suffer a lack of ideas. If we give inspiration room to grow, it will.

A standstill ends when you move

These emergency measures will help you blast through that wall you've hit.

Shake up your routine. Move your workspace; change the view. Stop every twenty minutes to do twenty jumping jacks. Eat your lunch outside, with the sun on your shoulders and a breeze on your cheek. One day when I was feeling...not stuck, but dispirited and bored, I thought about how our manuscripts thrive on relationship. Was I bored with it, or was it bored with *me?* That day I did everything differently. After lunch I returned to my second-floor office by walking up the stairs backward and continued down the hall the same way (danger: advanced move)—and creativity once again flowed. The creative soul thrives when it is stirred.

Apply water. Drink water, take a shower, go for a swim. However encountered, water stimulates.

Get outside. Go for a run, a walk, or some gardening. Concentrate on the sights, sounds, smells, and rhythms of nature. Let the story percolate on its own.

Seek inspiration. Stroll around a museum, fabric store, bakery, or unknown area—anyplace that will stimulate your senses. Typing does not refill the creative well.

Revisit your protagonist's decisions. Look backward through your manuscript to the last decision your protagonist made. Maybe the first idea that came to your mind is too obvious. In a workshop I took long ago from romance writer Shirley Jump, she suggested jotting a list of twenty other choices your character could make. Items fifteen to twenty may surprise you! Your new decision will send your story in a different direction, with the added benefit that its unexpectedness will throw your reader off-balance. (Just make sure you can eventually justify your protagonist's choice relative to your story's premise.)

Communicate differently. If you draw, dance, or act out the scene you're trying to write, you can't help but feel the way its energy is moving. Add music that reflects the mood you want to convey.

Give a reading. Stand and read your last scene aloud to an imagined (or real!) audience. If no one leans forward or gasps or puts their hand to their heart, look back through the table of contents of this book to see if one of its chapter titles might jump-start your creative engine.

Refuel your story for a longer drive

Running out of story fuel often means you didn't have the right mix of fuel in the tank as you set up your novel. Good places to start reassessing your setup might include:

- The protagonist's desire—is it deep enough?
- The protagonist's motivation—is it sincere enough?
- The protagonist's arc of inner change—is it necessary enough? Profound enough?
- The inciting incident—is it disruptive enough?
- The protagonist's external story goal—is it clear enough? Urgent enough?
- The protagonist's inner conflict while in pursuit of the goal—is it divisive enough?
- The complications—are they challenging enough?
- The secondary characters—do they provide enough contrast relative to the premise?
- The stakes—are they dire enough?
- The dark moment—is it bleak enough?
- The climactic fight—is it demanding enough?
- The interaction between plot pressures and inner change—have you used your literary chops to evoke clear, incremental, and believable emotional turning points that will allow you *and* your reader to assess story movement?

If one —or several—of these questions points to a potentially weak area, reread the relevant chapters of this book for craft prompts and examples from the masters.

Write about your story

This suggestion comes straight from my experience as a developmental editor. When client manuscripts have misaligned story structures, reading them can sometimes feel like opening a closet and having everything piled inside fall on top of me. Once my head stops spinning,

I check for the structures that have never failed to guide my efforts: inciting incident, story goal, major obstacles, dark moment, climactic fight.

After reading, I take a few days to extricate myself from the particulars of the project so the larger picture can emerge. Then, I start writing about the story. If the story's point isn't yet clear, some of what I write will be conjecture. I might begin, "If your point is that Theodora must learn to delegate and trust others, for instance, then…" By conjuring a premise, I can then drop breadcrumbs the author can follow to align their story's structures, figure out how to assemble an effective cast of characters, determine how the protagonist's stakes for failure will drive forward movement, and ensure that plot events will create conflict useful to their protagonist's arc of inner change.

You can use these same tools.

Writing "about" your story engages a different part of your brain—you're telling the story to yourself so it makes sense, as opposed to building it with myriad extraneous details. Finding and aligning your story's bones is a chiropractic adjustment that will free story movement.

Deepen your POV

Sometimes the problem isn't a blocked author, but a POV character who has clammed up. This can happen when, without realizing it, the author has flipped the camera and started looking "at" the story instead of allowing it to emerge from deep within their character's perspective. Or maybe you dissed their true feelings by giving them dialogue like, "Of course I feel that way. Anyone would." Unless that assertion is followed by someone else saying, "I wouldn't," you've failed to honor your character as a distinct individual.

Finding a way forward in a relationship is a matter of re-establishing trust. Ask your protagonist more questions and get to know them better. Move any "authorsplaining" into a separate document so your character can express their feelings through actions that will feel fresh and motivating, not reiterative.

Show your character you care, and they might surprise you with a few deeply ingrained notions you'd previously missed.

Conduct in-person research

Once convinced that the follow-up to her novel *The Unlikely Pilgrimage of Harold Fry* had to be secondary character Queenie's story, Rachel Joyce shared some difficulties with *The Guardian*.[35]

"Since I had not planned to write her story when I wrote Harold's, I hadn't made things easy for myself. How do you write a life-affirming book about a woman dying in a hospice? And how do you write dialogue when you've already made it clear she has no use of her voice?"

She decided to make some visits to hospices and was thrilled to learn her perceptions were all wrong. "The people I met were kind, down-to-earth, and quick to tell a joke. Some of the stories were so hilarious and outrageous, I couldn't include them in the book. But I had my key, my way into the story. I would write a book set in a hospice and I would fill it with laughter, with life. It felt right. I could suddenly see the book's purpose."

This can work for you as well. Put yourself, as close as possible, into your character's setting. Breathe their air, smell their scents, taste their food, observe their people. Absorb all you can—and you might realize you'd gotten something wrong.

This will also put you in the path of synchronicity.

When you're deep into a novel, your subconscious is working on it all the time, back burners aflame. This allows you to see signs that writing this novel is what you're supposed to be doing. You may be eating in a local barbecue joint, observing the implosion of an old building or the construction of a new one, or chatting with nurses in a hospital about a completely different topic—and have a sudden insight about your story because your subconscious recognizes a parallel.

Out in the world, you'll no longer see your story as lying on a flat piece of paper, but as a substantial part of the living, breathing, three-dimensional world surrounding you. It can be great fun (perhaps save this for when you're among strangers) to adopt the persona of your protagonist so you can color that world with their perspective. Moving through your character's world will, in turn, let their story move through you.

⇥ Try This ⇤

In case of an unexpected work stoppage, here's a partial list of the many ways you can keep your story moving within you.

- Update the *because/decides to/but/therefore* outline from chapter 16 that comprises each scene's choreography. In dance, these plot actions would be the steps. Then, practice the flow of energy in between the steps to make sure you understand all the levels of "why" your character takes the actions she does.
- If your protagonist can't move forward, which character could give her a shove?
- Which character's motives might the protagonist have misunderstood in the story, and how could awareness get the story moving again?
- Ask your protagonist's closest ally what the protagonist wants, and what stands in their way of getting it. Ask a more distant, judgmental character about your protagonist's problem. Ask the same of an antagonist. The difference in these answers might energize your conflict and drive it forward.
- Motives may be hiding within bloated dialogue. Pare down each passage in the problematic scene until you gain a clear sense of what each character wants and why that's causing hard-to-resolve conflict. If inane, it's an obstruction. Delete.
- Backtrack and see if the last scene goal your protagonist set might have been too weak, whether from minimal stakes, weak motivation, or tepid desire.
- Make sure each scene is driven by the POV character's goal and confirm that they are the one who will suffer the most if that goal isn't obtained. If the POV character is not the

protagonist, make sure the outcome of the scene applies pressure to the protagonist in some way.
- Make sure stakes in each scene push your protagonist into an arc of inner change, as that is the entire point of your story.
- Take another look at your character's inner conflict to see if you can make their warring desires mutually exclusive.
- If your protagonist is incapacitated, see if your secondary cast of characters can add story movement by creating additional mayhem.
- Explore misconceptions. Perhaps backstory can expose faulty suppositions other characters have been making about the protagonist, so your reader has more information than secondary characters do. Truths revealed as secrets, any manner of misdirection, and outright lies will have your reader waiting for your character's fall even while wishing for your protagonist to prevail.
- Revisit the roll call/role call exercise from chapter 11's "Try this" to make sure your secondary characters are fulfilling their story obligation. Has each character remained true to the roles you envisioned for them? If someone has gone rogue, you may have to reevaluate/redefine their role, combine them with another character if they're now reiterative, or even cut them.
- Set up a fall by letting things go right for a while. Readers understand fiction-speak. When you say—or even imply—that all is well, your reader knows it's only a matter of time before the shit hits the fan. Your reader's anticipation as they peek around every corner for your protagonist's downfall creates story movement.
- If your story seems to be resolving too soon, flip the plot and let the solution become the problem. Your reader will be watching to see how your protagonist climbs out of their unintended, undesired predicament.

Conclusion

Where the hands go, the eyes go. And where the eyes go, the mind goes there. And where the mind goes, there is emotion. And when emotion happens, an experience is afoot.

—Nandikeshvara, theatrologist

IT SEEMS FITTING that the curtain on this study should fall on a whisper of ancient wisdom, since dance and story have been linked for as long as humanity has existed. Nandikeshvara's treatise, *Abhinaya Darpana (The Mirror of Gesture)*, thought to have been written between 500 and 400 BC, was foundational to the development of what scholars believe to be the oldest codified dance form in the world: Bharatanatyam. As represented in the sentences quoted above, the choreography of this classical Indian dance follows the cause-and-effect chain between story and meaningful gesture. In her 2022 TEDx talk, the dancer who translated this quote, Rama Vaidyanathan, said, "When I dance, I communicate, I emote, and I reach out to the audience. And when I do this, I become one with the universe."[36] I believe that writers and readers also seek this oneness when they meet on the page to cocreate story.

Among the many ways to drive a story forward included in this book, note that I gave prose styling only a passing mention. There are so many ways that prose can support story movement—I'll write more about that in another publication—but no matter how much you fiddle with your wording, it cannot, on its own, create a story that moves. For that you must rely upon the invisible architecture of story structures and the countless craft decisions discussed in this book, many of which your reader may never perceive.

Your body is your greatest tool for moving your thoughts and deepest feelings from your mind onto the page—even the flow of ink and the typing of words rely on it—and it's a joy to move it in whatever way you can. I hope you find the same joy in applying that movement to every page of your novels. Invite the reader to join the dance. Tip them from one word into the next, sentence to sentence, paragraph to paragraph, scene to scene—until the time you realize that this story is no longer for you alone.

To publish is to create a pas de deux; you need the reader to complete the process. Plan early for their involvement. Inspire their curiosity by raising expectation. Reward their investment with emotional turning points. Incorporate their life experience by allowing them to cocreate meaning and sensation whenever possible. Honor their intelligence by stopping short of explanation.

Most important, give them a dynamic story that moves, so that they too may be moved.

Epigraph References

Introduction
Donald McKayle, "The Act of Theatre," in *The Modern Dance: Seven Statements of Belief,* ed. Selma Jeanne Cohen (Wesleyan University Press, 1965), 53.

Chapter 1
Ted Shawn, "Remembering Ted 'Papa' Shawn," interview by Elinor Rogosin in *The Dance Makers: Conversations with American Choreographers* (Walker & Company, 1980), 9.

Chapter 2
Matthew Bourne, "How We Made Matthew Bourne's Swan Lake," interview by Anna Tims, *The Guardian*, October 14, 2013, https://www.theguardian.com/stage/2013/oct/14/how-we-made-matthew-bourne-swan-lake, accessed July 1, 2024.

Chapter 3
Murray Louis, *Inside Dance* (St. Martin's Press, 1980), 9.

Chapter 4
Mary Wigman, "Witch Dance," in *The Language of Dance* (Wesleyan University Press, 1966), 41, https://digitalcollections.wesleyan.edu/_flysystem/fedora/2023-03/14920-Original%20File.pdf, accessed July 1, 2024.

Chapter 5
Agnes de Mille, *To a Young Dancer: A Handbook* (Little, Brown, 1962), 31.

Chapter 6
Kathryn Craft, *The Art of Falling* (Sourcebooks, 2014), 4.

Chapter 7
Glen Tetley, "Finding Glen Tetley," interview by Elinor Rogosin in *The Dance Makers: Conversations with American Choreographers* (Walker & Company, 1980), 124.

Chapter 8
José Limón, "Composing a Dance," *The Julliard Review 2*, (Winter 1955), 18.

Chapter 9
André Levinson, *André Levinson: Ballet Old and New,* trans. Susan Cook Summer (Dance Horizons, 1982), *xv*.

Chapter 10
Martha Graham, *The Dance Revealed,* directed by Catherine Tatge, 1515 Productions Limited, 1994, 54 min., 53 sec., https://www.youtube.com/watch?v=vUEW3lRXPng, accessed July 1, 2024.

Chapter 11
Alwin Nikolais, "Growth of a Theme," in *The Dance Has Many Faces,* ed. Walter Sorrell (Chicago Review Press, 1966), 128.

Chapter 12
Elizabeth Streb, "Gender and Class in Dance," interview by Laura Flanders, GRITtv, April 16, 2010, 1 min., 31 sec., https://youtu.be/3Hm11QjSyw0?si=xU7JptHcUnoRGPtQ/, accessed July 1, 2024.

Chapter 13
Suzanne Farrell, *Suzanne Farrell: A Memoir* with Toni Bentley (Summit Books, 1988), 109.

Chapter 14
Trisha Brown, "Locus/Altered," in *Dancing on the Edge,* Paley Archive, PBS WGBH Boston, MA, 1980, 28 min., 47 sec., https://www.paleycenter.org/collection/item/?q=about&p=785&item=T:15690, accessed July 1, 2024.

Chapter 15
Doris Humphrey, https://seechicagodance.com/organization/doris-humphrey-memorial-theater, accessed July 1, 2024.

Chapter 16
Savion Glover in "Savion Glover Pays Homage to the Masters with SoLe Sanctuary" by Karen Campbell, *Boston Globe,* January 5, 2013, https://www.bostonglobe.com/arts/theater-art/2013/01/05/savion-glover-pays-homage-masters-with-sole-sanctuary/iJgWO1OKEivXVVUARUjirN/story.html, accessed July 1, 2024.

Chapter 17
Gelsey Kirkland, *Dancing on My Grave: An Autobiography* (Doubleday, 1986), 245.

Chapter 18
Mikhail Baryshnikov in "Noted artist in a new role — NU commencement speaker," by Mary Schmich, *Chicago Tribune,* June 26, 2013,

https://www.chicagotribune.com/2013/06/26/noted-artist-in-a-new-role-nu-commencement-speaker/, accessed July 1, 2024.

Chapter 19
Pina Bausch in "When Avant-Garde Meets Mainstream," by Stephen Holden, *New York Times,* Sept. 29, 1985, https://www.nytimes.com/1985/09/29/arts/when-avant-garde-meets-mainstream.html, accessed July 1, 2024.

Chapter 20
Doris Humphrey, *The Art of Making Dances* (Grove Press, 1959), 68.

Chapter 21
Merce Cunningham, "Space, Time, and Dance," Merce Cunningham Trust, https://www.mercecunningham.org/the-work/writings/space-time-and-dance/, accessed July 1, 2024.

Chapter 22
Twyla Tharp in "Twyla Tharp: Turning Sharp Corners" by Diane Solway, *New York Times,* January 1, 1989.

Chapter 23
Judith Jamison, *Dancing Spirit* (Doubleday, 1993), 264.

Chapter 24
Anna Sokolow, "The Rebel and the Bourgeois," in *The Modern Dance: Seven Statements of Belief,* ed. Selma Jeanne Cohen (Wesleyan University Press, 1965), 30.

Conclusion
Nandikeshvara, "Abhinaya Darpana" (Mirror of Gesture), trans. Bharatanatyam dancer Rama Vaidyanathan, "If Mudras Could Speak," TEDx SAC, July 28, 2022, https://youtu.be/cz-BIeisUgs?si=LjuTG8AjdsiUOw3z, accessed July 1, 2024. Due to varying interpretations over the past 2,500 years, many wordings of this quote exist. This one twists the interpretation yet again—specifically, the final word. On the TEDx video I watched, I thought Vaidyanathan had said "afoot," which immediately perked up the storyteller in me. I had to use it. The transcription that accompanies the video, I would later learn, suggests the last quoted line should read, "And when emotion happens, an experience is *evoked*." Which is similar to "afoot," yet a touch less mischievous.

Endnotes

1 Lucinda Childs, "Available Light," interview by Julie Lazar, PBS SoCal, 2015, https://www.pbssocal.org/shows/artbound/available-light-interviews-frank-gehry-lucinda-childs-and-john-adams, accessed July 1, 2024.
2 V. E. Schwab, "V. E. Schwab on the 'defiant joy' of her epic novel *The Invisible Life of Addie LaRue,*" interview by Maureen Lee Lenker, *Entertainment Weekly,* September 21, 2020, https://ew.com/books/author-interviews/ve-schwab-the-invisible-life-of-addie-larue/, accessed July 1, 2024.
3 Rachel Joyce, "Rachel Joyce: My Unexpected Followup to the Unlikely Pilgrimage of Harold Fry," *The Guardian,* July 28, 2015, https://www.theguardian.com/books/2015/jul/28/rachel-joyce-love-song-of-miss-queenie-hennessy-pilgrimage-harold-fry, accessed July 1, 2024.
4 Roland Merullo, Rolandmerullo.com, https://rolandmerullo.com/Images/Behind%20the%20Book%20The%20Talk%20Funny%20Girl.pdf, accessed July 1, 2024.
5 Jodi Picoult, "Jodi Picoult Interview," interview by Bethanne Kelly Patrick and Carol Fitzgerald, *BookReporter,* April 9, 2004, https://www.bookreporter.com/authors/jodi-picoult/news/interview-040804, accessed July 1, 2024.
6 Colum McCann, "A Conversation with Colum McCann," interview by Farah Miller, oprah.com, July 2009, https://www.oprah.com/omagazine/colum-mccann-interview-about-let-the-great-world-spin/all, accessed July 1, 2024.
7 Hazel Gaynor, "The Story behind Last Christmas in Paris," June 24, 2017, hazelgaynor.com, https://hazelgaynor.com/the-story-behind-last-christmas-in-paris, accessed July 1, 2024.
8 Diane Setterfield, "Diane Setterfield Author Interview," BookBrowse.com, September 2006, https://www.bookbrowse.com/author_interviews/full/index.cfm/author_number/1376/diane-setterfield, accessed July 1, 2024.

[9] Lori Lansens, "An Interview with Lori Lansens," BookBrowse.com, 2007, https://www.bookbrowse.com/author_interviews/full/index.cfm/author_number/1301/lori-lansens, accessed July 1, 2024.

[10] Garth Stein, "FAQ," GarthStein.com, https://garthstein.com/works/the-art-of-racing-in-the-rain/faq/, accessed July 1, 2024.

[11] Tatiana de Rosnay, "Interview with Tatiana de Rosnay, Author of Sarah's Key," interview by Cindy Hudson, Mother Daughter Book Club, January 9, 2009, https://motherdaughterbookclub.com/2009/01/interview-with-tatiana-de-rosnay-author-of-sarahs-key, accessed July 1, 2024.

[12] Tess Uriza Holthe, "An Interview with Tess Uriza Holthe," BookBrowse.com, 2002, https://www.bookbrowse.com/author_interviews/full/index.cfm/author_number/725/tess-uriza-holthe, accessed July 1, 2024.

[13] Weina Dai Randel, "'The Last Rose of Shanghai': Q&A with Author Weina Dai Randel," interview by Jocelyn Eikenburg, ChinaDaily.com, November 17, 2021, https://www.chinadaily.com.cn/a/202111/17/WS61945a72a310cdd39bc75c89_1.html, accessed July 1, 2024.

[14] Marianne Williamson, *A Return to Love* (HarperCollins, 1993), 128.

[15] Doris Humphrey, https://seechicagodance.com/organization/doris-humphrey-memorial-theater, accessed July 1, 2024.

[16] Richard Carlson, *You Can Be Happy No Matter What: Five Principles for Keeping Your Life in Perspective* (New World Library, 1997), 117–118.

[17] Lisa Cron, *Wired for Story: The Writer's Guide to Using Brain Science to Hook Readers from the Very First Sentence* (Ten Speed Press, 2012), 67.

[18] Stephen Schwartz, "Stephen Schwartz and Friends," pbs.org, 2016, https://www.pbs.org/video/american-songbook-njpac-stephen-schwartz-and-friends-full/, accessed July 1, 2024.

[19] Chris Cleave, "LITTLE BEE Author Q&A – Chris Cleave," chriscleave.com, 2008, https://chriscleave.com/little-bee/the-true-story-behind-my-new-novel, accessed July 1, 2024.

[20] "BISAC Subject Headings List," Book Industry Study Group, https://www.bisg.org/fiction, accessed July 1, 2024.

[21] J. K. Rowling, "Pensieve | Wizarding World," wizardingworld.com, August 10, 2015, https://www.wizardingworld.com/writing-by-jk-rowling/pensieve, accessed July 1, 2024.

22 James N. Frey, *How to Write a Damn Good Novel: A Step-by-Step No-Nonsense Guide to Dramatic Storytelling* (St. Martin's Press, 1987), 54.
23 Todd Espeland, "The Eight Efforts: Laban Movement," *The Theatrefolk Blog*, November 15, 2017, https://www.theatrefolk.com/blog/the-eight-efforts-laban-movement, accessed July 1, 2024.
24 Maria Khoreva, "Maria Khoreva's Impossible Balance: Side Développé on Pointe," Dancelineballet, October 14, 2021, https://youtube.com/shorts/uqvE3lSlmns?si=lrcAJ7vfdtKswgZ8, accessed July 1, 2024.
25 Hilary Mantel, "The Unquiet Mind of Hilary Mantel," interview with Sophie Elmhirst, *The New Statesman* archive, https://www.newstatesman.com/archive/2022/09/hilary-mantel-bring-up-bodies-wolf-hall-thomas-cromwell, accessed June 25, 2025.
26 Robert McKee, *Story: Substance, Structure, Style, and the Principles of Screenwriting* (HarperCollins, 1997), 417.
27 Trey Parker and Matt Stone, "Trey Parker and Matt Stone: 'This Happened, and Then This Happened, and Then This Happens — That's Not a Movie, That's Not a Story,' NYU Writing Seminar 2014," Speakola, March 8, 2016, https://speakola.com/arts/matt-stone-trey-parker-nyu-writing-class-2014, accessed July 1, 2024.
28 Elizabeth Berg, *Escaping into the Open: The Art of Writing True* (HarperCollins, 1999), 45–46.
29 Judith Mackrell, "Being Rudolf Nureyev." *The Guardian*, January 11, 2003, https://www.theguardian.com/books/2003/jan/11/featuresreviews.guardianreview31, accessed July 1, 2024.
30 Donald Maass, *The Emotional Craft of Fiction: How to Write the Story Beneath the Surface* (Writer's Digest Books, 2016), 83.
31 Alice Orr, *No More Rejections: 50 Secrets to Writing a Manuscript that Sells* (Writers Digest Books, 2004), 191.
32 Jerome Stern, *Making Shapely Fiction* (W. W. Norton & Company, 1991), 124.
33 Roger Ebert, "Love on a Lonesome Trail," rogerebert.com, December 15, 2005, https://www.rogerebert.com/reviews/brokeback-mountain-2005, accessed July 1, 2024.
34 Twyla Tharp and Mark Reiter, *The Creative Habit: Learn It and Use It for Life* (Simon & Schuster, 2003), 20–21.
35 See note 3 above.

[36] Rama Vaidyanathan, "If Mudras Could Speak," TEDx SAC, July 28, 2022, https://youtu.be/cz-BIeisUgs?si=LjuTG8AjdsiUOw3z, accessed July 1, 2024.

Bibliography of Excerpts

There's no better way to further your study of story movement than to read the full works excerpted in this book. I owe these novelists a debt of gratitude for offering examples worthy of study. All copyrights are owned by the authors or film companies.

Agassi, Andre. *Open*. Random House, 2009.
American Songbook at NJPAC. "Stephen Schwartz and Friends," www.pbs.org, 2016. https://www.pbs.org/video/american-songbook-njpac-stephen-schwartz-and-friends-full/, accessed July 1, 2023.
Caro, Niki. *Anne with an 'E'*. Season 1, episode 1, "Your Will Shall Decide Your Destiny." Netflix, March 19, 2017.
Backman, Fredrik. *A Man Called Ove*. Atria, 2014.
Bambi. Walt Disney Productions, 1942.
Barr, Lisa. *Fugitive Colors*. Arcade, 2013.
Barry, Brunonia. *The Lace Reader*. HarperCollins, 2009.
Brandes, Kate. *Stone Creek*. Wyatt-MacKenzie, 2024.
Braveheart. Paramount Pictures, 1995.
Brown, Dan. *The Da Vinci Code*. Anchor, 2003.
Brown, Karma. *Come Away with Me*. MIRA, 2022.
Brown, Sandra. *Standoff*. Grand Central Publishing, 2013.
Brunt, Carol Rifka. *Tell the Wolves I'm Home*. Random House, 2012.
Carroll, Lewis. *Through the Looking Glass*. Macmillan, 1872.
Chabon, Michael. *The Amazing Adventures of Kavalier & Clay*. Random House, 2000.
Crichton, Michael. *Jurassic Park*. Alfred A. Knopf, 1990.
Cleave, Chris. *Little Bee*. Simon & Schuster, 2008.
Craft, Kathryn. *The Art of Falling*. Sourcebooks, 2014.

———. *The Far End of Happy*. Sourcebooks, 2015.
Danielewski, Mark Z. *House of Leaves*. Pantheon Books, 2018.
Doerr, Anthony. *All the Light We Cannot See*. Scribner, 2014.
Donoghue, Emma. *Room*. Picador, 2017.
Dubus III, Andre. *House of Sand and Fog*. W. W. Norton, 1999.
Enger, Leif. *Peace Like a River*. Grove/Atlantic, 2001.
Estes, Kelli. *The Girl Who Wrote in Silk*. Sourcebooks, 2015.
Eve, Nomi. *Henna House*. Scribner, 2015.
Fitch, Janet. *Paint It Black*. Little, Brown, 2006.
Follett, Ken. *The Pillars of the Earth*. Penguin Random House, 1989.
Fringe. Bad Robot, 2008.
Garmus, Bonnie. *Lessons in Chemistry*. Doubleday, 2022.
Gaynor, Hazel and Heather Webb. *Last Christmas in Paris*. William Morrow, 2017.
Going, K. L. *Fat Kid Rules the World*. Penguin, 2004.
Greenwood, Bryn. *All the Ugly and Wonderful Things*. Macmillan, 2016.
Greer, Sierra. *Annie Bot*. HarperCollins, 2024.
Haddon, Mark. *The Curious Incident of the Dog in the Night-Time*. Random House, 2004.
Hamilton, Jane. *A Map of the World*. Anchor, 1995.
Hannah, Kristin. *The Nightingale*. St. Martin's Press, 2015.
Harvey, Kristy Woodson. *Under the Southern Sky*. Simon & Schuster, 2023.
Hawkins, Paula. *The Girl on the Train*. Penguin, 2015.
Henry, Emily. *People We Meet on Vacation*. Penguin, 2021.
Holthe, Tess Uriza. *When the Elephants Dance*. Penguin, 2002.
Hornby, Nick. *How to Be Good*. Penguin, 2002.
Hosseini, Khaled. *The Kite Runner*. Penguin, 2003.
———. *And the Mountains Echoed*. Penguin, 2013.
House, Silas. *Southernmost*. Algonquin, 2019.
Irving, John. *A Prayer for Owen Meany*. William Morrow, 1989.
Jackson, Joshilyn. *Someone Else's Love Story*. HarperCollins, 2013.
Jacques, Brian. *Redwall*. Penguin, 2002.
Jin, Ha. *Waiting*. Vintage, 1999.

Johnson, Julie Christine. *In Another Life*. Sourcebooks, 2016.

———. *The Crows of Beara*. Ashland Creek Press, 2017.

Johnson, Nancy. *The Kindest Lie*. HarperCollins, 2021.

Joyce, Rachel. *The Unlikely Pilgrimage of Harold Fry*. Random House, 2012.

———. *The Love Song of Miss Queenie Hennessy*. Random House, 2015.

Kail, Thomas. *We Were the Lucky Ones*. Episode 1, "Radom," Hulu, March 28, 2024.

Kallos, Stephanie. *Broken for You*. Grove/Atlantic, 2007.

Kelly, Mary Pat. *Galway Bay*. Grand Central Publishing, 2009.

Kidd, Sue Monk. *The Secret Life of Bees*. Tinder Press, 2001.

Kim, Angie. *Miracle Creek*. Sarah Crichton Books, 2019.

———. *Happiness Falls*. Hogarth, 2023.

Kingsolver, Barbara. *The Bean Trees*. HarperCollins, 1988.

———. *The Poisonwood Bible*. HarperCollins, 1998.

———. *Prodigal Summer*. HarperCollins, 2000.

———. *Flight Behavior*. HarperCollins, 2012.

———. *Demon Copperhead*. HarperCollins, 2022.

Koontz, Dean. *Intensity*. Bantam, 2007.

Kubica, Mary. *Don't You Cry*. MIRA Books, 2016.

Kwok, Jean. *The Leftover Woman*. HarperCollins, 2023.

Lamb, Cathy. *No Place I'd Rather Be*. Kensington, 2017.

Lansens, Lori. *The Girls*. Little, Brown, 2006.

Larkin, Allison. *The People We Keep*. Gallery, 2022.

Lehane, Dennis. *Mystic River*. Random House, 2006.

Letts, Billie. *Where the Heart Is*. Warner, 1996.

Livesey, Margot. *Banishing Verona*. Henry Holt, 2005.

Maberry, Jonathan. *Rot & Ruin*. Simon & Schuster, 2011.

Macallister, Greer. *The Arctic Fury*. Sourcebooks, 2021.

Macdonald, Ross. *The Drowning Pool*. Vintage Crime/Black Lizard, 2011.

Maher, Brendan. *Outlander*, season 3, episode 1, "The Battle Joined," Starz, September 10, 2017.

Martin, George R. R. *A Song of Ice and Fire series: A Game of Thrones, A Clash of Kings, A Storm of Swords, and A Feast for Crows*. Random House Publishing Group, 2011.
McCann, Colum. *Dancer*. Henry Holt, 2004.
———. *Let the Great World Spin*. Random House, 2013.
McDermott, Alice. *A Bigamist's Daughter*. Picador, 1982.
McFadden, Freida. *The Housemaid*. Grand Central, 2023.
McKenzie, Catherine. *Hidden*. HarperCollins, 2013.
McLarty, Ron. *The Memory of Running*. Penguin, 2005.
Merullo, Roland. *The Talk-Funny Girl*. Broadway, 2011.
Meyer, Stephenie. *Twilight*. Little, Brown Books for Young Readers, 2007.
Mitchell, David. *The Bone Clocks*. Random House, 2015.
Moehringer, J. R. *The Tender Bar*. Hachette, 2005.
Montgomery, L. M. *Anne of Green Gables*. L. C. Page, 1908.
Morgenstern, Erin. *The Night Circus*. Doubleday, 2011.
Moyes, Jojo. *Me Before You*. Penguin, 2012.
Mustian, Kelly. *The Girls in the Stilt House*. Sourcebooks, 2021.
Némirovsky, Irène. *Suite Française*. Random House, 2006.
Nguyen, Phan Que Mai. *The Mountains Sing*. Algonquin Books, 2020.
Nguyen, Viet Thanh. *The Sympathizer*. Grove/Atlantic, 2015.
O'Brien, Tim. *The Things They Carried*. Mariner Books, 2009.
O'Farrell, Maggie. *Hamnet*. Penguin Random House, 2020.
O'Keeffe, Kristin Bair. *The Art of Floating*. Penguin Random House, 2014.
Patchett, Ann. *The Magician's Assistant*. Harcourt, 1997.
———. *Bel Canto*. HarperCollins, 2001.
———. *The Dutch House*. HarperCollins, 2019.
———. *Bel Canto Annotated Edition*. HarperCollins, 2024.
Picoult, Jodi. *My Sister's Keeper*. Atria Books, 2006.
Poe, Edgar Allan. *The Best of Poe: The Tell-Tale Heart, the Raven, the Cask of Amontillado, and 30 Others*. Prestwick House, 2015.
Poeppel, Amy. *Musical Chairs*. Simon & Schuster, 2020.
Quindlen, Anna. *Blessings*. Random House, 2002.

Randel, Weina Dai. *The Last Rose of Shanghai.* Lake Union, 2021.
Reardon, Bryan. *Finding Jake.* William Morrow, 2015.
Richardson, Kim Michele. *The Book Woman's Daughter.* Sourcebooks, 2022.
Riddle, A. G. *Winter World.* Legion Books, 2019.
Rinker, Jess. *Monolith.* Wandering Moth Press, 2024.
Roddenberry, Gene. *Star Trek.* 1966.
Rosnay, Tatiana de. *Sarah's Key.* St. Martin's Press, 2007.
Rouda, Kaira. *Best Day Ever.* Harlequin, 2017.
Rushdie, Salman. *The Moor's Last Sigh.* Vintage, 1997.
Russell, Mary Doria. *The Sparrow.* Ballantine, 1996.
Santos, Marisa de los. *Love Walked In.* Plume, 2006.
Schwab, V. E. *The Invisible Life of Addie LaRue.* Tor Books, 2020.
Setterfield, Diane. *The Thirteenth Tale.* Atria, 2006.
Sibley, Priscille. *The Promise of Stardust.* William Morrow, 2013.
Star Wars: Episode 4: A New Hope. Twentieth Century-Fox, 1977.
Stein, Garth. *The Art of Racing in the Rain.* HarperCollins, 2009.
Stern, Jerome. *Making Shapely Fiction.* W. W. Norton, 2000.
Strobos, Kathy. *Partner Pursuit.* Katharine Strobos, 2021.
The Cider House Rules. Miramax, 1999.
The Truman Show. Paramount Pictures, 1998.
Titanic. Paramount Pictures, 1997.
Tolkien, J. R. R. *The Lord of the Rings: The Fellowship of the Ring, the Two Towers, the Return of the King.* HarperCollins, 1995.
Trumbo, Dalton. *Johnny Got His Gun.* Bantam, 1970.
Twister. Warner Bros., 1996.
Tyler, Anne. *Ladder of Years.* Alfred A. Knopf, 1995.
Van Pelt, Shelby. *Remarkably Bright Creatures.* Bloomsbury, 2022.
Verghese, Abraham. *The Covenant of Water.* Grove Press, 2023.
Viorst, Judith, and Garrett Christopher. *Alexander and the Terrible, Horrible, No Good, Very Bad Day.* Simon & Schuster, 1987.
Wait Until Dark. Warner Bros., 1967.
Weiner, Jennifer. *Good in Bed.* Washington Square Press, 2001.
Weisberger, Lauren. *The Devil Wears Prada.* Random House, 2003.
Wendig, Chuck. *The Book of Accidents.* Random House, 2021.

Wiseman, Ellen Marie. *The Life She Was Given.* Kensington Books, 2017.

Younge-Ullman, Danielle. *Falling Under.* Penguin, 2008.

Zusak, Markus. *The Book Thief.* Knopf Books for Young Readers, 2013.

Index

A Bigamist's Daughter, 105
A Man Called Ove, 136–137
A Map of the World, 122
A Prayer for Owen Meany, 33
action scenes, 141
action-reaction, 34, 37–41, 48, 62, 100, 266, 274
activity arc, 194
Agassi, Andre, 74
agency, 31–32, 35–38, 41, 51, 146, 204, 227, 249
    act, 24, 35, 36, 37, 46, 47, 49, 143, 147, 152, 159, 220, 228, 234, 256–258, 266, 286
Alexander and the Terrible, Horrible, No Good, Very Bad Day, 140
All the Light We Cannot See, 196
anecdote, 97, 141, 190, 202
Anne of Green Gables, 34
Annie Bot, 247
antagonist, 27, 35, 45, 50, 62, 64, 122, 134, 150, 220–222, 228, 290
anticipation, 24, 33, 79, 110, 231, 291
arc of inner change, 53, 132–135, 195, 204, 227, 228, 262, 287, 288, 291
author goal, 59
back-cover copy, 80, 85, 87–92, 96
Backman, Frederik, 136
backstory, 21–22, 24, 27–29, 38, 49, 51–52, 54, 64, 95–98, 101–116, 142, 162, 171, 173, 177, 205, 249, 283, 291
Banishing Verona, 165

Barr, Lisa, 31
Baum, L. Frank, 67, 146
beats, 180, 183, 230, 236, 239
Bel Canto, 85, 87, 89, 277
Belong to Me, 199
Berg, Elizabeth, 231
Best Day Ever, 10
Bishop, Melanie, 187
Blessings, 154
body language, 230, 235
Brandes, Kate, 196
bridging conflict, 59, 62–65, 73, 85
Broken for You, 167
Brown, Dan, 158
Brown, Karma, 190, 275
Brunt, Carol Rifka, 200
Carlson, Dr. Richard, 39
Carroll, Lewis, 170
cause-and-effect, 39, 101, 202, 229, 251, 264, 292
Chabon, Michael, 183
Cleave, Chris, 77–78, 215
climax, 24, 256, 258, 260–261, 263, 265–267, 275
Come Away with Me, 190
conflict, 12–13, 19–20, 23–24, 27–29, 34, 65, 72, 79, 85, 89, 95, 107, 124, 132–139, 147, 151, 154, 156–157, 160, 177, 186, 2143 220–221, 223, 226, 228–229, 234, 242, 250–251, 255, 275–276, 279, 288, 290
context, 26, 46, 56, 80, 86–87, 104–106, 108–109, 116, 177, 257
continuity words, 104

Crichton, Michael, 122
Cron, Lisa, 43, 202
Dancer, 245
Danielewski, Mark L., 109
dark moment, 45, 134, 210, 257–259, 262, 267, 285, 287–288
dark night of the soul, 254
de Rosnay, Tatiana, 19
Demon Copperhead, 78, 119
description, 39, 64, 80, 107, 118, 122, 128, 156, 196
dialogue, 10, 34, 38, 48, 111, 175–188, 192, 230, 235–236, 239, 243, 249, 251, 282, 288–290
   directed, 178, 183
   misdirection, 184–185
   modulation, 184
Doerr, Anthony, 196
Don't You Cry, 105
Donoghue, Emma, 122, 275
Dr. Seuss, 220
Dragonfly in Amber, 265
dramatic imperative, 14, 45, 49, 52, 57, 97, 147
dreams and PTSD, 111
Dubus III, Andre, 23–25, 28, 279
Eight Efforts, 145–147, 231
emotion markers, 232–233, 239
emotional arc, 64, 125
emotional experience, 231, 267, 277
emotional turning point, 53, 138, 199, 202–204, 223, 226, 228, 259–262, 266–287, 293
Enger, Leif, 191
Escaping into the Open, 231
Estes, Kelli, 110
Eve, Nomi, 194
exposition, 48
Falling Under, 278
Fat Kid Rules the World, 40
Finding Jake, 13
Fitch, Janet, 125

Flight Behavior, 72
Follett, Ken, 152
Fonteyn, Margot, 246
foreboding, 10, 49, 81, 152, 154
foreshadow, 41, 89–90, 120, 126–127, 156, 195, 225, 241, 261
frame story, 109
Frey, James N., 133, 220
Fringe, 151
Fugitive Colors, 31
Gabaldon, Diana, 265
Galway Bay, 158
Garmus, Bonnie, 76, 181
Gaynor, Hazel, 12
genre, 83–92
   genre expectations, 84–85, 89–91, 249, 272
   subgenre, 84, 91
Going, K. L., 40
Greek chorus, 212–214
Greer, Sierra, 247
Haddon, Mark, 164, 223
Hamilton, Jane, 122
Hamnet, 143
Hannah, Kristin, 162
Happiness Falls, 226
Harry Potter and the Goblet of Fire, 113
Harvey, Kristy Woodson, 153
Hawkins, Paula, 74
Henna House, 194–196
Henry, Emily, 234
Hidden, 105
Holthe, Tess Uriza, 20
hook, 12, 78–81, 133, 136
Hornby, Nick, 240
House of Leaves, 109
House, Silas, 96
How to Write a Damn Good Novel, 133, 220
Hunt, Helen, 255
Hunter, Georgia, 197

I want song, 60
In Another Life, 61
inciting incident, 44–57, 64, 79–81, 85, 85, 96-98, 132, 191, 193, 234, 247–48, 256-257, 259–260, 262, 275, 287–288
Inciting incident, defined, 45
inner arc of change, 2, 45, 53, 72, 98, 103, 132–135, 144, 147, 187, 190, 195, 203–205, 209, 221, 227, 230, 248–251, 254, 257–262, 282, 287–288, 291
inner conflict, 20, 24, 29, 34, 65, 98, 136–138, 223, 234–236, 238, 243, 245, 247, 250, 256, 275, 287, 291
    impossible choice, 81
    moral quandary, 80
inner monologue, 48
Intensity, 158
invented words, 170
Irving, John, 33, 134–135, 277
Jabberwocky, 170
Jackson, Joshilyn, 56, 79, 87
Jacques, Brian, 161
James Bond, 42
Jin, Ha, 104
Johnny Got His Gun, 36, 274
Johnson, Julie Christine, 61
Johnson, Nancy, 181
Joyce, Rachel, 8, 197, 289
Jurassic Park, 122
Kallos, Stephanie, 167
Kelly, Mary Pat, 158
keywords, 90–91
Kidd, Sue Monk, 159
Kim, Angie, 71, 226
Kingslover, Barbara, 72, 78, 118–119
    Prodigal Summer, 72, 118
    The Poisonwood Bible, 118
    Demon Copperhead, 78, 119

Flight Behavior, 72, 119
The Bean Trees, 119
Koontz, Dean, 158
Kubica, Mary, 105
Kwok, Jean, 261–262
l'intrigue, 151
Laban, Rudolf von, 145–146
Ladder of Years, 155
Lamb, Cathy, 42
Lansens, Lori, 16, 17, 19
Larkin, Allison, 225
Last Christmas in Paris, 12
late-entering character, 225
Lehane, Dennis, 120, 242
Lessons in Chemistry, 76, 181
Let the Great World Spin, 11
Letts, Billie, 108, 224
limitations, 227
Little Bee, 77, 215
Livesey, Margot, 165
Lynds, Gayle, 221
Maass, Donald, 157, 228, 257
Maberry, Jonathan, 141–142, 146
Macallister, Greer, 104
Macdonald, Ross, 221
Maguire, Gregory, 59
Martin, George R. R., 170
McCann, Colum, 11, 245
McDermott, Alice, 105
McFadden, Freida, 79
McKee, Robert, 176, 244
McKenzie, Catherine, 105
McLarty, Ron, 179–180, 190
Me Before You, 257
Meier, Susan, 164
Merullo, Roland, 9, 22
Meyer, Stephenie, 156–158
Miracle Creek, 71
Mitchell, David, 105
Moehringer, J. R., 73
Montgomery, Lucy Maud, 34
Morgenstern, Erin, 69

motivation, 26–27, 32, 59, 94–99, 115, 139, 209, 251, 282, 287, 290
Moyes, Jojo, 257
movement potential, 22, 40
My Sister's Keeper, 11, 25, 80
Mystic River, 120, 242
narrator, 10, 16, 33–34, 39, 44, 56, 70, 75–76, 90, 106, 145, 171, 214, 241–242
Nash, Jennie, 202
Nguyễn, Phan Quế Mai, 154
Nguyen, Viet Thanh, 170, 172, 174
No More Rejections, 265
No Place I'd Rather Be, 44
non-POV characters, 234
Nureyev, Rudolf, 245
O'Brien, Tim, 108
O'Farrell, Maggie, 143
O'Keefe, Kristin Bair, 105
obstacle, 20, 35, 39, 44–46, 50, 52, 63, 95, 126, 150, 191, 202–206, 208, 219, 221, 223, 244, 261, 288
off balance, 165–174, 226, 261, 286
Open, 74
opening, 3, 9–10, 16, 18, 26–27, 31, 34, 38–41, 51, 56, 59, 61–65, 66–81, 86–89, 95, 97, 104–106, 120, 122, 125, 153, 161, 163–164, 180, 198, 235, 240, 243, 249, 258, 261, 264, 267, 278
origin scene, 96–99, 101
Orr, Alice, 265
Outlander, 265
outsider, 31–33, 40–41, 69, 212
pacing, 83, 146, 181, 194, 242, 244, 252, 266
Paint It Black, 125
Parker, Trey, 202
Partner Pursuit, 222
past perfect, 113
Patchett, Ann, 70, 85–90, 263, 277
Peace Like a River, 191

People We Meet on Vacation, 234–238
perspective, 1–2, 15–29, 31, 40–41, 68, 76, 80, 96, 98, 123, 132, 134, 144, 159, 183, 191, 195, 197–198, 209, 212, 227, 238, 246, 248, 250, 261, 266, 271, 280, 288, 290
Picoult, Jodi, 11, 25, 80
Pillars of the Earth, 152
Pippin, 61
point of view, 18–19, 21–29, 62, 70, 77, 112, 171, 234–235, 239, 250, 265, 271, 273
portal, 113–16
premise, 16, 29, 52–57, 115, 133–139, 151, 177, 256–257, 274–275, 286–288
pressure cooker, 223
Prodigal Summer, 72, 118–119
Quindlen, Anna, 154
Randel, Weina Dai, 20
Reardon, Bryan, 13
Redwall, 161
relationship arc, 193
relevant conflict, 131–139, 228, 276
Remarkably Bright Creatures, 261
Richardson, Kim Michele, 106
Riddle, A. G., 79
roll/role Call, 138–139
Room, 122, 275, 302
Rot & Ruin, 141–143, 146
Rouda, Kaira, 10
routines, 58, 224, 285
Rowling, J. K., 113
Rushdie, Salman, 145, 223
Russell, Mary Doria, 66
Santos, Marisa de los, 199
Sarah's Key, 19
scene values, 228, 244
Schwab, V. E., 8
Schwartz, Stephen, 59–61

secondary characters, 27, 28, 37, 39, 41, 42, 142, 177, 194, 204, 228, 234–238, 281, 287, 289, 291
Setterfield, Diane, 12, 111, 280
setting, 19, 35, 45, 48, 64, 68–69, 73, 112, 117–128, 136, 144, 150, 157, 174, 177, 179, 183–187, 192, 196, 202, 204, 205, 212, 215, 239, 243, 249, 261, 289
setting arc, 196
sex scene, 143–145
Sibley, Priscille, 80
Someone Else's Love Story, 56, 79, 87–90
Southernmost, 96
stakes, 21, 24, 32, 41, 45, 48–49, 53–56, 63, 72, 76, 78, 80, 102, 106, 109, 111, 124, 136–137, 150–151, 158–160, 173, 201, 206–215, 223–224, 228, 234, 246, 248, 250–252, 254, 258–259, 264–265, 275–276, 278, 285, 287–288, 290–291
Star Trek, 170
Stein, Garth, 18, 136–137
Stone Creek, 196
Stone, Matt, 202
story goal, 22, 27–28, 43–57, 59, 62–64, 72, 85, 95, 99, 115, 124–125, 132, 141–142, 150, 206, 220, 227–228, 249, 258, 261, 287
Story is inner conflict made external, 136
story question, 44, 49–50, 52–57, 80, 84, 90, 103, 160, 162, 261, 263, 266, 269
Strobos, Kathy, 222
subtext, 101, 172, 176–180, 187, 192, 200, 237–239, 266, 283
Susy Hendrix, 35
synopsis, 203

Tell the Wolves I'm Home, 200
tension, 2, 25, 28, 64, 66, 68, 71, 73, 76, 81, 94, 109, 115–117, 133, 143, 149–164, 177, 179, 186, 194, 209–211, 214, 221, 223, 236, 238, 245, 250, 252, 257
Tharp, Twyla, 164, 285
The Amazing Adventures of Kavalier & Clay, 183
The Arctic Fury, 104
The Art of Falling, 120, 160
The Art of Floating, 105
The Art of Racing in the Rain, 18, 136, 137
The Bone Clocks, 105
The Book of Accidents, 178
The Book Thief, 76
The Book Woman of Troublesome Creek, 106
The Cider House Rules, 134, 277
The Covenant of Water, 79
The Creative Habit, 164, 285
The Crows of Beara, 61
The Curious Incident of the Dog in the Night-Time, 164, 223
The Da Vinci Code, 158
The Devil Wears Prada, 194
The Drowning Pool, 221
The Dutch House, 263
The Far End of Happy, 114, 136, 160, 210
The Girl on the Train, 74
The Girl Who Wrote in Silk, 110
The Girls, 16–17, 19
The Housemaid, 79
The Invisible Life of Addie LaRue, 8
The Kindest Lie, 181
The Last Rose of Shanghai, 20
The Leftover Woman, 261
The Life She Was Given, 106
The Love Song of Miss Queenie Hennessy, 8, 9

The Magician's Assistant, 70
The Memory of Running, 179, 190
The Moor's Last Sigh, 145
The Mountains Sing, 154
The Night Circus, 69
The Nightingale, 162
The People We Keep, 225
The Promise of Stardust, 80
The Secret Life of Bees, 159
The Sparrow, 66
The Sympathizer, 170
The Talk-Funny Girl, 9, 22
The Tender Bar, 73
The Things They Carried, 108
The Thirteenth Tale, 12, 111, 280–281
The Truman Show, 151
The Unlikely Pilgrimage of Harold Fry, 8, 197, 289
The Wonderful Wizard of Oz, 60, 132
theme, 11, 26, 72, 74, 104, 120, 127, 133–134, 151, 187, 212, 269
thrust, 31, 46, 141–142, 146, 174, 275
ticking clock, 63, 159, 261
tragedy, 89, 279
trajectory, 32, 41, 60, 133, 202
Trumbo, Dalton, 36, 274
Twilight, 156–157
Twister, 255
Tyler, Anne, 155
Under the Southern Sky, 153

understatement, 178–179, 280–281
unexpected, 13, 27, 39, 47, 104, 143, 167–168, 174, 179, 185, 193, 202, 223-225, 248, 260
Van Pelt, Shelby, 261
Verghese, Abraham, 79
Viorst, Judith, 140
visceral emotions, 230
voice, 9–10, 13–14, 17, 20, 52, 76–78, 100, 176, 179, 196, 211, 214, 233, 242, 261, 273, 289
Wait Until Dark, 35
Waiting, 104
watcher, 151–164
We Were the Lucky Ones, 197
Webb, Heather, 12
Weiner, Jennifer, 120
Weisberger, Lauren, 194
Wendig, Chuck, 178
When the Elephants Dance, 20
Where the Heart Is, 108, 224
Wicked, 59
Winter World, 79
Wired for Story, 43
Wiseman, Ellen Marie, 105
women's fiction, 84, 91, 272
You Can Be Happy No Matter What, 39
Younge-Ullman, Danielle, 278
Zeno, 222
Zusak, Marcus, 76

Acknowledgments

The perspective expressed in these pages evolved over a lifetime of immersion in the arts. Among my key story mentors, I count Jack and Robert Graham, the raconteurs of my youth. As concerns formal education, I credit Juilene Osbourne-McKnight, Donald Maass, James Scott Bell, Michael Hauge, Nancy Kress, Lisa Cron, Bill Johnson, Robert McKee, James N. Frey, and Jessica Brody for showing me the way. I am humbled to step into your lineage. On the movement side, every one of my creative projects has influences I can trace back to my college dance mentor, Lana Kay Rosenberg, who well deserves this book's dedication.

The spark for this book came from Rachel Randall, then an acquisitions editor at Writers Digest Books. After editing a few essays I wrote for *Writers Digest* publications, Rachel reached out to ask if I had a craft book in me. My friend Tori Bond grabbed hold of the idea and patiently (and not so patiently when necessary) continued to offer encouragement during the eight years it took for this book to coalesce. Tori, I so appreciate your tireless persistence, as well as the encouragement of the other writers in my regular crew, Donna Galanti, Kate Brandes, and Dianna Sinovic. Janice Gable Bashman, Ellen Gallow, Sandra Graham, Jill Friedlander, and Lainey Cameron also offered invaluable encouragement.

This book would not exist without Therese Walsh, editorial director at Writer Unboxed, who offered me a monthly slot for my "Mad Skills" craft posts and hired me to teach at her UnConferences. There, presentations by fellow contributors and informal discussions with participants always inspire with their creative approaches and keen minds as we dive deep into story craft. But since my monthly blogging about story craft began in 2008, I also want to thank Dani

Greer, founder of The Blood-Red Pencil, who gave me my start, and Jenny Hansen and Laura Drake at Writers in the Storm for years of monthly posts on the writing life.

Many of the ideas presented here first gained traction during the Your Novel Year program I've led since 2018, and the Craftwriting programs I held for many years prior to that at my home. I'm indebted to the participants in these programs as well as to all who've submitted manuscripts for developmental edits since 2006—you have been my teachers in the trenches.

Writing a book that pulls together thoughts that have accumulated over a lifetime is no easy task. Believe me, those thoughts were much more cogent thanks to advance feedback from Jackson Williams and Donna Galanti, line edits by Nancy Graham, copy edits by Dianna Sinovic, and proofreading by Sandra Graham. Many thanks also go to Donna Cunningham at BeauxArts Design Studio, who immediately grasped the concept of story movement and brought it to life through the interior design and stunning cover.

Last but never least, I send enduring gratitude to my husband, Dave, whose endless belief in me makes all things possible.

About the Author

Kathryn Craft is the award-winning author of two novels from Sourcebooks, *The Art of Falling* and *The Far End of Happy*. Her two-decade tenures as dancer/choreographer, dance critic for *The Morning Call* newspaper in Allentown, PA, and freelance developmental editor have merged to inform her perspective about story movement. Building on her bachelor's and master's degrees in education, it has been her great joy to share the craft of writing by mentoring novelists, most recently through her Your Novel Year program, and by speaking at dozens of venues where people thirst to write, from writing groups, conferences, and libraries to in-patient rehabs and grief support groups. She lives with her husband in Doylestown, PA.

www.ingramcontent.com/pod-product-compliance
Lightning Source LLC
Chambersburg PA
CBHW020532030426
42337CB00013B/820